Losing Jessica

Robby DeBoer

Losing
Jessica

DOUBLEDAY
New York   London   Toronto   Sydney   Auckland

PUBLISHED BY DOUBLEDAY
a division of Bantam Doubleday Dell Publishing Group, Inc.
1540 Broadway, New York, New York 10036

DOUBLEDAY and the portrayal of an anchor with a dolphin are trademarks
of Doubleday, a division of Bantam Doubleday Dell Publishing Group, Inc.

Library of Congress Cataloging-in-Publication Data

DeBoer, Robby, 1957–
    Losing Jessica / by Robby DeBoer.
        p.   cm.
    1. DeBoer, Robby, 1957– . 2. Adoptive parents—United States—
Biography.   3. Adoption—United States.   4. Adoption—Law and
legislation—United States.   I. Title.
HV874.82.D44A3   1994
362.7′34′092—dc20
[B]   94-14740
CIP

ISBN 0-385-47458-x

10   9   8   7   6   5   4   3   2   1

Dedicated to Jessica Anne DeBoer

Acknowledgments

T HIS BOOK would not have been possible without the help of Angela Miller and Betsy Amster, my agents. It was their courage to pursue such a project, without a written proposal, that brought us to this point. With their wholehearted support we were able to present the concept to Doubleday and engage their assistance in bringing this project to fruition. The manuscript was expertly edited by Lori Lipsky and her staff. My sincere appreciation to Doubleday, David Gernert, William Barry, and Ellen Archer for recognizing the importance of telling this story.

Over the course of two and a half years Jan and I consulted with a number of therapists. Some directly assisted us in dealing with the expression of our own emotions and frustrations, while others, specializing in child development, helped us to define more clearly Jessica's needs and the impact that such a transition would have upon her. These people have been essential to our survival. We hope that if their advice is considered, it will positively impact upon Jessica's advancement over the next several years.

Stephanie's name has been changed for the purpose of confidentiality, but she knows who she is. Not only do Jan and I thank her, but our family appreciate her having been available to them as we all struggled through this trauma together. Kerry Novick helped us understand Jessica's world and to appreciate her even more in her time of need. Recognition must also be given to Sarah

C. Mangelsdorf, Ph.D.; Jerome Smith, Ph.D.; Paulette A. Day, A.C.S.W., C.C.S.W.; Jeree H. Pawl, M.D.; Jack Novick, Ph.D.; David Brodzinsky, Ph.D.; Albert Solnit, M.D.; Elissa P. Benedek, M.D.; Peter Ash, M.D.; Vicki Bennett, M.S.W.; and Irving G. Leon, Ph.D. Jan and I would like to also thank Dr. Allen Dumont for the loving care he provided to Jessica as her pediatrician.

In recognition of the extensive hours of legal research, writing, and dialogue in connection with Jessica's case, we gratefully acknowledge the legal and professional support provided by the following people: Glenna Weith of Meyer, Capel, Hirschfeld, Muncy, Jahn, Aldeen, P.C.; Golda Zimmerman, Michael Lunt; Kathryn Miller and Onita Mohr from the Youth Law Center in Iowa; Scott Bassett; Richard S. Victor; Peter P. Darrow, Jessica's Guardian ad Litem; Sally Rutzky, Jessica's Guardian ad Litem; the attorneys working on behalf of the National Council for Adoption; Michael P. Bentzen, Leslie Scherr, Robert L. Levin, and Susan L. Biro at Schweitzer, Bentzen and Scherr. And the many other legal professionals who contributed to Jessica's case.

We would like to thank Bernard Mercer and Steven H. Lytle for their efforts in the Iowa courts after Jessica's transfer. Thank you to Gary Robinson, Kim Ten Eick, John Monroe, Jeff Krausman and his wife, Susan Krausman.

Thank you to the counsel who helped in the preparation of the brief to the U.S. Supreme Court to request a stay for Jessi: John H. Pickering, Louis R. Cohen, Jane C. Sherburne, Margaret Ackerley, Patrick T. Connors, and Jacquelyn Ruff, and Charles Fried of Wilmer, Cutler and Pickering.

Thank you to Professor Barbara Woodhouse, Aaron Finkbiner, and other attorneys at the Philadelphia law firm of Dechert, Price and Rhoads. Thank you, Laurence Tribe, Martha Minow, Elizabeth Bartholet, Katharine Bartlett, Linda Silberman, Samuel Estreicher, Robert Mnookin, Joseph and Sonja Goldstein, and Joan Hollinger, for a brief submitted to the U.S. Supreme Court on Jessica's behalf.

We appreciate Professor Kent D. Syverud for stepping in and taking time to go to Washington to work on our case with Wilmer, Cutler and Pickering. Special thanks to Don Duquette for all his efforts in the trial preparation and the legislative action and in helping with the visitation process. Thank you to Cindy Kelly and Lou Anne Betts of the Child Advocacy Law Clinic for their long hours of support and for babysitting efforts during some of my meetings with Suellyn. Thanks also go out to the American Academy of Adoption Attorneys.

To the journalists across the country who wrote and spoke words of wisdom about Jessica's case, we applaud your courage. Thank you for standing against the biased opinions of our justice system. With your contribution, hopefully we have begun to change our court system to allow for a child's voice to be heard.

A special thank-you goes to Mary Beth Seader and William Pierce at the National Council for Adoption for all of their efforts involving Jessi and for their moral support.

A heartfelt thank-you to the attorneys from the National Committee for the Rights of the Child who spoke so eloquently at rallies and vigils sponsored by Justice for Jessi, and whose encouragement has meant so much: George Russ, Lewis Pitts, Gayle Korotkin, Judge Charles D. Gill, Nannette Bowler, and Shari Shink.

To Senator Jack Welborn, Representative David Gubow, and all the other legislators, past, present, and future, who work on behalf of legislative changes that benefit children, thank you from the bottom of our hearts.

To Joan Pheney Engstrom, thank you for starting Justice for Jessi and opening your home to meetings at all hours of the day and night for months on end. To all the members of Justice for Jessi, and to the members of the DeBoer Committee for Children's Rights, thank you for being part of a grass-roots organization which is growing steadily. Your selfless dedication will never go unrecognized. Please keep the light glowing inside of you, for it is you who will bring about change.

Thank you, Judge William Ager, for your dedication to Jessica, and to children in general. Jan and I believe that more judges should take a stand, and hear a child's voice.

Many thanks to Norm Nickin and John Israel of International Security Consultants Inc. for all the services they were able to provide for our family. We appreciate their friendship and guidance, but most of all we value the protection they were able to provide to our daughter, Jessica. Thanks should also go out to the Ann Arbor Police Department and all their officers for believing that Jessica was a person in her own right and that she deserved to be protected.

To all the people who have written Jan and me so many endearing, encouraging letters—you have given us hope. Thank you for your heartfelt words.

With the assistance of my sister Joan, Annie Rose, Janet Snyder, and their families, a diary of feelings has been magically transformed into Jessica's legacy.

We are eternally grateful for the help of Diane and John Riccolo and Cathy and Mark Gullickson and their nurturing powers to bring Jessi into a caring home.

There are no words, no matter how thoughtfully crafted, which can express our appreciation for the efforts undertaken by Suellyn Scarnecchia. She was not only an excellent attorney but also a confidante and friend. Without her love and commitment to her work and to children, the tragedy which children in this country suffer at the hands of the court would never have been so articulately argued. Suellyn listened to Jessica and in turn gave her a voice. We will be eternally in her debt, and we thank her for never giving up.

To our family and relatives, thank you for always being there for us. Together we laid the foundation for Jessica's life.

Finally, I would like to thank my husband, Jan, for encouraging me to write this book and supporting me through the heartache of reliving painful memories. He recognized that I would not have made it through this year without looking back and going over and over in my mind the events which brought us to that dreadful day, August 2, 1993. With his love and companionship I will be able to close the book, move down the road to healing, and remember my daughter in all of her glory.

Introduction

ARLY OCTOBER 1993:
I sat on the stool in our little kitchen, drinking a cup
of tea, rustling through pages of briefs, and trying to hold
back the tears. In the background, a conversation of Jessi and
Momma having a tea party played on the tape recorder.

Startled by the sound of the phone, I listened to the answering
machine to see who was calling before picking up the receiver.
Recognizing Suellyn Scarnecchia's voice, I answered, trying hard
to mask the sadness I was feeling that day. She spoke softly
about a speech she would be giving at the first national training
conference of the DeBoer Committee for Children's Rights. "Do
you know how big it's gotten, Robby?" she asked. I answered,
"Not really. Tell me about it."

"Twenty-one states will be represented this weekend at the
conference. They're holding it out near the airport. These people
are so dedicated. It's amazing. I've had letters from a lot of them,
and they say that their communities want to be involved in this
work. People want to make changes to help children.

"I'm really impressed. The people at headquarters in Ann
Arbor are working ten or twelve hours every day, answering mail,
returning phone calls, and connecting with lawyers and legislators
around the country. This weekend the chapter leaders will receive
information they need to run their own chapters."

"Sounds good, Suellyn," I said flatly.

Suellyn, quite adept at picking up on my emotions after representing us for months in the courts, said, "Robby, are you okay? You sound like you're having a hard day." The tears began to flow. I was distressed over the reality of Jessica's absence. I blurted out, "Suellyn, was this all our fault? Are we the ones to blame for all of this? I just need to know. Would the state of Iowa have given Jessica back to Cara without her having a hearing to reinstate her rights? Would Jessica have gone into foster care, as the professionals said, or would they have given Jessi to Cara? I need to know. I can't take this anymore. It is two and a half years later and we still don't know who was right. Would Jessi have gone into foster care?"

Suellyn responded, "Robby, that's hindsight. Who's to say what really would have happened? I don't think we can know. It's always easy to look back and see the mistakes that have been made, but that is not how things work."

In despair I hung up the phone. I was overcome with sorrow. I slouched into the old chair by the phone and wrote in my diary:

Dearest Jessica,

We are about to venture into a dark place, to turn back the pages of your life. It will be a sorrowful journey, full of pain, looking into the inner core of what has happened, somehow trying to explain it to you. I pray what we are about to do will be honest and clear to you. As I look around the house at all the legal documents and letters of comfort, I can only hope that someday you might be able to return to a place in your mind that tells you, "My momma and daddy loved me. They did everything they could to make me try to understand that I was an important person, that I was an individual and not a piece of property, and that I was worth fighting for."

Maybe one day you will be able to take in what we have written and weave back the broken threads of your tapestry so you may become whole once again. Dutchy lies on your bed, missing your great big hugs and kisses. Bearcha looks lonely. Pooh Bear sits on your wicker couch, almost asking me not to sail into the uncharted waters we are about to cross in writing this book. But we have to look back in order to move forward. Here we go into the dark place that seemed so wonderful at the time but only leaves pain upon my shoulders now.

God bless my little Sweet Pea tonight,
God bless your heart and soul.
Love, Momma

Losing Jessica

One

DRESSED in my white silk gown, I stood motionless at the altar. This was my wedding day. Happy, confident, and ready to take on a brand-new world, I looked out with love and gratitude at the church full of family and friends. I have always taken bold steps, but this time I went too far, giving a speech at my own wedding. My mouth opened as if I were a natural at this. "I've asked all my brothers and sisters about this thing called marriage and how to make it work. They told me that you must first truly love yourself and then you can love another." As I spoke I felt the steady presence of Jan, the man I already loved deeply, and would grow to love beyond measure.

I spoke of an Irish tradition in which a wreath, symbolizing happiness, health, security, and good fortune, is made for the bride and placed on her door the night before the wedding. I had not felt the need for such a wreath because I had found my happiness. I did find one that I had made long ago and brought it along to give to my father and mother. "I will not be by their side, and I hope that this wreath will take my place and watch over them." The church was transformed into a teary-eyed group that would switch from Kleenex to laughter at any given moment. We presented Jan's parents with a single white rose to symbolize love and the beginning of a new friendship.

Our kiss seemed to last a lifetime. Our marriage had been blessed, not only by the church but also by the people who had come to witness and support this union. They would later prove to be the backbone of our marriage.

After the ceremony, the band set up a stage on the porch of my parents' home, and music filled the air. The horse-drawn sleigh that I had tried to barter from my father for years stood as a basket for the wedding presents. The food fit the scene, with baskets of fruits and vegetables everywhere. The champagne toasts were given by my sister Joan—the youngest of us nine—and my cousin Bridget Connors. We raised our glasses to a new beginning and to the log cabin we would soon build in the hills of Colorado.

Among our many friends gathered on that beautiful day in May of 1982 were my cousin Diane Riccolo and her husband, John, as well as Cathy and Mark Gullickson, cousins of Bridget. Friends offered advice like "Keep it simple" and "Don't give in to thinking you have to be everything to everybody." Others said, "The first year is the worst. If you make it through that, you can make it through anything." The truest advice, which remains clear in my mind, was given to us by my mother. "If you handle hard times well, they can help to strengthen and solidify a marriage."

With all these words of wisdom in our back pockets, Jan and I got ready the next day to set off for Colorado, the place where we hoped our dreams would come true. With three thousand dollars in hand, we crammed the van full of all our worldly possessions. Jan protested as he tried to find a place for all the swatches of fabric which I had accumulated during my years of sewing. We were towing "Dee Dee Bugs," my bright yellow VW Bug. Dee Dee Bugs was a sanctuary for all of our wedding presents. Joan and Bridget, who had camped out in the backyard, tried to get us to wait a day or two, but Jan and I were impatient. "We've got to get going now," I said, promising to call when we were ready to start building our log home, hoping they might come to build it with us.

Our honeymoon promised to be adventurous and blissful as we traveled to the West Coast for a second wedding. Many of my relatives had been unable to travel to Michigan for our wedding, so we decided to have a small ceremony out West as well. It was important to me to share an affirmation of my love for Jan with all of the people who were dear to me. I wanted them to meet Jan and to welcome him into our family. As we drove west through the lovely roads of Michigan, I felt so alive! Every detail of the scenery was so vivid, every sound so clear. Jan's voice was full of love, his face animated, as he told me stories of the weddings he'd been to in the past. We talked on and on, thoroughly enjoying each other's company.

We drove from Michigan through Iowa to stay with my sister Sue, and then on to North Platte, Nebraska. One morning we decided to get an early start, to cover as many miles as possible while the roads were sparsely traveled. It was five in the morning and foggy when I mentioned to Jan that he should be wearing his seat belt, just in case we hit a deer. The wonderful thing about premonitions like that is that they have saved us so many times! Just after Jan hooked his seat belt, a deer loomed up suddenly in front of us. Jan had no time to swerve. We collided with the deer, smashing in the front of the van, leaving us stranded in North Platte for several days. A good chunk of our nest egg went into repairing the van.

Certain that the bad luck was behind us now, we continued on our journey to the West Coast. Introducing Jan to my relatives there was a wonderful experience for me. Jan was so good-hearted and friendly that everyone loved him right away. After spending several weeks with my family, we headed back to Colorado to settle into married life and build our home. What began as an uneventful drive ended up as a life-threatening emergency as my stomach started to distend and I went into shock. My temperature shot up to 105°. Jan pulled off the road and we raced to the nearest hotel. Quickly we called for an ambulance, which took us to a hospital in Boise. It turned out that my fever and shock were caused by a ruptured ovarian cyst. I spent the next two weeks in the hospital. When I was finally well enough to leave, the doctor told us I might never be able to have a child.

I imagine that many people would be devastated to hear this kind of news, but I was not. I have always been an optimist. When someone says, "You might not be able to . . . ," I say, "But then again, I might!" Although my energy was depleted a bit by the hospital stay, my spirits were high. Jan and I had each other, and we still believed we could have a child.

After putting our honeymoon behind us, we settled into life in Ann Arbor with a sense of optimism and confidence. Having spent all our savings, we gave up our dream of living in the hills of Colorado. Jan resumed his career in printing, and I went back

to managing an interior design company, a career I loved and had
spent several years searching for.

Jan and I always wanted a family. Still believing I could
become pregnant, we tried for years to have a child of our own.
Time and time again we used home pregnancy tests, hoping the
doctors were wrong in their assessment of my condition. We had
listed our names with several adoption agencies in southwestern
Michigan, understanding at the time that the wait would be four
to seven years. Contacted several times by attorneys specializing
in private adoption, we carefully reviewed the personal risks and
legal ramifications of the process of adoption. Presented with a
few potential offers, we assessed each one individually and chose
not to proceed, still hoping for an agency adoption. During all
this time we never stopped trying to conceive a child of our own.

At Christmas time in 1989, we adopted Miles—part St.
Bernard with the coat of a golden retriever—from the local
humane society. My sister Joan had been planning to buy us a
puppy, but when I saw Miles, all 110 pounds of him, I fell in love.
Miles filled our house with the craziness and hectic affection of a
puppy. We had begun our family.

Jan and I sat calmly in the doctor's office as he reviewed my
medical records. He had asked that Jan be present to hear his
diagnosis. Upon the advice of my doctors, I'd had a D & C in
August, hoping to put an end to the frequent bleeding I'd been
having for years. Now it was October, and the bleeding persisted.
We were facing our greatest fear. No longer could we delay the
inevitable. The doctor confirmed that I would need to be scheduled immediately for a hysterectomy.

Even in the face of this devastating news, Jan and I remained
optimistic about our chances to become parents, with the help of
an adoption agency. As I prepared for surgery, I tried to look at it
as the beginning of better health rather than the end of my dream
of motherhood. I spent the last few months of 1990 recovering,
and looking forward to a new year. Jan and I would concentrate
on each other for a while as I regained my strength.

Then, suddenly, everything changed. I was home alone on the
morning of January 17, 1991, when my cousin's husband, John
Riccolo, an attorney, called from Cedar Rapids. "Robby," he said,
"I called your mom last night to see how you were doing and to

ask her if she thought you were up to becoming a mom." The word "mom" echoed in my ear.

"John! What are you talking about?"

"Well, what do you think?" John asked. "A doctor I know here in Iowa has a patient giving birth to a baby girl sometime in February. She wanted to find a couple interested in adopting the baby." John had spoken with his wife, Diane, and they had immediately thought of Jan and me.

My first thought was that this was not legally possible. Michigan is one of only five states that do not allow private adoption, requiring that an agency mediate the relationship between birth parents and adoptive parents. We would surely not be allowed to adopt from another state. Could this adoption be worked out through our agency? When Jan came home we sat down and talked about it. Were we ready? We would not have much time, and we did not have a completed home study. We agreed to look into it. I had such a hard time sleeping that night! I felt twinges of excitement, sudden bursts of joy at the thought of having a little baby girl.

The next morning, we were off to the bookstore to do some research and try to figure out if any of this was possible. We discovered that it would be, as long as we worked with a licensed agency and followed the proper legal steps. We spoke with Anne Hacker, director of the Adoption Cradle in Battle Creek, where we had been registered since 1987. She agreed to work with us.

In the meantime, John Riccolo found us an Iowa attorney, John Monroe, who was known as an expert in family law. Our next move was to see if we could even afford this adoption. I called John Monroe, whose demeanor was calm. He explained that Iowa law prohibited charging adoptive parents for anything but medical bills and reasonable attorney fees. He spoke carefully and openly, and my worries diminished during the course of our conversation.

John Monroe said he would handle all the details from this point on. He knew of the doctor, and he would place a call to her. Then he would contact the agency and make the necessary arrangements. All that remained was our home study, and then, waiting for the baby to arrive.

Jan and I were lost in a flood of new emotions, from overwhelming joy to utter fear! Like other new parents-to-be, we were hoping that we'd be prepared in every way. Like other adoptive families, we were faced with the upcoming evaluations and a home study.

Anne Hacker made it clear that the home study could not be rushed, and that a child could not be placed with us until our home had been thoroughly evaluated. They had to examine everything, from the square footage of our house to the quality of our marital relationship, our health, our financial resources, and proof that we were law-abiding citizens. Jan and I had to get a police clearance, which meant checking for any criminal records, a standard requirement in the adoption process. We also obtained documents clarifying Jan's name change. Jan's parents had changed his name to John when they first came to this country from Holland, and he changed it back to Jan shortly before we were married. Everything was in order. Our papers had been on file with the Adoption Cradle for years, and I felt confident that everything would work out.

February 7 was a beautiful day. I had just stepped out of the shower when John Monroe called. "Robby, I got a call today from Cara, the birth mother. She wants you to know that she is going into labor." I was speechless.

"Robby, are you still there?"

"Yes! *Yes!*" John went on to say that Cara had named the birth father, Scott Seefeldt, who lived in North Carolina. John had spoken to Scott, who confirmed what Cara had already said. He also wanted to give the child up for adoption. I asked John, "What if they change their minds?"

"Don't worry," said John. "They won't." John explained that Scott and Cara were engaged, but they wanted to put off raising a family until they were settled. I understood how Cara and Scott felt. Jan and I had felt the same way in our first years together. Now we had a sense of security from what we saw as Cara's high level of commitment and responsibility to her child.

After the phone call, I became so anxious! I dashed outside to share the great news with our neighbor Jean. It was a warm, sunny day, and Jean was playing with her kids in their yard. "Robby," she said excitedly, "you'll have a baby by tomorrow!" She went inside to find several of her favorite books about what to expect with a newborn. Then she added, "You know, this could be false labor. It's sometimes hard to tell. Sometimes you just have to wait and see." Time dragged on. I tried to look at the books, but it was too difficult to concentrate.

Jan called a while later, and he was ecstatic when I told him the news. A friend of his at work later described Jan's reaction: "I have never seen him so happy." There was no update that day from Iowa, and we assumed it probably was false labor. Before turning out the light that night, Jan leaned over and gave me a kiss and said, "I feel like this is a new beginning for us."

All day Saturday we waited in vain for an update from Iowa. On Sunday, just as we'd concluded that it must have been false labor after all, the phone rang. "Cara's had the baby," John Monroe said. I felt my feet lift off the ground. My heart began to pound uncontrollably. Hearing my excitement, Jan dashed in as John was giving me the details: a healthy, beautiful girl with dark hair was born on February 8 at 7:02 in the evening at St. Luke's Hospital in Cedar Rapids, Iowa.

John went on to explain the rules on adoption and waiting periods that we would have to follow: First, there was a seventy-two hour waiting period before Cara and Scott would be allowed to sign off on custody of their child. Then they had an additional ninety-six hours in which they would be allowed to change their minds. Following that, John Monroe, the baby's legal guardian, would go to the hospital with Cathy Gullickson, who now lived in Cedar Rapids. She would be our baby's interim parent until Jan and I arrived and received permission to take her to Michigan. John went on to say that a hearing would be scheduled on February 25 to terminate Cara and Scott's parental rights.

"When can we come down?" I asked. John said that we'd be able to bring the baby home during the first week of March. In the meantime, he promised, he and Cathy would call when they got the baby home to Cathy's house on Monday, and we could come after the ninety-six hours had elapsed.

Jan and I tried to stay grounded, but it was hard to contain ourselves. We were overwhelmed with excitement. Strolling through the farmers' market that weekend, we ran into a friend, Nancy, a former social worker from Des Moines. She was excited to hear our news, but advised us to be cautious. I felt a momentary chill. "People don't realize that ten to twenty percent of birth mothers change their minds about adoption after the child is born," Nancy said. That was sobering advice that lingered in the backs of our minds.

That night, Jan and I went out to dinner with Joan and my cousin Greg. We discussed possible names for the baby. Jan and Greg suggested names like Jasmine and Chamomile, which sounded more like the teas I drink than a name for a baby! Joan and I favored simple names like Anna, Amy, Sarah, and Emma.

After dinner we sat around at my mom's going over the list of names one last time. Joan and I amused ourselves looking through magazines. Perhaps a name might just pop out at us. And then there it was, a beautiful photograph of a mother and daughter with their heads together. Underneath, the caption named the designer, Jessica McClintock.

There it was, a perfect name: Jessica. A name that would fit any personality, delicate or happy-go-lucky, tomboyish or a beautiful flower. Jessica would fit no matter who she was, whatever she wanted to be. Now, the name Jessica was like Cinderella's glass slipper: no other name would be such a perfect fit. Jan and I would name our baby girl Jessica Anne DeBoer.

In the meantime, the seventy-two hours had passed, and everything seemed right on schedule. The Gullicksons were calling the baby "Sweetheart." Cathy called on February 11. "Oh, Robby, you won't believe your eyes! This baby looks exactly like you!" Cathy went on to describe her features, her round face, her dark hair and beautiful eyes. "She's got that O'Connor look," said Cathy, referring to my mother's side of the family.

Looking for a distraction until I could meet Jessica, I went downtown to the Ann Arbor library. When the librarian offered to help me, I told her that I was about to be a mother. She looked at me strangely. I said, "I need baby books!" She helped me find four or five. That night, I said, "Jan, you don't know how to be a father yet, so you should read these." Jan looked at the stack and said, "Oh, Robby, do I really have to read these books?" I insisted he did. "Then you'll know something about little babies," I explained. "You know, that they're very tiny but it's okay to handle them?" Jan smiled and agreed to my suggestion of a chapter or two a night.

Valentine's Day arrived: the ten-year anniversary of our engagement and, we hoped, the day I'd get to meet our little Sweetheart. Because of his work, Jan wouldn't be able to come

until the next weekend, but my mom would come with me. It was
already snowing hard that morning as Jan left for work. Mom
wondered if we should wait, but I said no. If word came that the
documents and waiting periods were all taken care of, not even a
blizzard would hold me back.

Suddenly I realized I hadn't bought anything for the baby! I
put the answering machine on and took off for the Pied Piper, my
favorite nearby children's store. I had always loved the shop and
had bought presents for nieces and nephews there. My feelings
had gone completely topsy-turvy, and I felt as if I had never
shopped for a baby before. I had no idea what to buy! I tried to
slow down and think rationally. What did a baby need? A kind
saleswoman started up a conversation and helped me choose some
essentials, including assorted colors of onesies, several pairs of
stretchy pajamas, and two pairs of tights. As she guided me
around the store, she reminisced about her own children, whom
she had adopted years ago, and the tremendous joy they had
brought to her. I felt comforted by her loving words, and confident
that her advice was based on quite a few years of experience. I
chose a few more special things that I couldn't resist, including a
little sweater with Jemima Puddleduck on it, and a cuddly stuffed
Puddleduck to match.

Driving home, I felt happy and excited, expecting to find a
message when I got there. There was none. I began to pace the
floor. I called Cathy Gullickson and Diane Riccolo, but they knew
nothing. I was going crazy! Finally, at 3 P.M., John Monroe called
and suggested that we start our trip to Iowa. He had been waiting
for Scott Seefeldt's release to come by overnight express, and he
expected it to arrive the next morning. I called my mother and
said, "It's time to go, Mom! Everything is set! I can't believe this
is real!"

I called Jan, and as soon as I heard his voice, tears started
pouring down my cheeks. "Jan, you're a father, a real father!" He
said, "Oh my God, this is great!" He desperately wanted to come
with me, but he had to work over the weekend and through the
next week. He promised to come and join us right after work the
next Friday.

Half an hour later, Mom and I hit the road, heading for
Cedar Rapids in the biggest snowstorm I had ever driven through.
It took us hours to go just forty miles of the five-hundred-mile

trip. Disappointed, we stayed in a hotel. The combination of frustration and excitement made it impossible to sleep.

The next morning it was foggy, and the snow was two feet deep. At breakfast, the motel owner discouraged us from pushing on, but I was determined to try. The weather was still terrible, but we made it almost to Gary, Indiana, before it became impossible to see. We went into the McDonald's at the next rest stop feeling very discouraged. But there, a truck driver told us that just past Gary, it was sunny! So we made our way back onto the highway, and sure enough, the weather improved.

It was evening by the time we arrived in Cedar Rapids. My mom insisted that we stop at a mall and get a car seat for the baby. While we were there, she also bought a little jacket, size 3T. I said, "Mom, that's huge!" She said, "Robby, babies grow fast." I shrugged. Mom knew best; she'd raised nine of us!

Finally, we headed for the Gullicksons' house, but somehow we got lost and ended up in a different town. We phoned and they said, "Stay where you are. We'll come and get you." Apparently, they had been waiting all afternoon. John found us and escorted us back. When we got there, I opened the door to a roomful of cousins, with Mom by my side, and there was Cathy, holding a sweet bundle of joy. As I got closer, my palms began to sweat. Would this little infant feel the closeness that I was feeling?

Oh my, she was gorgeous. "Cathy, those eyes!" I wanted to hold her. Mark grabbed the rocker, and I sank into it, my arms extended. Cathy placed her in my arms. Jessica, my sweet Jessica! Jan, who had just called moments before we walked in, was on the phone with Diane. Now she passed me the receiver. "Jan, she's more beautiful than life itself. Oh! She's grabbing my finger. I wish you could be here!" I had begun crying and laughing all at once. Our dream was coming true, but Jan wasn't here to share it with me.

"I'm coming as soon as I can," he promised.

I said, "Jessi just motioned, 'I can't wait to meet you, Dad!'" I told Jan that Cathy and Mark were making a video as we spoke, and that we would send it the next day by Express Mail, along with some pictures of Jessi.

The Gullicksons were talking about Jessi's beautiful large hands, how calm she was, and how alert. One of the Gullickson children said that Jessi loved black-and-white pictures and would

smile at a panda they'd made for her. All the while, in the midst
of the commotion, loud voices, and laughter, Jessica stared at me,
calm and curious. "I'm your mom," I told her softly, trying on the
word. "Jessi's mother, Jessi's mom." I could feel my own mother's
eyes on me, and felt her loving understanding of this moment.
Her daughter was becoming a mother.

Cathy showed me the diary she'd started for Jessi and urged
me to continue it each day, so Jessi would have it to look back on
when she was older. I loved my own baby book that my mother
had prepared for me, and what a joy it had always been. I knew I
would write one for Jessi. I read Cathy's description of picking
Jessi up from the hospital on the eleventh, and who her first
visitors had been. Cathy had taken some pictures that day and
these were in the book. She noted that Jessi drank two and a half
ounces of milk but wasn't sleepy afterward. She liked her pacifier.
She liked the warm water in her first bath.

Cathy had written:

*Sweetheart enjoys multiple kisses and cuddles from Cathy
. . . Sweetheart earned her name by sleeping until 4:45 A.M. . . .
had full four ounces and went right back to sleep. Cathy feels
like a new woman, rested! Robby called. No word from John
Monroe. We're all having anxiety, except for Sweetheart, who's
sleeping peacefully . . .*

*Call from her new dad. Mom and Grandma on their way
from Michigan to Iowa . . . Sweetheart's one-week birthday: at
9:30 A.M., her first coo. She talked to Cathy. Must have been
saying how excited she was to meet Mommy and Grandma
later that day. At 10 A.M. she got a brand-new outfit from Aunt
Cathy and Uncle Mark. 4 P.M., had a nice nap, but now I'm
hungry again. I'm very careful to stay neat, so I'm clean to meet
my mom. 6 P.M., still waiting. Had a bottle. 6:30: Riccolos are
waiting, too. 7:30, they're nearby at last. Mark and John went
to bring them home. 7:50, met Grandma and Momma at last.
Dad is on the phone. Hello, my new life. I'm Jessica Anne.*

It was time for Mom, Jessica, and me to move out of the
Gullicksons' house; I gave Cathy a grateful hug and took the
diary, along with Jessi and our things, to the Riccolos' house,
where they had a nursery set up in the basement, a little home
away from home. A cozy fireplace warmed the room. A wooden

cradle sat beside the couch that opened up into a bed. The wet bar had been magically transformed into a changing table, and Jessi's little clothes, which Diane had borrowed from a neighbor, sat neatly folded and ready to use.

I had borrowed a monitoring system from my neighbor Jean. I was setting it up when John came down and said, "What do you need that thing for? Put it away!" I said, "What do you mean?" He said, "Oh, you'll hear her. You'll hear her because you're not going to be very far away from her." Of course he was right! But it would take some getting used to. John said, "Now just put her in bed, and she'll be fine. You might want to go to say good night to your mom, Diane, and the kids."

Upstairs, my mom said, "Is she down? That's great. Well, you might want to follow soon."

I said, "Hey, it's early. I'll be okay."

"Well," Diane interjected, "she's a pretty good sleeper, but all the same, it's a big change from what you're used to. She'll be up in another two hours or so for a feeding." I got the picture. I wasn't going to get any sleep! "Welcome to motherhood" was what they were trying to say.

I laughed and said good night, but downstairs I had to call Jan once more, just to tell him again how beautiful our daughter was. Jan said, "Tell me exactly what she looks like!" He was so happy, so excited. He couldn't wait to see her in person.

I gazed at Jessi, unable to take my eyes off her. Finally I lay down to sleep, but it was no good; Jessi was too far away. I gently picked her up and put her next to my chest. Feeling her heartbeat and listening to her breathing soothed me to sleep.

Suddenly I was awakened by *crying!* What was that noise? It was only two hours since we'd gone to bed, but Jessi was hungry. Fortunately, Diane's daughter Jennifer had made up several bottles before we'd gone to bed. It took me a couple of minutes to warm the bottle, and Jessi howled. Finally, as she sucked on the bottle, she calmed down and fell back asleep.

In the morning, John and his three daughters, Jennifer, Erin, and Megan, came down to see how I'd survived the night. The girls jumped on the end of the bed and peered under the covers at Jessi. John just grinned. "So how was your night?" he asked. I looked at the clock. It was six in the morning. I said, "What night? I feel like I'm just beginning to get some sleep!" John just laughed and headed upstairs, while the girls stayed to help me get Jessi ready for the day.

In the days that followed, I got used to Jessi's pace and settled in for the weeks that we would be in Iowa. We would stay there until all the necessary legal proceedings had taken place that would allow us to go home to Ann Arbor as a family. I met John Monroe for the first time in person when he stopped by for the first of a few visits with us at the Riccolos'. One day when he was there, the family was gathered downstairs playing with Jessi. He said, "I spoke with Cara, and she likes Jessica's name. She misses her." I felt Cara's presence for the first time. John also mentioned that Cara's mother was upset about Cara's having given Jessi up, and wanted to know if she could see her. Apparently, she had learned about Cara's pregnancy only four days before the baby was born! That seemed so strange to me, because as we understood it, Cara lived with her parents. John went on to say that Cara's mother had been upset at the hospital, not wanting Cara to give the baby up for adoption.

I felt very uncomfortable. I said, "I think you should go back and tell Cara that if she would like Jessi back, she may have her. I'll try to look at this as a babysitting job and get on with my own life." My throat tightened. It would be hard waiting for Cara's response, but I couldn't bear to think of this going on and hanging over our heads. I said, "I will also talk to Jan when he gets here and see what day would be good for us to go and meet Cara."

That afternoon, I took Jessi to her first doctor's appointment—with Dr. Wendy Burish, a family practitioner who was also Cara's doctor. I asked Wendy if Cara really wanted to give the baby up. She assured me that Cara had been very definite in her decision. Then my mother said, "Cara is lactating now, and probably depressed. This is a difficult time for her right now." That made sense, and helped to put my mind at ease.

When Friday finally came, Jan hit the road right after work and drove most of the way to Cedar Rapids. He slept in the car at a rest stop. On Saturday, he woke up very early because it was so cold. As Jan got close to the Riccolos' house, he stopped to get a cup of coffee to calm himself down—it had started to hit him that he was about to become a dad! "One thing's for sure," Jan confided to me later. "This little human being had a father who was just as scared as could be!"

When Jan finally arrived at the Riccolos' house, it was very early morning. Jessi was still asleep. Jan was scared at first to pick her up. She was so tiny, her hands and feet so small, her head and neck so fragile. Tenderly he picked her up, and he started to cry. He said, "Oh my God, I've fallen in love all over again."

Jan doesn't usually verbalize his feelings very much. He's an articulate man, but he's usually somewhat reserved. Later in the day I found him writing in the new diary.

> *Jessi, asleep in her little crib, is the most beautiful thing I ever saw. She is so tiny, so small. Her skin so soft, her hand the size of my thumb. I just looked at her face and her fingers and her hands and her little puggy nose. I must have kissed her a million times. I lay down with Jessi and dozed off. When Jessi started to wake up I awoke, and that was the first time she saw me. She looked at me as if she didn't know what a beard was. But right away, she knew she was safe with me. It was like we had waited forever to meet, and finally found one another.*

We had become a family! It was a joyous new chapter in our marriage. That weekend, the Riccolos went away on a ski trip. They left a message to take it easy and enjoy the hot tub, and we took them up on it. The hearing for the Termination of Parental Rights would be on Monday, the twenty-fifth. As long as nobody contested, everything would be fine. Jan had gotten back to John Monroe and told him that we would be happy to meet with Cara or Scott on Monday, the day of the hearing. That Sunday night was tense, haunted by a fear that all this joy would somehow slip through our fingers. What would we do if something were to go wrong? Once again the answer came gently from my mother. We would pick up the pieces and move on. As hard as it would be, we would still survive.

On Monday morning, as Jessica splashed in her bath beside the fireplace, her umbilical cord fell off. The moment it happened, I saw it as a positive sign. This was the twenty-fifth of February, the day our dreams were coming true. Jessica would meet her birth mother after the hearing. She would be kissed by the very woman that made all this possible. The admiration I felt for Cara today would be eternal.

The hearing came and went without a hitch. Neither Cara nor Scott showed up for the hearing, and neither one protested it.

Then we had another hearing, to turn in our adoption petition. Again, there were no problems. Things were moving along as we had hoped.

John Monroe stopped by to see Jessica and to have us sign a final set of papers before Jan went home. He told us that Cara had decided it would be too hard for her to meet us that day. We were disappointed, but we knew she was in a lot of pain, so we didn't push the issue.

Jan had to leave the next day, to return to work. Jessica and I would have to stay in town for a few more days while the paperwork made its way past several desks, including Iowa's Department of Social Services, the Social Services of Michigan, and the adoption agency. The papers would then be given back to John Monroe before we could take Jessica across state lines to Michigan.

I said, "What happens after that, John?" He explained that we would wait the mandatory six months for the Adoption Cradle to complete our home study, which would verify that Jessi was in a safe, loving environment. Then in the summer we'd come back to Iowa for Jessi's "finalization." Just as we were leaving, I couldn't help asking John one more question: "But what if something goes wrong?"

John looked stunned. "Robby," he said patiently, "all the *i*'s are dotted and *t*'s are crossed. All the statutes have been followed, and nobody has contested the proceedings. Everything is fine." That was all I had to hear. Now I felt safe. Saying goodbye to Jan, I made sure that he had a piece of Jessi's clothing to bring home for Miles so that he would get accustomed to her. Jan kissed Jessica on the cheek and said, "I love you, little sweetheart." Jessi stared up at him and gave him her first smile, her first! I felt sure it was a real smile—and not just gas, as the old wives' tale goes.

We would see Jan in a few days. Now my mom and I had to tell our family and friends that Jan and I had just had a beautiful little girl, officially named Jessica Anne DeBoer. That afternoon, we went out and bought baby announcements that read: "There's someone new to cuddle and love, to spoil just a little and think the world of."

At last, on March 1, we were given the go-ahead. All the necessary papers had been filed. It was raining outside as Mom and I packed our bags and headed out the door for home. Home!

I could hardly wait to show Jessica her new home! She was an angel in the car, as Mom and I took turns driving. Securely strapped into her car seat, she slept almost the whole way, crying only when she needed a bottle. Every time it was my turn to sit in the back seat with her, I got out my camera and took pictures of her from every angle. Studying her sweet face was such a luxury. I was glad that Mom could do a good bit of the driving.

We arrived at seven o'clock that evening to a "Welcome Home" sign hung on the porch outside our front door. Aunt Joan and Uncle Barry had been waiting. Jan was by the door. I felt so supported and loved! Jessi began right away to draw out the best in everyone. Gazing at her became a family pastime. Taking photos of her gave Joan the idea of bringing out our baby books to see how we had come into the world. Jessi looked as if she had been woven out of the same cloth. My brother Barry loved holding Jessi in his arms and whistling to her softly. Jessi was totally fascinated! That night, I wrote in Jessi's diary:

> *You're a wonderful baby, Jessi. I love that you look just like me. You never cry except for when it's feeding time. You sleep through the night until it's 4. Then you come into bed with Mom. Your father adores you. I've never felt so blessed in all my life as the day you were born.*

Three days later when the mail arrived, there was a large envelope addressed to the DeBoer Family and postmarked March 1. It was from Cara Clausen. Jessi was napping, so this was a good time to open it. Inside, this first letter was addressed to "Dearest Baby Boo." Written on February 9, it began:

> *As I am writing this, I realize you are nearly twenty-four hours old! Quite a birthday, little one. This letter is so very difficult to write. I want to tell you, you are loved so much and releasing you for adoption is by far the hardest thing I have ever done, or will ever do. But because of the love I have for you, it is by far the best decision.*
> *I think of the love that surrounds you now. And I think of the overwhelming joy you brought to your mom and dad. They are blessed with a truly beautiful child. And you are blessed with people who can give you what I cannot. And I am blessed with the time I spent with you. The memories will always be*

clear and remembered with much love. Memories of your first bath. The nurse said most babies scream and cry during their first bath. I told her you wouldn't because your biological daddy is a fish—he loves to swim—and we both like waterskiing and being around and on the water. I was right! You only cried once for a very short time. You were almost six hours old. Memories of feeding you, and holding you and staring at you while you sleep. And telling you, "I love you," over and over again.

Memories of uncurling your fists to look at your long, long fingers. You got those from me—they are great for the piano, and basketball, too. Looking at your long skinny toes—those are from your daddy, I'm glad to say! Wee one, the world is yours. And it is full of wonderful things and wonderful people and love. We love you—God bless you and keep you always.

Mom

Beneath that, dated February 25, there was a letter to us:

To the DeBoar Family:

I wanted to write so many things in this letter, but it is still so painful for me. There isn't a minute that goes by I don't think of Jessica and I will for a long time to come. I try to find comfort in the thought that my pain brought some very blessed people joy and happiness. This doesn't always help. This was the most difficult and emotional decision ever made and there are times I wish I could turn back the calendar. But right now all I could have given her is love. I want her to have the kind of childhood I had. Not only filled with love, but also never needing or wanting. I just want her to have all the opportunities I may not have been able to offer.

Please let her know I will always love her—she was never unwanted. I know you will treasure her and surround her with love. Support her, encourage her to dream, to reach for the stars. Be there for her—good times and bad. Teach her to pray, to live, to laugh, to love. Take good care of her—love her—and kiss her—hold her close for me. She will always have a very special place in my heart, my thoughts, my prayers. God Bless and Keep You All. You may think these letters "strange" but they do help somewhat. Help me feel closer to her and it does help me to talk about her, too. I want to be open if it isn't too painful for you. I would like an occasional "progress report" if it wouldn't be too hard on you.

Cara Clausen

There were also photographs with a note:

I wanted you to have some pictures of her when she was "brand-new"—just minutes old. In the first ones she is being held by my mom. (You could probably cut her off if you need to.) The others were taken Sunday 2/10/91 before I left the hospital. She is a beautiful girl.

Cara had written this second letter on February 25, the day her parental rights were terminated. The love she had for Jessi was deep, unconditional love. Cara was willing to do everything she could to make sure that her child had the best in life. For that, I thanked her from the bottom of my heart. She was validating Jan and me as Jessica's new parents, asking only that we give Jessi the best love and care in the world.

For a moment, I felt as if I had taken something away from Cara, and I felt a need to reach out and let her know that we would always love and cherish Jessica. That night, I started a letter in response. The words came flowing out. I was full of questions, wanting to know everything there was to know about Cara and Scott. My mom and Jan felt that the questions might be too much for Cara to deal with while she was still grieving over the loss of Jessi. I decided they were right. So together, Jan and I expressed our gratitude to Cara and our love for Jessi, and promised to honor the precious gift of trust that she'd bestowed on us. I tucked the letter into my pocket with the intention of mailing it the next day.

Now we felt so comfortable with Jessi, so attached to her. It was hard to remember our lives before she came. Simple things meant so much: just sitting around, having tea and holding Jessi, feeding her, introducing her to the rest of the family. Life was secure and wonderful. Jan worked and I stayed home with Jessi, just as we had planned, nurturing our little seedling. This was something I had always dreamed of, and I felt extremely confident in my role. It was like finding a hidden part of myself. It was a job I could put my whole self into and come up with only rewards.

My mom was enjoying her role, too, and Jessi seemed to

enjoy seeing another face. We called her "Grandma Jo," a name I just loved. My father had nicknamed her "Jo" years ago, and now calling her by Dad's pet name made me think of him. He had died nearly six years ago, and I still missed him very much.

Like all mothers and daughters dealing with a newborn, Mom and I had some adjusting to do. For instance, Mom objected to Jessi's pacifier. She tried to tell me that it wasn't good for Jessi, but I disagreed, and stood firm. Mom was able to stand back and let me make my own decisions. That helped to reinforce my self-confidence, and it made me respect my mother even more.

Jessi awoke to a bright sunny day and a blanket of snow on her one-month birthday. "Little Pooh Bear, you look so big!" I said to her. "Look how you lift your head now!" Her eyes were so bright, so intelligent. She had been holding her head up very well for about a week. When I had taken her for her immunization the day before, the nurse practitioner had opened Jessi's mouth and said that she had never seen a mouth quite like Jessi's, with all the teeth in place, just waiting to pop out.

The day was filled with anticipation of a family gathering at Grandma Jo's, which would start around four-thirty. After that, Jan and Barry would be heading up to what we called "the North Forty" for the weekend. Together, the men had become tree ranchers and had built some rustic cabins on their property in northern Michigan. It was their "home away from home," and neither of them could live without their bimonthly dose of that special freedom.

But first there was Jessi's party at Grandma Jo's. I dressed Jessi in red cotton overalls and a white turtleneck for the occasion. A very large crate of gifts had arrived for Jessica Anne from her cousin Riley Connor Long. He was twenty-four hours younger than Jessi, and lived in California. Riley's parents, Colleen and Jeff, had shopped till they dropped and bought boxes and boxes of gifts for our one-month-old. The crate looked tempting, but we decided to save it for the next day. We already had enough excitement to look forward to at today's party.

Jessi enjoyed all the attention at the party. She loved Pinky, her brightly colored new bunny from Aunt Joan. Uncle Barry's gift was a brand-new dollar bill to be saved in Jessi's baby book.

After dinner, the boys headed for the North Forty and we made our way home. My friend Maura and her husband, Bob, had said they might stop by that night to see Jessica. I put Jessi down in her little crib and went to see if Maura had called and left a message on the machine. There was a message, but it wasn't from Maura. It was from John Monroe. His voice sounded calm, but the message was unsettling. "I'm in Florida. It's important. Call me back."

Puzzled, I dialed the number he had left. John answered. He got right to the point. "Robby, something's gone wrong," he said. "They want Jessi back."

Two

LIGHTNING HAD STRUCK. I stood there trembling, feeling totally isolated. I could feel my heart pounding. John said, "Cara has raised some procedural question, something about that first seventy-two hours. I haven't seen all the paperwork yet, but I'll be back in the office on Monday. I'll know a lot more then. Robby . . . Robby?"

"John . . ." My voice seemed to come from far away. "What's going on? I can't believe this."

His voice began to quiver. "I'll know more on Monday, Robby." He paused. I heard him take a deep breath. "There's more, Robby. Cara lied about the father."

"*What?* How can that be? Why would Cara do that?" My mind flashed to the letters Cara had sent us. "This doesn't make any sense, John."

"What do you want to do?" John asked.

"I don't know. I'm here by myself. Jan's away until Sunday. John, I just can't believe what you are telling me."

"Robby, let's try not to make too much of this just yet. It's just another step we have to take. Are you okay, Robby?"

"John, just call me first thing on Monday, please!" I hung up and dropped into the chair, weeping. Why? Why would Cara do this? What on earth could have changed? Had Cara forgotten all the things she had just written about Jessica? Why had she lied about the father? If Scott wasn't Jessi's father, who was?

I thought of Jessi sleeping in her crib. She had seemed so big to me yesterday, lifting her head to look at her family, smiling, being loved by an ever-widening circle of friends and family. Now she seemed so tiny, so vulnerable.

I suddenly felt exhausted. I couldn't bear to be alone any longer. I called my mom, but her phone was busy. I knew Joan would not be home yet. I ran upstairs to Jessi's room, picked her up, and held her in my arms. The tears fell on her fragile little cheeks. What would we do?

I snuggled Jessi up in a shawl and carried her downstairs, thinking we would go to my mom's house. When I opened the door to leave, there were Maura and Bob. I almost collapsed in Maura's arms. I couldn't speak. Maura and Bob took us back inside.

"Robby, what's happened? You're white as a ghost." Maura led me to the living room. "Here," she said, reaching for Jessi, "let Bob hold her. Sit down and tell me what happened."

"They want her back."

"*Who* wants *who* back?"

"Cara wants Jessi back. Cara lied about the father. John Monroe just called and told me. I'm scared to death, Maura! I don't know what to do. How am I ever going to break this to Jan?"

"Robby, now hold on." Maura placed a steadying hand on my shoulder. "You signed all the papers correctly and the court gave you custody, right?" I nodded. "Okay, then," she went on. "So the court will look at the adoption petition you filed, and then everything should be okay. Right, Bob?" Maura turned to her husband for confirmation.

"Well, none of this makes sense," said Bob, frowning. "It sounds like Cara committed fraud, and I don't think the law takes kindly to that. Think about it, Robby. If there weren't rules, a birth mother could come back at any time and say, 'I lied; give me back my child.' That would put the whole adoption process on very shaky ground. There would be no protection for the child. That's why the court set up all these procedures, all that paperwork. That's why they have certain time limits and requirements. You had to stay in Iowa for a long time. But once they let you take Jessi out of the state, the court was saying in effect, 'That's it.'"

"Yes. But John said something about some procedural problem with the seventy-two hours."

"Well, did John wait the seventy-two hours?" Bob asked.

"I think so," I said. I knew from Cathy's entry in the diary that John did not take Jessi out of the hospital until Monday.

Maura and Bob were able to calm me down for the moment. They told me not to panic and to share all of this with Jan when he called. I had no way of getting in touch with him, since there are no phones at the property up north. I couldn't fall asleep that night. I held Jessi close to my breast. She had no idea of what had just happened to her life. She was my only comfort.

The phone rang before daybreak. "Oh, Jan . . ." I cried.

"Robby, what's wrong? Why are you crying?"

"John Monroe called. Cara wants Jessi back. She lied about the birth father. She wants Jessi back!" There was silence. Then I could hear Jan moaning.

"I'm so sorry, Jan. I hated to tell you." My feeling of panic was back. "I just don't know what we are going to do."

"What *we* are going to do? What about Cara? She committed fraud! Did John say anything about that?"

"John's in Florida and he hasn't seen the documents yet. He'll be back on Monday and he'll give us a call then. I'm sorry I ruined your weekend, Jan."

"Robby, this isn't your fault. I love you. I miss you and Jessi." His voice broke. "Kiss Jessi for me, will you?" I hung up and heard the sound of Jan's wounded voice echoing inside of me.

Saturday was difficult. I called Joan and told her what had happened, but I didn't have the heart to tell my mom, at least not until I had more information. Joan came over and spent the day with me, holding my hand and telling me that things would be okay. I called John Riccolo to see if he knew anything—and he did.

John Monroe had called John Riccolo on March 6, two days prior to his call to us. He told John Riccolo that Cara was filing an action in the Juvenile Court in preparation for a lawsuit. This was all news to me! I felt my stomach in a knot. "Go on, please."

John Monroe had asked John Riccolo to break the news to us, but he had declined, saying that he wasn't familiar enough with the case and wasn't sure what Cara's arguments would be. "What will happen now?" I asked.

"Maybe nothing," John Riccolo replied. "It might be nothing

more than a matter of John Monroe finding the other father and having his parental rights terminated." It was all too complicated for me to grasp. I would have to wait for John Monroe's call to fill in the missing pieces.

He did call Monday morning and faxed me all the documents. Reading them was so difficult, not only because we had never read court documents like these before, but also because the contents were so disturbing. Even though I didn't have all the information yet, I felt I should tell my mom what was going on. We went to her house that night. We told her everything we knew, including the fact that we were expected in court in Iowa ten days later, on March 21. My mother's eyes filled with tears and she left the room to compose herself. Upon returning, she went to her chair and asked if she could hold Jessi. She got down a little musical clown and played it for her, much to Jessi's delight.

We all went over and over the same questions. Hadn't Cara just sent loving letters full of kind words for us and Jessi? She had our address and phone number. Why didn't she contact us directly to talk about this? Why would she initiate legal proceedings without talking to us? It just didn't make any sense. What could have happened to change her mind and her behavior? Was this really what Cara wanted? Who was behind this? Would she change her mind again?

We had many conversations during the next few days about the request Cara had filed in court. Cara had accused John Monroe of fraud, coercion, and misrepresentation. She stated that she had been forced to sign legal papers before the end of the seventy-two-hour waiting period and that she had not consulted with a social worker. Cara mentioned that she was never made aware of any part of the termination process either orally or by letter. She "let everyone assume that Scott was the father" and she just "went along with the flow."

The documents that Cara filed went on to say that the new father was a man by the name of Dan Schmidt, a co-worker of Cara's at the trucking company where she worked. John mentioned that Dan and Cara had dated for four months, and on their last date in April, they had conceived Jessica. While Dan first observed Cara's pregnancy in November 1990, it wasn't until February 23, 1991, that he learned that Cara had delivered on February 8. On that same day, he had heard from a friend that

Cara wanted to talk to him. He counted up the months and realized that they had been sleeping together when Jessi was conceived.

The documents took our breath away. Cara's allegations were full of falsehoods. When I checked through John Monroe's affidavit to the court, many things that I knew to be true were confirmed, disproving Cara's allegations. She had said that she was under the influence of medication when John came to bring her the papers to sign. We were able to investigate this claim, as Jan and I had paid all the medical bills for Cara and for Jessi, so we had a record of the medications. In consultation with a pharmacist, we found Cara had not been given any narcotics. Jan and I assumed that whatever medication Cara was given, it would not have caused any loss of her faculties. Cara had wanted to leave the hospital early, but was told by her physician that she would have to sign a release for the child first. Cara did have a consultation with a social worker on the phone for twenty minutes over the weekend, in which she described her feelings about giving up her child. Although she stated that she had not received documents about the termination, she had in fact received copies and had signed for them. John Monroe had talked to Cara "on the 11th, 15th, 18th, and 25th . . . and at no time did she indicate that she had any questions with regard to the release [of her parental rights] or desire . . . for custody."

One of Cara's letters to us had indicated that Jessica's "biological daddy is a fish—he loves to swim—and we both like waterskiing." We questioned if this statement was referring to Dan, a man whom Cara had dated for only four months, primarily during the winter.

Nothing Cara said made any sense. It still seemed so unreal, even with all those documents in front of us. We had seen Cara as a friend, an insightful and loving woman. We had felt a unique bond with her. Suddenly she had initiated litigation, and this loving woman was saying things that were not true. Where would this lead? Would we always have to be in this adversarial relationship that she had created, or could we somehow resolve this? And what about Jessi? Where did she stand?

No matter what, we would have to wait approximately ten days to see what would transpire. Cara's parental rights had been legally terminated on February 25. The judge was the only one with the power to resolve this case.

We learned more about Dan Schmidt through the documents as well. In his affidavit, he stated that he "could have prevented Cara from making the mistake she did in giving up the baby." Our minds kept drifting back and forth between November 1990 and February 1991, when Dan and Cara were working together. Dan knew that Cara was pregnant, and had figured out that this might be his child. The sad part was that he knew that Cara had given the baby up for adoption before the date of the termination hearing. This was a perfect scenario for playing the "if only" game. Why didn't Dan get back to Cara until February 28? Why was it that Cara made no move to contact him even though she had known all along, since the conception of Jessica, that Dan was the father?

The pressure mounted: John Monroe would no longer be able to represent us. Instead, he had to be a witness at the trial. Cara had made serious charges, and his reputation was on the line. With only ten days, finding a new attorney was going to be difficult. I called Betsy Petoskey, our family's lawyer in Ann Arbor, to see if she had any suggestions. She didn't know anyone directly, but she referred me to Glenna Weith, an attorney who not only specialized in adoption but also sat on the board of directors of the American Academy of Adoption Attorneys, based in Washington, D.C.

I called Glenna. She was interested in our case, but because she lived in Illinois, she couldn't represent us. However, she promised to find us someone. I waited nervously. Finally, at the end of the day, Glenna called back with a sad conclusion: "I'm sorry, Robby," she said, "I don't know of any attorney in Iowa whom I can recommend."

Discouraged and worried about Cara's claim, I asked Glenna what she thought about the seventy-two-hour question. Did she feel that John Monroe had interpreted the statute correctly? I faxed Glenna all the information, and she immediately started phoning lawyers in Iowa, asking them to try to figure out the statute and give their interpretation of it. The consensus was more or less what John Monroe himself had said in our last conversation: that a judge could go either way.

Glenna sympathized. "If the judge did cancel the adoption, it would be based less on Cara's claim than on Dan's. Even if Cara's claim amounts to nothing, just the fact that there was another father could disrupt the adoption." The bottom line was that we'd just have to wait until the trial, and whatever was going to happen would happen.

The next days were tense, as Jan and I were haunted, day and night, by the question of what would happen to Jessi. Having no idea what would come to pass, we imagined every possible scenario. Should we give Jessi back to Cara? How could we do that? Her rights had been legally terminated. Was Dan really the father? Or had something gone wrong with Scott that might have prompted Cara to claim that he was not the father? Was someone else behind this?

One thing was clear: we could not make any sudden decisions. We were dealing with the future of a precious, unique child. We had to proceed slowly to protect her. No matter how things might turn out, for now we were responsible for Jessi's well-being.

We had to decide how to handle the days until the court hearing. Maura, Jean, and Joan had already planned Jessi's baby shower for March 17—St. Patrick's Day. I wondered if we should call everyone we'd invited and cancel. On the basis of Glenna's survey, Jan and I understood that Jessi might not be with us much longer. On the other hand, our relatives and friends deserved a chance to meet our little Pooh Bear.

In the end, it was family wisdom that guided me. When I was growing up, my parents taught me to live in the moment, to enjoy what we had and not take anything for granted. Now our situation was very uncertain, but Jan and I had to put aside our own insecurities and just enjoy Jessica. She deserved all the love we had to offer, no matter what the outcome of the hearing. Instead of canceling Jessi's baby shower, we would have it—and make it a joyful celebration.

Getting Jessi dressed for her first real party was important. She had to look just right. Tights were essential. My sister Pam, in California, had just sent the perfect gift for Jessi: a beautiful green velvet dress with a big white collar—so perfect for St. Patrick's Day. Still, I felt that something was missing. Then I realized what it was. My Aunt Mary Jane always used to say, "Every girl needs a slip; you can't wear a dress without one."

Off we went on Jessica's first outing to the Pied Piper. All the women gathered around to admire Jessi as I found the perfect slip, a little white one with lace. Then, all dressed for the shower, we went to Grandma Jo's. Joan and Maura were in the kitchen, cooking up a storm. "Ohhh!" they both cried when they saw Jessica. Aunt Joan had to hold her little angel. Maura exclaimed at how lovely Jessi looked in her special new outfit.

The last step was to lay Jessi on her grandma's bed and slip on her new pair of strictly-for-show black patent-leather shoes. She was a knockout! Suddenly Jessi saw her hand. She picked it up and gazed at it, as if to say, "What is this and who does it belong to?" Then she bonked herself on the head with it. She picked her hand up again and looked at me, as if to say, "What do you do with this thing, Mom?"

I gave Jessi a big hug, and then I turned her over onto her tummy, so that she could lift her head. My little Sweet Pea wriggled with excitement—and smiled: a real smile *for sure* this time!

Jan had borrowed a video camera to capture the day. Friends and relatives started arriving. I felt so happy, introducing Jessi to her extended family as well as to all our dearest friends. The feast Maura provided was incredible. Gifts were piled high in the living room sleigh, just as they had been at our wedding reception, each one specially wrapped, with bows and rattles and little stuffed animals attached.

However, at a prearranged time, I had to slip away from the party to my mom's bedroom to call our new Iowa lawyer, Gary Robinson. He had been recommended to us by John Riccolo. I picked up the phone and began to shiver. The shock of leaving the festivities and plunging back into this horrible dilemma was overwhelming. As soon as I reached Gary, I thanked him for taking our case on such short notice. I said, "I have all the documents here. I know you've spoken to John Riccolo. What can I do to help?"

Gary explained that he would need more time to familiarize himself with the documents. He would ask the judge to postpone the hearing. That way, Gary could find out all he needed to about the case and prepare for the trial. "You see, I'm involved in a trial now with another case," Gary said. "I'm just hoping that it will be over by the twenty-first so I'll be able to help you." Gary asked me to fax him all the files right then, while he was still at his office, so he could look them over. He also needed a letter from me stating that I had hired him to take on this case.

I promised to send Gary what he had asked for. Then I tried to pin him down about what he really thought. "I need time to look everything over." Gary refused to be pressured. I was disappointed that it all seemed so vague, so murky! I wanted a concrete "This is what will happen" answer, but nobody was willing, or able, to give me that.

After the conversation, I returned to the party while Jan slipped out to fax all the documents to Gary. The guests were in such a festive mood! Only Joan and Maura knew about the hearing coming up, so I had to mask my own fears. Live in the moment, I struggled to remind myself. I opened another gift. It was a hand-knit sweater with an Irish shamrock, a lovely piece of work and such a thoughtful gift. Then I flashed on an image of myself after the hearing, having to pack up and return every gift. It was terrible! Still, I was able to draw comfort from knowing that if everything did fall through, I would still have all these wonderful people to fall back on.

The next day, Anne from the adoption agency called to see how Jessica was doing. I told her the horror story of what was happening. I asked her if she could give me any advice. Anne said that she had never dealt with a case like this before. Like everyone else, Anne said, "You'll just have to wait for the hearing, Robby. It will be up to the judge to decide where Jessica belongs."

By then, Gary had read the material. Because of his other case, he had asked the judge to postpone the hearing, but the judge had denied the request. At least the suspense would be over sooner. Two days after Jessi's shower, Jan and I drove to Iowa, our first time ever leaving our Sweet Pea with anyone. Gary recommended leaving her at home for this trip. Of course, we knew that Jessi was in good hands at Grandma Jo's. Barry was there to help, Jean planned to bring her children over there to play with Jessi, and after work Joan would take over and bring Jessi back home to her own bed. Still, it was very hard to say goodbye and know that we might be returning in a day or two with an order to bring Jessica back to Iowa.

We left right after Jan got home from work. As we drove, I noticed that Jan's sweatshirt smelled like Jessica. What a glorious fragrance it was! That night Jan and I slept holding the shirt close to us. I don't know if we could have slept at all without the comfort of that shirt.

We arrived the next morning just in time for an appointment with John Monroe and Gary in John Riccolo's office. Jan and I listened nervously as John Monroe explained that he had made a thorough search, but he'd found no case that legally resembled ours. No birth mother in the state of Iowa had ever terminated her rights, allowed an adoption petition to be filed, and then come back and said that she had lied about the baby's father. John Monroe explained: "This is why I wasn't able to give you a concrete answer." In effect, Jessi was in legal limbo.

Nor was there a precedent to guide the court in assessing the birth father's claim. As Glenna had told me on the phone, it was in the judge's discretion to make sense of this case and come out with the right solution. What would that be?

Gary had three possible scenarios in mind. First, the judge would throw the case out. A second possibility was that the judge would look at the fraud Cara had committed and respond by having a full trial on the issue.

"If that happens," John Monroe cut in, "then you'd better be prepared for a full investigation, which will take time and money, not to mention all the emotional upheaval." Jan and I looked at each other. We were both thinking: Please, not that.

"The third possibility isn't any better," Gary said. "On the basis of the evidence presented by Dan Schmidt at this hearing, the judge could decide that Dan is the biological father. If so, this will stop the adoption petition from ever being completed." Gary went on to say that if that happened and we wanted to challenge it, our only hope would be to go into full litigation to try to prove that Dan was not the biological father.

It was grim. All these scenarios led to only one conclusion: that Jessica was coming back to Iowa.

Should we simply give her back to Cara now? We didn't want to hurt Jessi. She was our number one consideration. What would be best for her? What would happen to her? The best advice we could get was this: we could not give Jessi back to Cara now, because we were her legal guardians. Cara had terminated her rights. There was no proven birth father. If we were to try to give Jessi back now, she would go into foster care with an entirely new set of guardians. We could not bear to do that to Jessi. We had no proof that this action of Cara's was coming from her heart. Her previous actions had been so loving. We were confused, but remained clear about one thing: Jessi came first. We had to make all of our decisions based on our commitment to her.

The next day we headed for the stately pillared courthouse. All three attorneys were with us; still, Jan and I were terrified. He held my hand. John Monroe told us that he had witnesses on call if we should need them, including the nurses who had witnessed Cara's signature on the legal papers and the social worker Cara had consulted with while in the hospital.

Jan and I were told to wait in the courtyard on the first floor while the lawyers went down into the judge's chambers. As we stood waiting in the courtyard next to a marble pillar, I suddenly looked across and saw Cara's mother, whom I recognized from the photos that Cara had sent us. I assumed that the man with her was Cara's father. Then I saw Dan and Cara. I was glad they didn't see us behind the pillar as they went downstairs.

Suddenly I felt so anxious, I was afraid that I might faint. I headed for the bathroom to splash some cold water on my face. When I came back out, I was surprised to see Jan talking to our lawyers. "What's going on?" I asked as I approached them.

John Riccolo said, "So far, so good!"

I said, "What's happened?" It hadn't been more than five minutes since Dan and Cara had walked into the building. Gary responded, "Never in my life would I have predicted this outcome. I've been a litigator for a long time, but most of my cases don't have such happy endings."

"It *was* pretty unusual," John Monroe agreed. He seemed a little confused as to how the judge had resolved the problem. He said the judge looked at the statute and read: "The Juvenile Court shall retain jurisdiction . . . to allow a Terminated Parent to request [reinstatement of one's right] vacating the termination order if . . . a Petition for Adoption of the child is not on file." Of course, in this case, our adoption petition *was* on file! The judge had dismissed Cara's request because he felt the Juvenile Court did not have jurisdiction.

Nor had Dan managed to get his parental rights reinstated. The judge found that Dan's rights had never been terminated, so there was nothing that the judge could reinstate. There was no proof that Dan was the father. The adoption petition had listed a different father, so Dan's request was held to be moot.

Jan looked relieved, and so did Gary. John Riccolo seemed a bit subdued. "Aren't you pleased?" I asked. Hesitantly, he said, "It's good. But it's only a small victory." I felt a chill. Small victory? What did he mean? John patted my shoulder. "It's just that there might be more litigation ahead," he explained. "Let's hope not."

Then Gary started to describe the way Jackie, Dan and Cara's attorney, had behaved in the courtroom. As soon as the ruling was announced, she became very agitated. We wondered what this might indicate about her future actions.

Jan and I shook hands with our lawyers. Gary said, "There's a small chance that they will appeal, but I can't imagine it. If they do, of course I'll let you know." John Monroe was still in a quandary. He felt that the judge's determination that the case was outside the jurisdiction of his court could be challenged, and I could see that he was worried about it. John Riccolo's phrase "small victory" popped back into my mind. Once again, Jan and I were confused. Yet the lawyers were confident that, for now, everything was okay.

We celebrated over lunch that day with the Riccolos and Gullicksons. They invited us to stay for the night, but we couldn't wait to get home to Jessi.

On the road, I thought of Cara. She must have had a terrible sense of loss. It had to be very hard—maybe the hardest thing in the world—to give up a baby. I hoped that at some point she'd feel again the way she had felt when she wrote us those beautiful letters: resolved that she had done the best thing for her daughter.

I thought of the crate at home filled with presents from little cousin Riley. Now, I'd finally feel safe in opening it. I saw it as a symbol that things were normal at last, and that Jan and I could settle back and enjoy being Jessica's parents.

Diary entry from Aunt Joan, March 21, 1991:

> *Everyone pitched in to take care of Jessica while Mom and Dad went to Iowa. Each of us has cherished the time we have been able to spend together and also learned a few things at the same time. Jean found out she is more than capable of taking care of seven kids at the same time. What energy! Grandma*

learned that Jessi is a mover—it takes her no time to get across a king-size bed. Joan learned about the responsibilities of parenthood and what it would be like to be a working mom. Jessica "talked" to Barry. She loves his whistling. All the neighbors came to see Jessica at Jean's house. Good news from Mom and Dad. They are on their way home.

Our drive home was long, but well worth the effort. We stayed up late, loving Jessi. What a gift! She seemed even more alert than when we left, and wanted more attention than ever. "She wants me to hold her every minute," I wrote in the diary.

We hoped we wouldn't see Iowa again until August 3, the finalization date for Jessica's adoption. The next five months would go smoothly. The Adoption Cradle had been authorized to supervise Jessica's placement by Judge Van D. Zimmer of the District Court of Iowa.

I looked forward with pleasure to the finalization of the adoption and, of course, another celebration with the Riccolos and the Gullicksons. It would be such a joyous day, signifying an end to all the red tape and allowing us to move forward like any other family. The Juvenile Court of Linn County, Iowa, had just ruled that Jessica was well on her way to becoming a DeBoer.

Three

CARA APPEALED HER CASE to the Supreme Court of Iowa on March 26, 1991. It is difficult to convey in words our feelings of remorse and betrayal. Jan and I had fallen in love with a little child named Jessica. She had stolen our hearts.

Cara asked the court to assess her constitutional rights with regard to the seventy-two-hour statute. Cara had signed the papers forty hours after Jessi's birth because she had wanted to leave the hospital and could not do so until after the papers were signed. The statute stated that she couldn't sign until seventy-two hours after the birth. Dan also intervened in the adoption, but at the District Court level. He agreed to submit to blood tests to prove his paternity, but in the meantime he wanted his daughter turned over to his "custody and control."

There was no way that Jan and I could turn Jessi over to Dan. If we were to give her up now, we were told, she would not even go to him. We believed she would go into foster care, since there was no proven biological father. That went completely against what Cara had said she wanted for her child. The words she had written to us still reverberated inside of me: "I want her to have the kind of childhood I had. Not only filled with love, but also never needing or wanting. I just want her to have all the opportunities I may not have been able to offer . . . I know you will treasure her and surround her with love." We assumed that Cara was still engaged to be married to Scott. Who was to say what might happen? Would they marry? Would Scott or Dan turn out to be the biological father? We could not let Jessi end up in further limbo while all of this was resolved.

We tried so hard not to let any of this happen. Did we try hard enough? We did our best. Believe me when I say that there was nothing gained by anyone after this terrible day. All of us were sucked into legal quicksand with nothing to grab on to.

Our attorneys had no idea what the final outcome would be for Jessi. There wasn't one professional I contacted who could tell me exactly how this would unfold. There was not a single case history in Iowa to show us a clear path. Since each state has its own set of laws, case histories, and legal precedents, it would do us no good to research similar cases in other states. John Monroe tried to put an end to the legal entanglement before it went any further. His research of Iowa case law indicated that since Cara had failed to attend the termination hearing to argue her claim, the seventy-two-hour question was moot; her rights had in fact been terminated. He wrote a letter to Jackie, Dan and Cara's lawyer, asking her to outline the legal basis for her appeal. John had done extensive research and saw no legal merit to it.

Pointing out that without concrete arguments, it made no sense to subject everyone to the time and expense of an appeal, John wrote in his letter: "If you have any authority which indicates that my position is wrong or that there is a good faith argument for the extension, modification, or reversal of existing law, I would appreciate your notifying me accordingly." John was hoping, as we all were, that the legal battle would end then and there.

But Jackie had a different agenda in mind. Refusing to disclose any arguments supporting her case, she nevertheless claimed that several points could be made on Cara's behalf which had not been addressed earlier. She said she intended to proceed vigorously on account of Cara's wholehearted commitment to the appeal. John had tried to be a mediator, putting an end to the litigation, or at least initiating some conversation between the parties, but Jackie just said no. They were pressing ahead no matter what the consequences.

In a court document, Jackie mentioned that Cara had gone to a meeting of a group called CUB (Concerned United Birthparents) on March 4. The meeting was held at St. Luke's Hospital, where Jessi was born. Cara, grieving over the loss of her child, had seen a notice of the meeting, and attended, hoping that the group would help her through this difficult period. It was this group that put Cara in touch with Jackie, who had a reputation of being a persistent, aggressive "for cause" lawyer. As I saw it, Cara had gone to the CUB meeting looking for support for the enlightened but difficult decision she had made. Instead, she was encouraged neither to mourn nor to recover, but to retrieve Jessica.

Our household was overflowing with tension. The fear of losing Jessica was overwhelming, but not knowing for certain who would be taking care of her was unbearable. We needed a break. Easter had arrived, and Pooh Bear was eight weeks old. I focused on the fun of the season: baskets of candy and our traditional Easter egg hunt at my mom's. It would be a warm family time, a perfect escape from the turmoil. The weather cooperated with a crisp sunny day as we waited for my brother Jim, who was coming down from Grand Rapids with his fiancée, Gerri, and her young son, Jordon.

Jessi was precious in her white cotton sailor dress, a gift from one of my aunts. Nestled against my chest in her Snugli, she cooed and laughed as we walked around the yard hiding the brightly colored eggs that Jessi and I had helped decorate the day before. I talked to her all the time, certain that she heard the love in, if not the meaning of, my words. "Here's the pink one, Pooh! Where shall we hide this one? How about under this branch? Now, don't tell anyone where we put it!" She watched me and listened, laughing whenever I paused. Our rhythms were totally in synch.

The combination of fresh air in my lungs and my baby close to me helped me to focus on the one most important person of the day, my daughter. Sitting on a boulder overlooking the rolling hill, a beautiful row of pines isolating us from the rest of the world, I cherished our moments together. This was the yard I had run through to find our Easter eggs, hidden by a brother or a sister. This was my heaven. I pictured Jessi running through the yard and rolling down the hill someday. "Please, God," I whispered. "Don't take away what you've just given us."

Diary, March 31:

Jessi, you are a very pleasant baby, with a great personality. You laugh and coo. You are a cruiser, wanting to crawl. Jessi

*can't figure out who Miles is, or what he is, but he likes to lick
your head. You think that's funny. Miles cries right alongside
of you when you are upset. I have never seen such a pair, made
for each other. After church today, we went out to brunch. We
had a wonderful time! Even I was able to let go and forget our
troubles enough to laugh.*

My sister Pam, a paralegal, called during the Easter holiday.
She had done some research, and told me that it would cost in the
range of thirty to fifty thousand dollars to go to the Iowa Supreme
Court for Cara's case alone. My heart sank. I knew that Pam was
trying to be helpful, but that was the last news I needed. There
was no way Jan and I could ever pay that kind of money. We were
barely meeting our current financial obligations. We did not have
the resources to go through litigation. If we were to try, we would
lose everything. We felt trapped.

John Monroe was fairly confident that Cara would not get
her rights reinstated, because she had not shown up for her
termination of parental rights hearing. That meant that Jessi
would go to Dan, if he could prove his paternity. As I tried to fall
asleep that night, questions swirled in my head. What was Cara
doing? How could anyone who loved Jessi do this to her, deliber-
ately tossing her into this legal limbo? Awakened by my restless-
ness, Jan tried to comfort me: "Honey, it will be okay." I whispered, "I'm so mad at Cara." Jan listened as I talked it out, first
blaming Cara, then blaming myself. I wanted so badly to stop
what was happening. I felt responsible for making sense out of
everyone's actions and for keeping Jessi's future from careening
out of control. Jan reminded me that the judge was the only one
who could change the course of events at this point. "How could
any of this be your fault?" Jan asked. "What about Cara's lies?
You can't blame yourself for other people's mistakes."

I told Jan, "Deep down inside of me I feel that if Cara and I
had met, none of this ever would have happened. She never
would have gone to the CUB meeting, and she would have felt
comfortable calling and talking to us."

Jan said firmly, "This isn't just a matter of our needs, our
wants, our desires. We have made a commitment to protect and
care for Jessi. That is what we have done, and it's what we will
continue to do." Jan never wavered in his position. "If we don't
look out for Jessi's interests, who will?"

I thought about what Jan was saying, but I still wished that Cara had not canceled our meeting on February 25. I wished with all my heart that she had not gone to the CUB meeting. I had begun to read a bit about CUB. Their literature explained so much about what Cara had run into at that first meeting: ". . . coercing women to surrender their babies. Why not shoot the mother in the head, grab her baby and run, as criminals do in some South American countries, to fill this selfish, arrogant demand for other people's babies? Why waste the mother's and everyone else's time killing her slowly with subtle brainwashing and years and years of being separated from her child? Short of kidnapping and murder, this is the most horrible, unnatural loss a mother can endure."

This was what had happened to Cara; there was no doubt in my mind. She was swallowed up into this group. She went to them at the most vulnerable moment of her life, and gave up everything she had believed in about what was best for Jessi.

I could not get back to sleep. I was happy to see Pooh Bear stirring in her crib. I picked her up and took her downstairs for a bottle. Jessi and I enjoyed these times together. A sweet lullaby played in the background as we rocked, soothing me as well as Jessi. She fell asleep, and I carried her back to her crib. Unable to shake my disturbing thoughts, I went back downstairs to make a cup of tea. As I sat in the dimly lit kitchen waiting for the water to boil, I fumbled through the drawer and chose a box of tea. I read the side of the box:

Thought and Purpose

Until thought is linked with purpose there is no intelligent accomplishment. A woman should conceive of a legitimate purpose in her heart, and set out to accomplish it. It may take the form of a spiritual idea or it may be a worldly object but whichever it is, she should steadily focus her thoughts. Focus upon the object which she has set before her. She should make this purpose her supreme duty, and should devote herself to its attainment, not allowing her thoughts to wander way into ephemeral fancies, longings, and imaginings.

It went on a bit more, but this was the gist. It was signed: Dorothy J. Hulst. Jessica was my focus. I would never give up on her or her life. I would do whatever it took to protect her.

In the days and weeks that followed, Jessi continued to grow more aware of herself, her surroundings, and her family. She would stare at the lights, waving her fists as if trying to reach up and grab them.

Sleep was becoming more regular. Before going to bed, Jessi loved to listen to stories. She would never grow impatient as we slowly turned the pages, describing everything in great detail. The colors, the expressions, our laughter, would keep her captivated.

As spring arrived, with its promise of renewal and hope, we were preparing for Jessi's baptism. One day my mom arrived with a beautiful baptismal bonnet and gown. It was the same one that many of us had worn. Meticulously packed away many years ago, the gown retained its grace. It was pearl-white hand-embroidered silk, with lace finishing the hemline. As I dressed Jessi in it, I felt her connection to me, to my family, my brothers and sisters who had worn the same gown. How can you put these feelings into words? To look into your child's eyes and see eternity there—it is so profound that it defies expression.

The morning of April 7 was exquisite. The radiant sun welcomed us to St. Patrick's Church. Jessi looked like a porcelain doll, so fragile and fair. Jan and I had chosen Barry and Joan as the godparents. Jessi entered into the world of God as the priest poured water over her brow. She was content, not shedding a single tear. Barry, a strong man, held her so gently in his arms, looking proud as he whispered to his precious little niece.

I know that it was a very important day for Mom. With her strong religious convictions, nothing could have pleased her more than seeing one of her grandchildren being brought into the Church. I think she also felt a strong connection to Cara's mother, who wasn't there in person, but was in spirit. She had written a nice letter to my mother, back on February 25, asking her to love Jessica and care for her, and to have her baptized. Mrs. Clausen lovingly asked that when the time came to tell Jessi that she was adopted, we would make sure Jessi knew that it was because her family in Iowa loved her so much that they were able to let her go. The letter was very much appreciated by my mother.

The next days yielded to a more mundane, everyday concern of raising an infant, Jessi's first cold. Nursing a tiny child through an illness can be very unsettling, especially when you're brand-new at it, as we were. Jessi awoke one night with a stuffed-up nose. She was gasping for air. Frantic, I called our neighbor Jean, who suggested using an aspirator to suck up the mucus. We tried, but it didn't work. While I walked Jessi, Jan went to the drugstore for another brand of syringe. That didn't work either! After several hours Jessi was still crying, unable to find comfort in our arms. I called my mom, who suggested contacting Pediatric Urgent Care at the hospital. I phoned them, but they were closed. We finally ended up talking to our pediatrician's nurse, who suggested a simple nasal solution. This gave Jessi enough relief so that she could finally sleep.

Jessi was getting bigger now and outgrowing the old infant crib. Joan and Maura had offered to buy a new, bigger crib for Jessi as their shower gift, and we had spent some time discussing what kind of crib would be best. We had even gone shopping a couple of times, looking at the various styles and safety features. Now it was time to buy the crib. Joan, Jessi, and I went to a store that is about an hour's drive from Ann Arbor. We picked out a perfect crib, and I felt comforted. I couldn't control the tenuous legal position that Jessi was in, but as long as she was with us, I could make sure that she would feel safe and secure.

As we were driving home, Jessi suddenly started to cry. Joan, who had been sitting up front with me, got in back to try to comfort her. Nothing that Joan did had any effect. Jessi was so upset, I had to pull over. I was worried that she was getting sick again. I had never heard her cry so much. But as soon as I picked Jessi up, she stopped crying. Jessi just wanted her momma. That was what she needed. Joan drove the rest of the way home, while I sat next to Jessi, holding her hand. There was no question, even then, that Jessi knew who her mother was.

On April 24 our Iowa attorney, Gary Robinson, called. "Robby," he said, "I've done some investigation of Dan. He has a criminal record."

"Gary," I said, "say that again." I couldn't believe what I was hearing. At this point, we weren't even sure if Dan was the father, but hearing that he had a record was still very upsetting. Later, we were to learn that Dan's so-called record consisted of only minor charges such as speeding, nonpayment of fines, and writing bad checks. The most distressing information was that several civil lawsuits had been filed against him, including two paternity cases and two child-support cases.

Jan and I were furious! How could the court take Dan seriously in his pledge to support Jessica when he hadn't been willing or able to support his other two children, a boy of fourteen and a girl of twelve? Gary indicated that the child-support suits against Dan were eventually resolved through garnishment of his wages. It seemed that the more information we received, the worse we felt. That night, I wrote in Jessi's diary:

> *Dear Jessi, I feel like I'm going to break into a thousand pieces. I can't let you go through this. It's just too much to ask anyone. I want you to have a good healthy life, not one that tears at the heart of you. You are too special.*
>
> *Love, Momma*

Gary moved ahead with the procedure of paternity determination. The judge had issued an order, stating, "It is possible to safely draw the necessary five cc's of blood from a two-month-old." We appealed, quoting Jessi's pediatrician, Dr. Allen Dumont, who advised against it. We also submitted literature from the lab which was to perform the analysis, stating that drawing blood from a child under six months of age was not recommended: ". . . a young infant tends to have threadlike veins that are small and fragile. It is extremely difficult to extract the minimum of 5 cc's of blood before these veins collapse. Even skilled phlebotomists, qualified in pediatric vein puncture, experience problems with very young children."

The court was potentially putting this child in danger. Jan and I could not just sit back and let that happen! What if her veins collapsed? Was this something that any informed individual would have wanted? Jessi would be the only one who would suffer from this decision. In response to our appeal, the judge held another hearing and maintained her decision to have Jessi's blood drawn. The court ordered the Guardian at Litem, an attorney representing Jessi's interests, to make the necessary arrangements to have blood drawn from all the parties, including Jessi, Dan, Cara, and Scott Seefeldt.

Meanwhile, our expenses were beginning to mount up. A bill from Gary for three thousand dollars added to the strain and fear. We were just getting started, and already we were close to being out of money. Jan and I began to fight about how we would make it for one more day. Concerned, Barry stepped in and lent us some money to help us get by. He lectured us about how money wasn't worth fighting over, and how we needed to get beyond this. In the following months other family members, both immediate and extended, helped us out. It was an enormous relief to have their support.

Every afternoon after Jessi's nap, we loved to open our front door and look in the mailbox to see if the mail had come. I always opened the mailbox cover and held Jessi up so she could peer inside. We would take out the letters and I'd count them, saying things like "Here's a letter for Daddy; let's put it in his pile. Look! A magazine for Mommy! Let's put it here." One day we were surprised to find a letter for Jessi. It was from Jan. He had found a card with a beautiful picture of a child on it. Inside, he'd written:

> *Dearest Jessica Anne,*
> *Went out today and picked up some flowers for you and your mom and Miles the wonder dog. I just wanted you to know how much I love you and care about you. You'll always be Dad's sweetheart and a warming of my spirit and soul . . . in other words, you're my everything! I love you, Jessi!*
> *Love, Dad*

We put it up on Jessi's wall so she could see it all the time.

Jan began to work a second job. Now, instead of coming home for the evening, he would come home for fifteen minutes to see his little Sweet Pea. Then he'd go back out to his second job. I could see that the strain on him was overwhelming. I wanted to get a job to help, but Jan felt strongly that I should stay home to take care of Jessi. Jan insisted that it was his responsibility, and his alone, to care for his family. I was not accustomed to such rigidity in Jan, or even in my childhood home, a generation earlier. My mom, a nurse, had worked professionally while we were growing up. Jan remained adamant. His upbringing had convinced him that the man is the breadwinner in the family. Finally, I found a compromise. Having worked most recently in interior design, I started sewing at home, making window treatments. Making a little bit of extra money was better than letting Jan carry the burden alone.

From then on, while Jessi and Jan slept, I would stay up and work. I'd begun to relieve some of my frustrations by writing them down. Thrashing out the issues on paper seemed better than having my mind constantly cluttered with these thoughts. I wrote:

This is a very hard day. I know in my heart that we don't stand a chance without more money. I guess I'm still praying for a miracle. I woke up at 5 A.M. to give Jessi a bottle. She wouldn't go back to bed, so I took her downstairs and looked at the pile of bills which I hadn't dared to confront in days. Jan and I are now $3,400 in debt with little hope of repaying it, and the bills just keep coming. As I held Jessi in my arms and watched the sun come up, I thought I must have been out of my mind to think that we could keep her.

But each time I resolved to tell Gary that we couldn't go on, I just couldn't do it. The thought of turning Jessi over to Dan was impossible.

Mother's Day had arrived. I had once thought that this day would never be a part of my life. I was more than grateful to have Jessi; I never thought that one person could bring so much joy. Her daddy had been busy preparing for the day. Jan, a true romantic, loves cards, and carefully picked out a card from Jessi and one from himself. We spent the day just lying around in the sun, and having a picnic with Grandma Jo in the backyard. It was a warm day; the sun was rejuvenating. Jessi, dressed in her sunsuit and bonnet, was a delight. We could spend endless hours just watching and enjoying her. What a gift that day was!

That night, I gave myself a special treat. After Jessi and Jan had both gone to bed, I got out some letters that I had not looked at in a long time. They were from the nurses at St. Luke's Hospital, where Jessi was born.

Hello there! I just wanted to write you a note to let you know what the first few days of my life were like . . . I had been warm and comfortable before my birth. It had been dark, then suddenly it was bright. I could hardly open my eyes. I felt cool. The nurses dried me off and wrapped me in warm soft blankets. The nurse who took me to the nursery told me I had a pretty face . . . I got poked in the leg with a shot to get some vitamin K. I yelled. Then I was wrapped up and rocked for a while. She sang me a song . . . I liked being held . . . I had my first bath at 25 minutes after midnight on February 9, 1991 . . . I like to

*look at my bull's-eye or my panda bear. My nurse is feeding me
again. I took 2¾ ounces. I like to hold my burps. My nurse
wishes I wouldn't do that!*

*It's 2:15 P.M. on February 11, and I think something is
happening. I'm getting dressed in clothes I have never worn
before. Some man and two women are walking me away from
the nursery. My nurse whispered in my ear, "Goodbye, bright
eyes." She says I get to see you soon, Mom. I can't wait.*

I walked up the stairs slowly and went to Jessi's crib. "Thank
you," I whispered, "for coming into our lives. We love you so
much." When I looked at Jan lying in our bed, I could see tension
in his face even as he slept. I placed my hand on his forehead and
let it rest there. As his tight brow yielded to my touch, I silently
prayed that soon life would touch all of us with its healing hand
as well.

The brief oasis of Mother's Day ended with an early-morning
call the next day to Gary. He told me that Dan had not completed
the interrogatories that Gary had sent him, asking for personal
information. Dan provided only his name, address, and little else.
In response to the questions about his marriage and children, he
said, "I decline to answer the questions since neither they nor my
answers are relevant to the subject matter." Dan was given another week to respond, but he failed to complete the papers again.
Gary had to take Dan back to court in order to enforce the
request for information. The judge ordered Dan to provide the
information, but again it was incomplete. We were worried about
what Dan might be trying to hide. Jan and I agreed to keep
fighting for Jessi, at least until we found out more about Dan.

Diary, June 1991:

Dear Jessi,

*You have begun to make sounds, babbling, screeching. Oh,
how you love to screech! You have so much to say. I love our
conversations. You have started to kiss. Well, that's what I call
them. It's more that you like to suck on Mommy and Daddy's
face. You can pick up most things, and you're learning to crawl.
Your favorite book is* The Real Mother Goose. *You love your
tubby time and Daddy coming home. You spend a lot of time
in your swing talking to Miles. The thing you hate the most is*

when Mom is talking on the phone. You have begun to sit up
without any support, and you still hate to go to bed by yourself.

We planned our first picnic of the summer for Father's Day,
a day to have fun, relax, and celebrate. Our neighbor Randy and
her husband, Richard, came over to join us with their three young
sons—Ben, six; Nick, five; and Graham, who was one. The boys
and men played ball in the backyard while Randy and I fed Jessi.
Jean had just moved away, and I missed her. Her new house was
only a few miles away, so we could arrange times to see each
other, but the convenience of walking out our front doors and
sharing time spontaneously was gone.

I felt very lucky to have Randy and her family close by.
Randy and I had a lot in common and we were already friends,
sharing our lives over tea as we sat in each other's kitchens.
Richard had grown up nearby, and was in my brother Jerry's class
in school. With all our legal and financial problems, Jan and I felt
rich and blessed when it came to the people around us.

After everyone had gone home and Jessi was tucked in, Jan
and I sat and reminisced about when Jessi was a newborn. He had
been so proud to take her out. He wanted the whole world to
know he was a father. I felt so good about his whole approach to
"fathering." He was warm and caring, relaxed and tender with
Jessi. She adored him. You could see it in her face whenever Jan
was with her.

At the end of June, we had a big family gathering in Grand
Rapids for my brother Jim's wedding. Our car was all packed,
with Jessi's portable crib in the back, and we were just pulling out
of the driveway when the mail was delivered. There was a large
envelope from Gary's office. After having had a few months to
compile the information on Cara's case, Jackie had filed a brief in
the Supreme Court of Iowa. "Don't read it now," Joan advised.
"You don't need this grief right now." But I couldn't help it. I had
to know what Cara's claims were.

She stated that John Monroe had misrepresented her, that he
had not informed her of her rights, or told her that she was
allowed to change her mind. Cara denied that she had ever been
counseled by a social worker. I felt my anger rising. The court
documents filed with the brief were enough to disprove her
statements. A judge could not possibly entertain her claims! The

process had been overseen by a lawyer, and the courts themselves had approved all of the documents. How could Cara draw all of us into this—and how could the system allow her to do it?

Although the seventy-two-hour statute had not been met, Cara's failure to attend the termination hearing meant that her rights were legally ended. The judge at the hearing had said that the releases were "in proper form." Even Jessi's Guardian ad Litem, Rick Boresi, had stated, "I've reviewed these documents and it appears to me, your honor, that everything has been done correctly and the proper procedure has been followed in this case." The paperwork had also passed over the desks of Iowa's Department of Social Services, and Michigan's, too! How was it possible that so many professional people could have been wrong?

With Jessi sleeping peacefully in the back seat, Jan and I talked about this latest bit of news as we drove to Grand Rapids for the wedding. We had to talk ourselves into rallying for this happy family occasion, no matter how overwhelmed we felt. As it turned out, just seeing everyone and sharing Jessi with them were enough to change our mood. After the wedding, many members of my family read through the brief, trying to familiarize themselves with Cara's claims. I hoped that Pam would be able to give me some answers, but after reading the documents she felt she would have to read Gary's brief before commenting. No one had the answers, but the love and concern shown to Jan and me by the whole family gave us the strength we needed to go on.

Jessi and I spent many long summer days at the pool in Joan's apartment complex. Cara had mentioned in her letter that Jessi might enjoy the water, and she was right. Jessi loved the pool. Her little body would just start wriggling in eager anticipation when she saw the big blue pool of water in front of her. She hated the kiddie pool, insisting on going in the big pool with the rest of the family. When she wanted to rest, she would lie under the umbrella and snooze to her heart's content. Everyone who saw her smiled. She was a bathing beauty!

On July 8 we had to take Jessi for her blood test. I had told Jan that I could handle it on my own, and I was surprised when I heard a knock on the door in the late morning. It was Joan. I stood at the door with tears streaming down my face when I saw her. I was so grateful that Jan had ignored my words of independence and called Joan to accompany me and Jessi.

We drove in silence to the doctor's office, and when we arrived we were the only ones there. Jessi's doctor laid her on the table. She felt safe with him, and seemed very interested in what he was doing. He looked at me and said, "Robby, I have been informed that they need fifteen cc's of blood for this test." I was furious! The lab had said that five cc's were dangerous, and they had tripled it! I put my foot down. "You'll have to stop when Jessi can't take it anymore!" He agreed. He ended up stopping at nine or ten cc's. Joan stood next to me as Jessi screamed. I'll never forget that day. When they took the required fingerprints and pictures of Jessi, I felt like asking for a copy of a picture of Jessi screaming so that I could send it to Cara.

After that, I began to spend many afternoons at the University of Michigan law library. I felt that if I could learn more about the law, I might be able to participate in a more helpful way in discussions and decision making in Jessi's case. Packed in her Snugli, Jessi dozed on my chest as I waded through law books, hunting for any case history that might help us understand what was happening. The library had a policy prohibiting babies, but Jessi was so quiet that they made an exception for her.

With his two jobs, Jan had no time to get involved in hunting down a legal precedent for our case. But I had the time to do it, with the support of a friend named Mary Anne, who had once thought of becoming an attorney and had spent a lot of time in the law library. She led me through the legal maze, spending hours with me, going over the case and searching out information that might help Gary if there was to be a trial. After trying to understand the scope of the legal barrage we were under, I started investigating Cara's claims in her brief to the Iowa Supreme Court. We still hoped Dan's case would fall away when it was proved that he wasn't the father of our six-month-old daughter.

On the morning of July 22, Gary called. His voice was low. He said, "Bad news, Robby."

"What?" I felt my heart pounding.

"Dan is the father."

Four

I T TOOK ME A MOMENT to realize the impact of Gary's words. Scott Seefeldt, who had legally signed away parental rights, was not Jessi's birth father. I started crying, tasting my own tears of bitterness and anguish. I looked at Jessi in her walker playing with the camera bag. I reached over, picked her up, and held her close. "I love you, Jessica," I said. "I love you so much." I couldn't bear the thought of losing her, or the thought of her losing Jan and me. "You've just started to say 'Mama' and now they're going to take you away," I whispered to myself as I rocked her.

I spent most of the day in tears. By the time Jan came home, my eyes were red and puffy, and I was cried out. "You'll never believe what happened," I told him. "Scott's not the father. Dan is." Jan shook his head in disbelief. Kicking the door open, he stepped outside and lit a cigarette. He smoked it in silence. When he came back in, his face was tense and his voice strained. "Robby, it'll work out. It just has to. We'll take care of it."

Jan has always taken care of people and things around him. Whenever someone is in need, Jan is there. Everyone trusts him. He has the knack of recognizing a person's need and answering the call before it is even made. Many times he has hopped in the car and driven for an hour to help a friend with a project or bring a tool that was needed.

Jan's generosity was one of the things that drew me to him

right from the start. I remember one evening on our honeymoon when we were on the road and nearly out of gas. We'd been driving for a long time and were anxious to find a place to stay. We pulled into a gas station and Jan got out to pump the gas. It seemed to be taking an awfully long time, so I got out to see what was going on. Jan was at the other pump, helping another couple pump their gas! I felt almost annoyed at first, thinking that he must have forgotten that we had just been saying how tired we were and that we really needed to be done with the driving for that day. Then I realized that he was just being Jan, a man who sees someone in need and responds. I got back in the car and closed my eyes, thinking that I might as well rest while Jan took over the pumping responsibilities for all the late-night travelers!

Now I saw the vulnerability in Jan as we dealt with the reality before us: Dan was Jessi's biological father. Jan repeated his words to me, as if saying them might make them come true: "Don't worry. We'll take care of it." It tore me apart to see him in this position of helplessness, of waiting for the next bit of information that would come from a lawyer, a judge, a document in the mail. We were all in that position, wanting so much to do the right thing, to feel some sense of understanding and control of the situation, yet feeling increasingly powerless and vulnerable as time went by.

Jan and I had a bad night, although Jessi slept quite well and awoke as bright-eyed as always. I was filled with joy at the sight of her, yet my heart was deeply troubled. I thought about how nice it would be to get away for a day or two, away from the phone and the mail and the worry. As if I had spoken my thoughts aloud, my Aunt Irene called and invited Jessi and me to join her for a few days at the family cottage on Lake Michigan. Her daughter Colleen would be coming with her children, Riley, now six months old, and Michael, ten. Colleen's niece Caitlin, also ten, would be there, as well as my mom. I couldn't wait to go.

Packing for a six-month-old is quite a funny experience. I packed just about everything that Jessi owned. We had beach toys, indoor toys, summer clothes for the hot days, winter clothes for the cold days, and even a few outfits for the in-between temperatures. Colleen, on the other hand, was the veteran mom. She packed only a few T-shirts and shorts for Riley. She even forgot diapers. Luckily for her, I had packed a trunkful.

It was a wonderful family time. I loved having three generations of us around, sharing our varied impressions of motherhood. Grandma Jo and Aunt Irene discussed the difference between raising girls and boys and how fortunate they were to have daughters. Colleen and I shared many funny stories about our six-month-olds. All of us felt that familiarity and security of family that have always been so important in my life.

Each morning, Colleen would wake at the crack of dawn and head down to the water with Riley in his stroller. They would sit on the deck together and watch the sun rise. Jessi and I would soon follow. The peaceful silence restored my spirit. Watching the loons floating on the water gave me a sense of calm that I had not felt in some time.

As we sat there feeding yogurt to our babies, who babbled happily to each other, Colleen and I reminisced about our own childhoods. We were the same age, and had been close since we were five or six, when our families both lived in Madison, Wisconsin. During summer vacations together at another lake cottage, we would walk on the beach, collect rocks, play with dolls, and giggle endlessly.

Colleen had always taught me new jokes and games when we were kids. Now she taught me a great mother's trick: fast food works even before a child has any teeth! She and Riley took Jessi and me to a fast-food restaurant, where she ordered french fries for the kids. Oh, how Jessi welcomed that change in her otherwise careful diet. She and Riley gnashed and gnawed at them, having a great time. Jessi grinned at me as if to say, "Where have the fries been all my life?"

On the way back from the family cottage, Jessi and I took a detour. We went to meet Jan in Hart, Michigan, where Joan and her friend Chuck had gone up to a softball tournament. Chuck had a passion for sports and played on a team sponsored by Casey's Bar and Grill, one of our favorite restaurants. Chuck's eight-year-old son, Scott, who also loved sports, had come along to the tournament with Chuck and Joan.

Chuck's teammates and their wives were there: Steve and Wendy, Jeff and Colleen, Dave and Helen. We spread a blanket out so that the women could sit and talk during the games. Jessi and Scott played in the sand at the base of the field, and every once in a while Scott would stand up and cheer his dad on. Each

On my wedding day: from the left, Joan, Maura, me, my niece
Renee, and Bridget. May 22, 1982.

All packed up and ready to leave Colorado to head home to
Michigan from our honeymoon. October 1982.

Here I am talking to Jan
as I held our newborn
daughter for the first time!
February 15, 1991.

Jessi's first Easter—seven weeks old.

Jessi's christening. April 7, 1991.

Jessi already loved the water at twenty weeks!

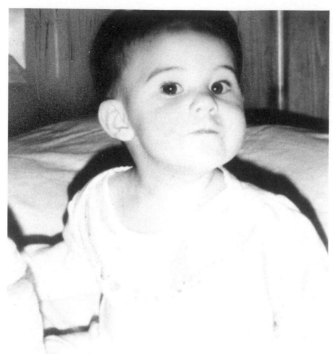

"I've got spunk, Momma!"

"I love my 'Gamma Jo.' "

Jessi with Oma and Opa, Jan's parents, at eight months.

"She's my sweetie,
I love her so." Jan
and Jessi at the pool.

"Feed me, Mom!"—eight and a half months old.

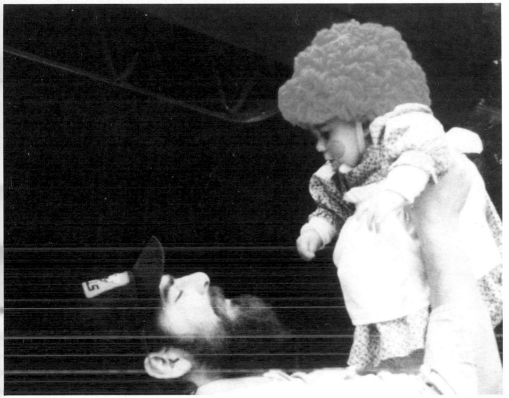

Jessi's first Halloween, with Uncle Barry, at eight and three-quarters months.

Jessi and her great pal Miles, who followed her everywhere.
October 1991.

Jessi's first Christmas. December 1991.

Jan helps teach Jessi
(twelve months) to walk
at Oma and Opa's house
in Florida.

time he did that, Jessi just gazed at Scott with wonderment. The two children became very close that weekend. Scott kept trying to lift Jessi up. He couldn't quite do it, but Jessi was very amused by his efforts, laughing and smiling at him. I thought to myself: If Chuck and Joan get married, Scott and Jessi will be cousins.

After the game, Jessi had her first real swing ride at the playground. She seemed to enjoy the motion and the wind blowing through her hair. Jessi would have swung all evening if she could have, but the sky darkened and it began to rain. That didn't stop the softball crowd at the campground from having a great time. The men struggled to keep a fire lit, and through trial and error they managed to erect a makeshift plastic canopy over the picnic table. The grilled hot dogs on toasted buns and the ice-cold beer tasted great.

All the others were camping there, but Joan and Chuck had a surprise for Jan, Jessica, and me: a prepaid room at a charming Victorian bed-and-breakfast. The room was beautiful, with a big brass bed covered with a pretty lace bedspread, sturdy oak furniture, a bay window, and pale floral-printed walls. It seemed like the perfect refuge from the storm—and our worries.

The best part of the trip was having the time together as a family. We shared a delightful discovery before heading home: Jessi had sprung her first tooth! I couldn't believe how excited Jan and I got. We wanted to tell everyone about it right away. Jessi kept pushing her tongue against it, as if she might like to push it out. I thought of Colleen and the french fries. I'd have to call her right away and tell her about this tooth!

Almost as soon as we were home again, Jan and I felt the weight of our legal problems and the tremendous financial burden bearing down on us. We had to come up with money. After weighing the possibilities, we decided to sell Jan's truck. Jessi and I would take Jan to work and pick him up. At least he was only working his regular printing job now. He had quit the second job in order to spend what little free time he had with Jessi and me. Surprised and dismayed to hear that the truck was gone, my family urged us to try to get a clear picture of where we were going in terms of financial commitment.

I called Gary, and with his permission I taped our phone conversation. That way, my family could hear the explanation in Gary's own words and figure out what help they might be to us financially. We could not keep this up on our own. In tears, I explained to Gary that we had sold the truck and would begin to sell other items in the house. "We can't go on, Gary," I said. "There is no way any of us will survive. This whole thing seems to be getting out of hand financially, and it scares us."

He was reassuring. "Don't worry about it. We'll sort it out once we're done," Gary replied. "You can't quit now. We've come too far. This whole thing is about to be wrapped up. Dan's hearing will be held soon, and we'll know something shortly. Just pay us a hundred dollars a month when you get the bills, and we'll sit down when this is all over and work something out."

His kindness in dealing with us somehow made me cry even more. I thanked him. "Gary," I said, "I also need to ask you about some legal issues. What is this Adjudication of Law Points hearing on August 2? If it goes in our favor, what happens?"

Gary replied, "We have asked the court for guidance as to whether it's a termination proceeding . . . or whether the adoption case will just handle the best interest of the child. We want the court to tell us what hoop to jump through next, and tell us what the rules of the game are."

I asked him, "What would happen as far as Jessi goes? Where would she go in the process?"

"I can't honestly tell you, Robby, because there's no authority one way or the other."

"Okay, say that everything goes in Dan's favor and we try to appeal it to the Iowa Supreme Court. Is there much chance at all, or are we just wasting time?"

"There's no real case authority in Iowa. I think, and this is my opinion, that the Iowa Supreme Court is going to say that the best interest of the child controls. Historically, that is what they have always said."

Jan and I understood what Gary had explained. We were becoming well versed in legal terms and procedures, but when my family listened to the tape, they couldn't understand what Gary meant.

"Robby, I still don't know exactly why you need this hearing," Mom said. "Why on earth does it take all of these court proceedings to determine what will happen to Jessi?"

I explained to her that since there was no precedent in Iowa that could determine what should happen next, this hearing would tell the attorneys how to proceed.

"Are they going to consider what would be best for Jessica?"

"Well, Mom, we pray that they will. Gary thinks they will. We'll just have to wait and see." I said what I thought might keep my mother from worrying too much. Yet deep inside I knew she could read the truth in my face and my voice.

The adjudication hearing took place on August 2, 1991. Judge L. Vern Robinson stated in his order: "There will be no jury trial relating to paternity . . . The court will first make a determination if he is the father . . . The proceedings shall immediately proceed to the termination hearing. The court determines that this is a matter *not* to be decided under the general 'best interest of the child.'"

We were outraged that the judge had decided not to consider Jessica's best interest. Wasn't Jessica a person? Didn't she have rights, just as adults do?

Back on the phone to Gary, I asked about the termination hearing and what we would have to do there. Gary went on to tell me about the statutory grounds for termination of parental rights, one of which was abandonment. He thought the argument would be that Dan had no intention of being a father to Jessica in any event, and the only reason he was involved in this was so that Cara could use him as a straw man. I asked Gary what Dan and Cara's relationship was. He said they had none. I wondered if that meant that Jessi would go to Cara's mother to raise, if not to Dan.

I remembered that Dan had lied on his interrogatories when he claimed that there were no civil suits against him. That would go into the court record. Gary drew a parallel to the two paternity proceedings that Dan had fought. The question, obviously, was why would Dan fight paternity in those two cases and want to prove it in this one, particularly when he had no intention of staying in a relationship with the mother? Gary said, "We can also play against what he has done historically; we can see how involved he is in the lives of his other children, and if he's abandoned them, we can assume that he is likely to abandon this child."

I asked Gary why Rick Boresi hadn't stepped in. Wasn't his role to look out for Jessica's best interest? He was Jessi's court-appointed attorney and it seemed to me that he should be looking out for her. "Well," Gary replied, "Rick has basically washed his hands of it . . . He just doesn't want to have anything to do with it. I think he feels that it should be litigated by the parties who really have the interest . . . and besides he's not in our corner. By the way, Robby, we've also talked to Dan's ex-wife. She's going to testify . . . Dan allowed his son to be adopted . . . and didn't support him."

The fear mounted daily; it became hard even to pick up the phone only to hear one more terrible thing, and we had no power to do anything about it. It seemed to us that Jessi was all on her own if Rick Boresi had dropped the ball, and we felt that we had to do something. We were Jessica's parents and we were not going to just sit back and let the court pull another fast one on us. We had to get prepared for the trial on Dan's case coming up on September 24, 25, and 26. The judge had allowed three court days in order to assure ample time for the trial.

I called my sister Pam to see what I could do to make a difference. She thought I might be able to call the University of Michigan's Department of Psychology and ask for an affidavit about bonding. Dr. Dumont's office connected me with a child therapist at the university, Sarah Mangelsdorf, Ph.D. She was a professor who specialized in research on the emotional development during the first two years of a child's life. I asked her if she could prepare an affidavit for the court explaining what an eight-month-old would go through if she were to be separated from her parents.

When I called Sarah, I had no idea what Jessi would be up against emotionally. I just wanted someone who was a professional in this field to tell us what would happen to her. Sarah said she would be more than happy to but she could not take sides in the case. I told her that was exactly what I was looking for: someone who would deal with Jessica's needs only.

Jessica's needs. I spent endless hours worrying about what Jessica's needs might be in the long run, but her daily needs were so simple now. She was not terribly demanding, although she knew how to let us know when she did want something. She was so inquisitive and responsive. I talked to her all the time, and she "talked" back. She had certain mature facial expressions that made her look as if she understood every word I said. And she did understand so many things. Mom always said that she understood so much because I talked to her all day long about everything that was going on.

She carried on conversations with Miles, too. She would sit in her walker and watch Miles go by, chirping and chortling at him. He would stop and lick her and wait for Jessi to pat him. Sometimes when he was lying in the corner sleeping, Jessi would suddenly call to him as if to say, "Okay, Miles, it's time to come see me!" Miles, ever the good friend, would come over right away and give her a lick.

I received a letter from Gary in early September:

> *Since I last spoke with you on the phone there have been some further developments in the case. We have located and spoken with Barbara [Schlicht], the mother of a now 12-year-old girl whom Dan has fathered. Mr. Schmidt and Barbara were never married, and when their daughter was about 5 years old, Barbara filed paternity action, was successful, and Dan was ordered to pay child support in the amount of $100 per month. While the child support has been paid, it appears that this has been through . . . garnishment procedures. Mr. Schmidt has neither voluntarily offered to support the child nor made any effort to contact her to date despite knowing her whereabouts.*
>
> *Also, we are continuing, through Rick Boresi, the Guardian ad Litem, and Cara Clausen's obstetrician, to determine whether there is any truth in the rumor that your daughter's gestational period was something less than 40 weeks, which may support our argument that Mr. Schmidt is not the father.*

Hanging on to the slim remaining hope that Dan was not the father seemed futile. The blood tests were 96.9 percent accurate. In Iowa, blood tests are just evidence; Dan would have to establish that by a preponderance of evidence, he truly was the father. This was an issue that we'd been discussing for a long time. I had a friend with a baby born on the same day as Jessi who was conceived, not in April, but in May. It was just another angle that Gary was pursuing, along with all the others. As far as I was concerned, it didn't seem all that promising.

The information about Barbara and her daughter may have helped our case, but it hurt Jan and me. It caused us such distress to think that Jessi's birth father had not voluntarily supported a daughter he already had, yet now was asking for custody of his other daughter.

The impact of our legal problems was quite strong, but somehow we managed to preserve a happy and loving day-to-day existence with Jessi. She was such a miracle. Every day there was something new about her to celebrate. She would have a new facial expression or a new sound; she would figure out a new "dance" in her walker; she would clap along with Jan as he sang a song. One day when Joan was over, we sat at the top of the stairs with Jessi. Joan held on to the back of Jessi's shirt to steady her as she sat and peered down the steps. I got a box of little rounded blocks that Jessi loved. Jessi discovered a lot about the laws of gravity in this adventure—she took the blocks, one by one, studied them for a moment, gazed down the steps, and then let them roll. She made a great experiment out of it, throwing some as hard as she could, gently rolling others, and simply tapping a few off the top step and watching them bounce-bounce-bounce down the whole flight. Each time she smiled up at Joan and me as if to say, "Hey! Did you see what that one did? Wasn't that exciting?"

Soon we had great family news. Joan and Chuck were engaged! We all went over to my mom's house, where everyone was hugging and congratulating Joan and Chuck, including Jessi, who seemed to understand that this was a very important occasion.

I knew I would be happy to put all my efforts into Joan's wedding. Since Joan didn't have time for a lot of details, I was eager to do all I could to make sure that my baby sister had a magical wedding day. The following weekend, my mom, Joan, Jessi, and I went to inspect a very special place for the reception, Wellers Carriage House. It had a beautifully landscaped yard with a river running through it, and a couple of large barns that had been turned into an elegant restaurant and banquet hall. Mom and I had always wanted Joan to get married in a special place, and this seemed to fit the bill.

As Mom and I looked at the room and discussed flowers and other details, Joan swished up Jessi in her arms and started waltzing around the dance floor. Aunt Joan and Jessi had a very close relationship; it was as if Joan were Jessi's second mother. She took Jessi in her stroller out to the courtyard where the wedding would be held and wheeled her around by the river.

Jessi's eyes widened with excitement and her little feet began to flutter as if she thought she could fly over into the water and have a swim.

There was much more fun in store for us that weekend; the North Forty awaited us. Jan and Barry had planted a grove of trees in Jessica's honor and christened it Jessi's Grove. Jan was so proud that we would come all the way to see the grove and the work that they had accomplished. In the past few years, they had put in roads, planted over ten thousand white pine trees, and built a cabin, an outhouse, and a barn, which they called the Timberwolf Barn. The buildings were built primarily out of recycled crate wood. Inside the barn they had built a stone fireplace that reached sixteen feet into the air. I loved seeing these products of my husband's and brother's labor.

The leaves had turned bright red, orange, and golden yellow, and a crisp wind blew through the trees. It was a perfect time to be up north, in the glorious Michigan fall. Jessica loved it so much, just being outside, with Miles diving in and out between the trees, trying to show us the way around the property. She was becoming quite mobile and wanted to be able to stand on her own. Her cute little legs, so pudgy and full of life, filled out her corduroy overalls. Jessi sat on the ground next to Miles and rummaged in the fallen leaves, having the time of her life. Her spirit of adventure was contagious, and as I looked around me, I began to see things through Jessica's eyes. It all seemed so new and fresh and alive.

Our ride home was a funny and memorable experience. The men went together in Barry's van, leaving the car for Joan, Jessi, my mom, and me. Jessica couldn't tolerate sitting in her seat after so much fresh air. The only way to keep her from crying was to sing her two favorite songs, "Old MacDonald" and "The Itsy-Bitsy Spider," over and over again. Grandma Jo sat in the back with Jessi. As soon as Jessi started to get fussy, my mom would motion to Joan and me to sing the songs one more time. "Faster!" she ordered. Or "Slow down! Stop laughing, be serious!" As we sang the songs over and over, the whole situation became funnier and funnier to Joan and me. We were almost in tears from laughing so hard, but my mom kept on insisting that we sing. Jessi finally fell asleep, thank heaven. Our voices were completely gone.

Soon after we returned home, the trial date arrived. Jan and I would have to go to Iowa. It would be hard to leave Jessi one more time. She was becoming such a little person, and leaving her behind was like leaving a part of us. "Hey, little one, talk to Daddy," Jan said as he changed her diaper on the morning we were leaving. Jessi looked into his eyes and chortled, waving her arms and legs with glee. "That's my girl!"

"We're going to miss you, Pooh," I told her. "But we'll be back soon." Randy and Aunt Joan would be the main caregivers while we were away.

The drive seemed to take forever this time. We had hoped that we could make the trip all in one night, but things didn't work out that way. The more we drove, the hotter the car got. We couldn't figure out what was wrong; the car was only five years old, and we had just gotten it out of the shop. We pulled off the road at a rest stop and called our mechanic to find out what the problem might be. On the mechanic's advice, Jan rigged something up to the fan belt. That helped for a while, and we approached the Chicago area. We decided to spend the night there, too afraid to drive the car at night. The next morning we made it to Moline, Illinois. The car started to smoke and the engine was ready to blow. We had almost made it to an exit when there was a horrible loud noise.

The car stopped. The radiator blew and started smoking. We could barely see through the windshield, but we were just a mile from the exit. We tried to drive. A rod went through the engine, and then the car wouldn't move. At that moment, Jan lost faith in everything. We had no money, and now we had no car! "Why? Why does everything always happen to us, Robby?" he muttered as we walked to the nearest service station. I didn't even try to answer. My mind was focused on the trial. We had a meeting in a few hours, and I was afraid that we might not make it to the hearing.

In the next several minutes, we were able to call a tow truck, use our credit card to rent a little blue Colt, one of only two rental cars available, and phone Gary. "Oh my God!" he said when I told him that we wouldn't be there for a few more hours. "You guys always run into problems." When we finally got into the rented car, heading to Iowa, I looked out the window and my eyes filled with tears. Jan was right; just when it seemed that everything was going along okay, the whole world would come crashing down on us. I wondered if the days ahead would be unlucky, too.

We spent that night at the Riccolos' house. Diane was sweet and tried to keep us distracted from our problems by talking about her children's swim class and their other activities. But it was impossible to forget that we were in danger of losing Jessi that weekend. This trial was meant to produce the final decision. We didn't know if we would hear the outcome right away or if we'd have to wait. We were very tense.

The next morning, Diane drove us down to the courthouse and stayed with us to be our silent support system. It was difficult to find ourselves back in the same courthouse where the judge, just months ago, had told us that Jessi belonged with us. We could see Cara and her parents standing near Dan on the second floor. Kim Ten Eick, Gary's assistant, a tall woman of thirty with shoulder-length hair, stood waiting for us. When we got into the courtroom, we took our seats up front. Diane sat in the spectators' section in the rear. Finally, everyone was seated, except Cara, who stood right behind my chair.

Judge William R. Eads presided over the hearing. Jackie, the Schmidts' lawyer, immediately asked to approach the bench, and then proceeded to enter a Motion of Limine, an action meant to stop information from coming into the court. Jackie asked the judge not to allow any of our witnesses into the courtroom. Nor did she want Cara's letters admitted.

Gary stood up. He said, "Your honor, we ask that this be a closed hearing." The judge granted Gary's request, asking everyone who was not a party to this case to leave the room. Cara and her parents and Diane filed out of the courtroom.

"Your honor," Jackie began, "this man has not abandoned any of his children." I found the strident sound of her voice to be very offensive.

Gary remained calm. "Your honor, that is a falsehood. We know for a fact that this man has other children, a daughter he has never seen and a son whom he has allowed to be adopted." Judge Eads paused for a moment. Then he asked to see both attorneys in his chambers. The courtroom remained completely silent. Moments later, Gary and Jackie emerged. Approaching the bench, the judge announced, "We will recess to determine Jackie's motion to the court." Jan and I stood up. The delay was disconcerting. I wasn't sure how much longer I could take the tension.

As we walked out the door of the courtroom, we saw two women: one only five feet three and very thin and fragile, with short brown hair; the other sturdy, about five feet nine, with short, curly blond hair and wire-rimmed glasses. They both looked uncomfortable. Jan said softly, "Don't look now, but I think they might be Dan's ex-wife, Joanne, and his ex-girlfriend Barbara." I looked at them. Barbara looked back. I asked if they'd like to join us for a cup of tea.

In the courthouse cafe, Jan started up a conversation with Barbara, as the two of them smoked one cigarette after another. Joanne and I sat quietly, drinking our tea. Barbara was talking freely about her relationship with Dan, which sounded terrible. She told of the trouble she had had delivering their daughter, Amanda, who was born very sick and needed surgery when she was just a few days old. Barbara was angry that Dan had not been around for her at that time or since. I gripped the handle of my teacup so hard, my knuckles were white. I had never heard this before. Jan lit a cigarette and exhaled slowly. "That is unbelievable," he said to Barbara. "Once the judge hears you, there is no way he'll give Jessi to him."

Finally, Joanne spoke up. She was trembling, her whole body shaking in anger. "Don't ever let this man get your child," she warned.

"That's right. Don't let him get her!" Barbara echoed Joanne's warning. That was all I needed to hear. Before I could reply, Kim appeared and sat down beside us. She said that the recess would take a while, and that maybe we should go out and walk around the town. She and Gary would come and hunt us down when it was time to come back.

Jan and I went outside with Barbara and Joanne. We walked around and listened to the women describe the painful details of their lives with Dan. It was hard to listen, knowing that Dan might end up with custody of Jessi. Nobody was calling us back to court, so we went into JCPenney and looked at clothing.

Needing some joy in my day, I knew just where to find it—with Jessica. I called home to see how she was doing at Randy's house. Randy had just come in with the children when I called. "Hi!" she said. "What are you doing calling in the middle of the day? Did something bad happen? What's wrong?"

"Nothing's wrong," I assured her. "We're just waiting for the judge to rule on whether we'll be allowed to have witnesses at the trial. What are you guys up to today? How's little Pooh holding up? Does she miss us?"

"Well, we've been out all morning," Randy said. "I took the kids to the petting farm. Jessi loved it there, and she loves being around Nick. He spends a lot of time with her. In fact, they're playing the piano even as we speak."

"Can I say hi to her, Randy?" Randy put Jessi on the phone. "Hi, sweetie!" I said. "Momma misses you. How are you doing today? Did you like the animals you went to see?" Jessie babbled excitedly. Randy took the phone back. "She was kicking her little feet when you talked to her, Robby. She misses you. Hurry home." I felt so empty after hanging up the phone.

Barbara's feet were killing her, so she bought a pair of red tennis shoes for two dollars at a drugstore around the corner. Then we decided to head back. By then, the judge had taken five hours, but he was ready to come down with his ruling. We entered the courthouse with Dan behind us. Everyone else had to sit outside. When the judge came in, he explained that he felt we deserved a jury trial to settle the issue of whether or not Dan was the father. He postponed the trial until they could find a jury.

Jackie went screaming out of the courtroom. You could hear her running down the hall. We saw Cara, who must have been upset by the postponement, running down the stairs and out the door by herself. Dan stayed, talking calmly to his mother. None of this made sense. It seemed that Dan and Cara had no relationship at all. In their brief to the court, they had said that they wanted Jessi returned to both of them, as if they were a couple. But from the look of it now, Dan wasn't supporting Cara at all. Unlike the rest of us, he seemed entirely detached.

All that day, Jan and I couldn't get Joanne's chilling words out of our minds: "Don't ever let this man get your child." Neither Gary nor Kim had any idea why the judge had ruled for a jury trial. We had already had the Adjudication of Law Points, in which both sides had presented the judge with the most important issue to consider, as we saw it. And the judge in that hearing had said there would be no jury trial. It amazed us that the law could have so many contradictions. We left town not knowing what would happen next. Diane drove us halfway to Chicago. Then Grandma Jo picked us up and drove us the rest of the way home.

Jan and I should have felt relieved: we still had Jessi. But instead we were so frustrated by the drawn-out and now contradictory process. Gary's bill was out of control, and on top of that, we had no car. The mechanic working on our car said that he could repair the engine for around three thousand dollars, or he would give us four hundred dollars for the car. We had just made the last payment on the car. We took the four hundred dollars.

We were in a state of shock: our lives were torn apart, and we had no idea what would happen next. My mom dropped us off at Randy's to pick up Jessi. Mom wanted us to come and have dinner over at her house, but we couldn't. We felt so used, so worn out from the contradictions of this case. We just wanted to be with Jessi and crawl into our little cocoon. My mom picked up on our mood and warned us that we should snap out of it and not let this carry over to the next day. And, of course, it didn't, because as soon as we saw Jessi we felt better. She looked as excited as we were when we picked her up, wiggling and chortling and smiling.

Our spirits lifted further with the arrival of Jan's parents, whom we called Oma and Opa (Grandmother and Grandfather in Dutch). They had spent the summer visiting relatives in Holland, and thought they would come and meet Jessi on their way back to their home in Florida. I had always loved Jan's parents, though we didn't get to see them very often. Opa, tall and thin like Jan, gray-haired and bespectacled, was a typical European husband: very dominant, concerned and protective of his family. Oma was warmhearted, jolly, and loving. Now, as they met Jessi for the first time, Oma and Opa both fell in love with her. Right from the start, Jessi loved the new faces and liked playing with Opa's glasses. Oma loved picking Jessi up to give her tickles and hugs. Seeing that our house had been transformed from the home of two adults to the home of a happy family of three, Oma and Opa expressed admiration and delight as we proudly showed them Jessi's room.

We had decided on the colors for Jessi's room on the basis of her personality. I'd painted the walls a pale corn-yellow, a calming color—with a cheerful bright green floral border. The painted trim was a pearl-white, with eyelet curtains to bring in the sunshine. The color scheme was a vision from my past: Bridget and Colleen's bedroom, a home away from home where I'd always found love and happiness. The corner-cabinet hutch in Jessi's room had once sat in my cousin's room and was on loan from Bridget. The water pitcher and basin were from my father's past. A forest-green jelly cabinet sat in the corner, filled with art materials for Jessi to use when she got older. Grandma Jo had let us borrow the family infant crib, while Jan's "first bed in America" stood covered with a soft yellow patchwork quilt. Maura and I had painted a row of violets under the windowsills, while a matching shelf and chair carried the violets across the room. On one wall, I had sketched a little Peter Rabbit trying to escape from Mr. McGregor's fence as he lost his shoe. The last decorating step had been the chair: Maura had painted Jessi's name on the back of the chair in violet. It had taken six months to do it all, but the room was finished—and well worth the effort.

It was during Oma and Opa's visit that something really wonderful happened. Randy was surprised to hear about the engine in the car, but she had a solution to our immediate problem: a 1976 Ford Granada. It was amazing that Randy and Richard would just give us a car! Jan and I were moved to tears. It wasn't just the car, it was the Dishmans' generosity in making such a gift. Jan and I knew we'd gained more than a car. We had two of the best friends in the world.

Jan spent some time with his dad cleaning the car up and getting it road-ready. But Opa was concerned with the thought that if there was an emergency and I needed a car quickly while Jan was at work, I wouldn't have one. And what if we had to go to Iowa for another trial? The car might not be able to make such a long trip. At Opa's suggestion, all the family members took up a collection to help us with a down payment on another car. Then Jan's parents offered to send us a couple of hundred dollars a month to cover a payment plan. Jessi, Grandma Jo, and I went shopping for cars and ended up with a Ford Taurus that was about a year old. It made us all feel safer.

Oma and Opa enjoyed sharing our simple pleasures, like going for walks down our tree-lined street and seeing the beautiful array of colored leaves. One afternoon, we stopped by Randy's for tea, and Jessi played with the boys. Oma and Opa loved watching Jessi playing with her "brothers," Nick, Ben, and Graham. Jessi just loved all three of them. The two older boys showed her all kinds of new things, like Ben's art supplies and Nick's piano. Ben was a fine artist, and Jessi was fascinated watching him paint and draw. Of course, she wanted to join in the fun! He was very generous with her, offering paper, markers, paints, and a lot of help.

Nick was quite musical and very creative. Jessi adored his piano, and proudly demonstrated her own skills at the keyboard in long duets with Nick. Graham, only a year older than Jessi, gave her a chance to see what she could be doing soon. Everything he did interested her, and as she watched him, she would shriek with delight, as if to say, "I'll be able to do that soon, Mom!"

One day, Jessi and I took Oma and Opa for a picnic at Gallup Park, a beautiful place with a river and ducks to feed. Jan was able to come down from work for a few minutes. Jan and Opa proudly took Jessi for a walk, while Oma and I sat on the blanket and talked about the glorious day and how grateful we were that they had been able to stop and see us. Oma said, "I would have it no other way!" She took my hand and promised to pray for us daily. "I hope all this ends soon," she said.

We all felt a little bit sad when Oma and Opa left. Jessi was especially sad to see them go. She'd had a special time with them, and for several days after they left, she would look for Opa, as she crawled from room to room, with a questioning "Pa? Pa? Pa?"

Five

DIARY, OCTOBER 1:

Is it possible to capture in words the essence of your child's spirit, or the way you feel inside when she looks into your eyes? Any mother who has ever written about her child must have wondered the same thing. The feelings are so profound that they seem weakened when put into words. I wish I could create a whole new vocabulary to use when I describe Jessica.

She is so beautiful. Her dark eyes dance with life and vitality. She never seems to have an expression that one might call "dull." It's as if the flame of life inside her is constantly refueled, so that she never runs out of her commitment to the moment. She is engaged and engaging, impossible to resist. I can't wait until she can talk, and yet I treasure this special time in our relationship, when we communicate so well without words.

Jessi has mastered the art of the screech. I don't want it to seem like an unpleasant sound; to Jan and me, it is more beautiful than the greatest symphony ever composed. Her screech has personality and meaning, reflecting her mood and her intent. When she wants to ask a question about something, her screech goes up at the end, like an adult's inflection. When she is excited, you can almost hear the exclamation point at the *end of the screech. Joan says that when she starts talking, we'll never have a moment of silence! She just has so much to say.*

The art of parenting seems to be something that just evolves with time. If you try hard enough you can master it, with love and deep commitment. Jan and I had definitely committed ourselves to Jessi. She was a piece of our soul, and with her pain came ours. An experience that was especially painful for all of us was trying to get Jessi to learn to go to sleep on her own. We felt a lot of pressure from friends and relatives. Some friends told us that their children learned in three to five days. Others advocated reading the books that teach you to break them into it slowly by letting them cry it out. Still others suggested the family bed concept.

None of these methods seemed ideal for us. We loved the thought of the family bed, and always loved snuggling up with Jessi. But neither of us could sleep soundly when she was in the bed. We tried the "cry it out" method, too, and that was especially painful for us. Following the guidelines in the book we read, we were supposed to let her cry for a certain number of minutes before we went to comfort her. Jan paced as I sat there watching the timer. It seemed so unnatural, so unlike anything else we did in parenting. The worst part of it was what the sound of her crying represented to us: what she would sound like if she were being taken away from us. That prospect was all too real. We just couldn't bear to put any of us through that crying.

In the end, Jan and I started to trust our own instincts, working out a technique of our own. At seven-thirty or eight o'clock we would both read Jessi a book in our bed. Then Jan would kiss her good night and head downstairs, and I would rock her while she had a bottle. I played a tape or sang softly to her, and when she fell asleep, I would put her down in her own bed. She would stay asleep until early in the morning, then join us in our bed for her morning bottle. This way we all looked forward to bedtime and to waking up together, and all of our needs were met. Trusting ourselves was the most important thing we ever did in parenting Jessi.

Cara's oral arguments were heard in the Iowa Court of Appeals on October 2. Gary said it might take months for an opinion to come down, and there was no telling what the opinion might be. We felt so lost in this seemingly endless process. Gary felt that Cara's case would not hold up after he filed a decisive brief to the court. In it, he explained that Cara had a full seventeen days to change her mind about the adoption after Jessi was born. If she had really felt the way that she now claimed she felt, then she should have gone to the termination hearing and said, "I want my baby back." The Iowa statute dictated a seven-day period between the birth of a child and the termination hearing. Cara had seventeen days. The termination hearing was supposed to be the end of it.

Meanwhile, Sarah Mangelsdorf had completed her affidavit and sent it to the Linn County Courthouse in Iowa. Glenna Weith thought it was an excellent idea to have an expert opinion on Jessi's welfare. I couldn't wait to read it when Sarah came by to drop a copy off for us. After the opening paragraph listing her qualifications, Dr. Mangelsdorf wrote:

> *If the child Jessica DeBoer were removed from her current caregivers (Roberta and Jan DeBoer) I would anticipate that she would experience a number of emotional difficulties.*
>
> *Because Jessica DeBoer has been cared for by the DeBoers since she was a newborn infant she has become "attached" to them. All infants become attached to the people who care for them, and these attachments develop gradually over the course of the first year of life . . . By the second half of the first year . . . the child has formed specific attachments to the caregivers.*

She went on to list how Jessi might respond if she were separated from us:

> *a. Stranger Anxiety . . . it is likely that Jessica DeBoer would respond very fearfully to strange adults to whom she has no attachment.*
>
> *b. Separation Anxiety . . . a series of phases:* Protest—*the child tries to regain attachment figure by crying.* Despair—*the child becomes apathetic and unresponsive to other people . . . appearing to be in "mourning."* Detachment—*the child shows renewed interest in the environment, but shows indifference to caregivers.*

She concluded by saying that if Jessi were to be taken from us she would definitely experience acute distress, with possible long-term detrimental effects.

I wasn't prepared for the grim picture that her affidavit painted. I'd had no idea what Jessi would be up against if she were taken away from us. I cried for hours after reading it, I was so distraught.

Once again Jan tried to comfort me. "There is no way the court will take Jessi away from us, Robby," he said gently. He held me and stroked my hair. "They just wouldn't take her away." I knew Jan was as scared as I was, but he was doing his best to steady me, as he always did. This time his words of encouragement would do no good. We were the parents she knew and depended on. No matter who might await her as a future mother or father figure, Jessi would suffer long-term as well as immediate harm. I just couldn't bear it. Of all the pain in this whole ordeal, the idea of Jessi's suffering was the hardest to bear.

Diary, October:

> *Dad has taken a couple of days off just to spend some time with his little Pooh. You've been showing him how you love to crawl, and stand up and hold on to furniture, or grab your dresser drawers upstairs in your bedroom. Peekaboo is your favorite game and you pull the blanket over your head and wait for someone to whip it off and say "Pee boo!" You've gotten so good at saying "Ma-ma-ma" and "Da-da-dee." We've been to several movies this month. You're so good when we go. You just stare at the screen. The highlight of the month was going to the apple orchard with Randy and the boys, and Joni's day-care group. You've been spending a lot of your time with your cousin Will, over at Annie Warner's house (Mom's cousin). Will is about 6 months older than you, but you enjoy playing with his toys. Dr. Dumont measured you. You're getting so tall, 27 inches, and you weigh 18 lbs. 4½ oz.*

The days were growing shorter and chillier. I loved to stand outside holding Jessi as the wind shook the branches and brought down the leaves around us. She loved the feel and the sounds of our outdoor adventures. One day we watched a squirrel on a high wire. Every time it moved, Jessi screeched. Then it would stop and flick its tail a bit. Jessi studied the squirrel as it sat there looking down at us. Suddenly it would dart across the wire again and Jessi would squeal again. She could concentrate on that squirrel for long periods of time, never taking her eyes off of it.

Halloween would be here soon, so Randy and her kids came over to brainstorm about costumes. She had always made terrific costumes for her kids, managing to create unique outfits to suit their personalities. Now I had a chance to do that for Pooh! I had some blue calico fabric that Jan had given me back in Colorado after our honeymoon. Jan and I had no money back then, after the hospital bills and our other troubles ate up all our savings. We were living at a campground while we waited to move into an apartment. With no cash to speak of, we lived as frugally as possible on credit cards, waiting for Jan to get his first paychecks. On my birthday, Jan drove to the other side of Denver to buy me whatever he could find at JCPenney. He came back with a strange assortment of gifts, one of which was a couple of yards of this calico fabric. It wasn't the kind of fabric I'd use to make clothing for myself, but I always knew I'd find just the right use for it. When I pulled it out and held it up to Jessi, Randy and I said in unison, "Raggedy Ann!"

I had a marvelous time making the outfit and the wig of red yarn. Jessi looked so cute; I couldn't take my eyes off that feisty little red head, with the red striped socks, white apron, and red shoes to match. Randy and I also designed some great outfits for her boys. She had gotten red felt, black fabric paint, and royal-blue sweats to make Ben's Spider Man outfit. Nick was a black widow spider, with fake black fur and a couple of tubes painted black. Graham was a little red devil, with red sweats and a red winter ski mask with little horns sticking out of it. The finishing touch was the pointy tail.

I'll never forget Halloween night. Once out on the street, we met up with another neighbor, Joni, and her three little children: a clown, a cowboy, and a ghost. Then another family with little children joined us, and another. We had the time of our lives! Jessi wasn't sure what was happening, but she enjoyed reaching into the bowls of candy and putting what she got into Nick's bag or Ben's. Meanwhile, I carried Jessi's bag and ate most of her candy!

Dan's case was set to come to trial on November 4. It would not be a jury trial; Jackie had petitioned the court to assign one judge to handle Dan's case. We had heard that the new judge, James Kilburg, had an adopted son. I asked Gary if he thought we should fight having him assigned to the case; I could only foresee Jackie protesting that the judge was biased if things went in our favor. The last thing we needed at that point was an additional complication. Gary didn't think it made much difference whether we had Kilburg or another judge.

The real bombshell was the news that Jackie had petitioned the court to have Jessica brought to the trial. Apparently Dan had maintained that his daughter looked just like him and that the judge would need to see Jessi to observe the father-daughter resemblance. Jan protested, "It's ludicrous! Did they think we'd actually put this little girl in a car and drive for twenty hours round-trip just to show the judge what she looks like?" He insisted that there was no way we would drag Jessi into this nightmare until the court decided her best interest.

I spoke to Gary the next day and asked him to respond to Jackie's motion. Gary felt there was no way the judge would order us to bring Jessi, and we shouldn't worry; but he would respond to her motion anyway by offering to provide pictures of Jessi if the court wanted to see the likeness.

That evening, Joan and I took out our baby pictures. We found one of me when I was six months old and held it next to one of Jessi when she was six months old. The likeness was unreal, as if these were pictures of the same person. Jan took five photos to a camera department and blew them up into eight-by-ten glossies. The photos proved that a strong physical resemblance does not necessarily prove a blood relationship. Clearly, there was no need to haul Jessi into court. Jan, feeling the need to make his own contribution to our case, was more than determined to bring the photos to court.

Anne Hacker from the Adoption Cradle was asked to come to court to give the judge her evaluation of our care of Jessica. Anne had come to Ann Arbor to finish the home study and had evaluated the bonding that Jessi had experienced. She was very positive about it, and was willing to testify in court on our behalf.

As November 4 approached, we waited anxiously for word on whether Jessi would have to come to court with us, but word never came. Judge Kilburg never responded to Jackie's motion, as far as we knew. As we packed our bags for one more trip to Iowa, we tried to tell ourselves that everything would be fine and we'd be back in no time. But it just felt so wrong. It was harder than ever to leave Jessi. I couldn't help crying as I held her one last time before leaving the house. Aunt Joan had taken a few days off from work and had come to stay with Jessi in our home. Joan tried hard to hold back the tears as she said, "You've done your best, Robby, and don't ever forget that. Jessi will be fine and we'll all take real good care of her." Just a few days before, Grandma Jo had taught Jessi how to wave "bye-bye." Now, as we drove away, Jessi and Aunt Joan stood at the door waving, and I could see the smile on Pooh's face. She was so proud of what she had accomplished! Our tears began to fall as we watched Joan close the door.

Once again we found ourselves in a closed trial. This time, the Clausens and Schmidts were all there, as were Barbara and Joanne. First, the judge would deal with the issue of paternity. Dan had to establish, by a preponderance of evidence, that he was truly the father. After that, there would be a hearing on whether or not Dan's parental rights should be terminated. Jan and I would have to prove that Dan had abandoned his two other children and was likely to do the same thing to Jessi. If we made it through all of this, we would go on to the adoption hearing.

Cara was the first witness. Under oath, she stated that she had dated Dan until May. This contradicted what she and Dan had said in their affidavits, that they had dated till mid-April and that Cara had started dating Scott at the beginning of May. Gary was trying to prove that the gestation period was too long for Jessica to be Dan's child. At first, Cara had claimed that the gestation period was forty-four weeks; but on account of her testimony, it was now changed to forty weeks, the normal gestation period. Gary found out from Cara's doctor that her last period had been in May. She said that she had never used birth control because of an article she had read in *Reader's Digest* when she was in high school. According to Cara, the article said that X rays make a person sterile. Since she'd had a number of X rays, she erroneously believed that she could not become pregnant.

This new image that Cara presented of herself was so different from the one we'd seen in her thoughtful, mature letters. She spoke of how she had broken up with Dan and neither one of them knew why; they just separated. She sought no prenatal care until one month before Jessi was born. Cara went on to say that she named "Scott [the father] because I was with him and everyone assumed, everyone knew that I was pregnant, including Scott, just assumed it was his, so I said Scott Seefeldt." This, too, contradicted her affidavit, in which she had stated that no one knew she was pregnant.

Cara went on to say that she told Dan that he was the father on February 27 at Spike's Tavern. She then spoke of going to a CUB meeting, during which the members told her that adoption just isn't right. They put her in touch with an attorney, who in turn introduced her to Jackie. Finally, Cara told the judge that she was engaged to marry Dan! She said that if Jessi were to be returned to Dan, Jessi would live with Cara's parents until Dan and Cara were married. After they were married, Cara's mother would take care of Jessi while Dan and Cara went to work.

Gary had the opportunity to question Cara. He said, "So, as I understand what you're telling us today, you told Mr. Monroe that Mr. Seefeldt was the father?"

"Yes."

"And you knew when you told Mr. Monroe that, that was not true?"

"Yes."

"But you wanted the adoption to go through, and you needed to give Mr. Monroe a name of someone so that the adoption could go through?"

"I guess."

"So it's Mr. Monroe's fault that the name of Mr. Seefeldt was used?"

"I gave it to him."

"Are you saying that Mr. Monroe forced you to lie?"

"No."

"Okay. That lie is something you did on your own."

"Yes."

Then Gary showed Cara the eight-by-ten photos that Jan had brought. Cara stated that all the photos were of her child, even the ones of me! Gary then moved on to Dan. He asked Dan about his contact with his other children. Dan admitted that he had had no contact with his son, Travis, from 1978 to 1990, except for three occasions. It seemed that he did get reacquainted with Travis in 1990, and saw him four times in the next two years. Dan had given up his rights to his son. Gary had told us that Dan's rights were terminated on grounds of abandonment. Gary then asked Dan, "Do you think you have treated Travis properly?"

"No," said Dan quietly, looking at the floor. "I have not

behaved right." I could hear the pain and regret in Dan's voice. He was sincere.

Joanne was next on the stand. She was so nervous that her hands shook and her voice was unsteady. She had brought the documents concerning Dan's termination of his parental rights to his son, Travis. The order implied that Dan had abandoned his son and had neglected his duties as a father, and that he was $9,342 in arrears in child support payments which he had refused to make as previously ordered by the court. This was enough to take our breath away. Dan stared hard at Joanne, as if trying to intimidate her. Joanne's voice wavered in and out. It was clear to me that she was scared to death of Dan and that there were other things that Joanne didn't want to say in front of him.

When it was Barbara's turn, she testified that Dan had never even met his daughter, Amanda, even though they all lived in the same area. Dan's paychecks had to be garnished to get him to pay child support for Amanda.

We were disappointed that the letters from Cara were never entered as evidence, and that the judge said there was no need to have Anne Hacker come to the trial. He had accepted her affidavit as evidence, and that was all he needed.

We left the trial feeling utterly discouraged. How could we possibly trust Dan to take care of Jessi? Aside from all the other problems we'd just heard about, he was on the road most of the time with his job as a long-distance truck driver. He would never be around to care for Jessi, even if he did get custody of her. Cara seemed cold and very impersonal. She never asked how Jessi was doing or even asked for a photo of her. They both seemed so detached from Jessi's life. Jan and I never could figure out who really wanted Jessi. Was it really Cara who wanted the baby, or was it her parents?

It was such a relief to come back home again after the trial. Reunions with Jessi were always thrilling for Jan and me. As we drove, we kept constructing scenes aloud about what she would do when she saw us. Talking about her made the time go more quickly. We were able to laugh as we talked about her screech, her captivating smile, her energetic legs. We imagined that her face would light up and she would babble away, kick her legs, and reach out for us. She seemed a bit bigger than when we left only a few days before. Joan said that she had crawled to the door a lot, as if to say, "Where are they?" Scott came over to play with Jessi twice while we were gone, and he introduced her to a Nerf basketball set. Jessi couldn't manage to get the ball into the basket, but did learn to throw the ball high into the air. For Jessi, the most fun was clapping along with Joan as Scott managed to make basket after basket!

Our legal bills were mounting every week. Jan and I decided to have a garage sale to try to make at least a little money. Even though Randy was there to help me, the preparation for the sale took so much effort. I was overwhelmed by the emotional burden of thinking that we could lose Jessi any day. I wanted to be with Jessi every minute that we had left together. Somehow I felt I was neglecting Jessi as I prepared for the sale, even though she was with me the whole time. I packed up our wedding presents to sell, the silver platters and some crystal. Some of the furniture would have to go, too, because it would bring in the most money. It was a painful process, but we would do whatever we had to do to keep Jessi. Gary had said if the ruling came down in Dan's favor we could appeal the case to the Supreme Court, but if we did that, we would have to sell the house and everything in it.

Diary, November:

> Something is strange about this week. I feel as if I'm going to lose you, Jessi, and I've wasted this whole week on the garage sale. What have I done? I didn't mean to take that time away from you. The one good thing was that we made enough money from the sale to be able to buy a good Thanksgiving dinner.
>
> The other day we borrowed a George Winston tape from Aunt Joan. On it was the song that I heard as I drove away from the hospital on the day my father passed away. Does this mean I'm losing you, too? I love you so much.
>
> I also just got a call from Patti Carrigan, my roommate from college. I haven't spoken to her in years, and Susan Clark, an old neighbor that I haven't seen in years, stopped by the same day. It's as if God is sending me a support system in preparation for losing you. I can't lose you, Jessi. You've just learned to clap your hands and you've begun to learn to go up the stairs. Your little body just scurries across the floor and your eyes open so wide when you see the stairs. You don't want

any help and your little pudgy legs master the first step and then the next. When you reach the top you sit and start clapping, so proud of your accomplishment. Maybe the stair climbing will teach you enough confidence to try to master walking. You also have learned to hug Nick and have begun saying his name in your sleep. Your first crush.

At a baby shower the other day for Maura you cried so hard just having me leave the room—how will you ever be able to survive losing us? Can't the court see this? Why aren't they protecting you? Annie says that no one in the court could care less what happens to you, that biology is more important. I hope that's not true.

Thanksgiving was a somber time. Jessie didn't feel good; she had a terrible ear infection and a high temperature. We dressed her up warmly in an outfit that was handed down from one of my cousins, white legging tights with rose-colored polka dots and a rose sweatshirt dress with two little gray mice on it. Jessi loved the button eyes, and she felt proud to show them off to Grandma Jo. It felt good to just sit around at my mom's and watch *The Quiet Man,* an old John Wayne movie, and play with Jessi. Her cousin Jordon was down for the holiday, and playing with him seemed to help her feel a bit better. I made a tunnel for them out of sheets and blankets which they found thoroughly fascinating. They played in it for hours, keeping Jessi distracted from her ear troubles.

After the holiday Jan and I both felt very depressed. We decided to go and see a therapist who specialized in grief work. If we were going to lose Jessi, we would need the best help we could get to survive that loss. My doctor recommended a therapist named Stephanie. I went to see her first.

Stephanie is a wonderful woman. I spent the first visit crying almost the whole time. I didn't cry much at home unless it was late at night and Jan and Jessi were asleep. It felt so good to just sit with someone else and cry. We talked a lot about Christmas, which would be here soon. Jan and I had no money to buy presents. Stephanie explained that it was probably best to put up a tree and try to get in the mood for the holiday. She urged us not to minimize or throw away a single moment of the time we had left with Jessi.

On subsequent visits Jan and I sometimes went together. Stephanie would always ask us if we had bought any Christmas presents yet for Jessi. We had to admit that we hadn't bought anything. She suggested wrapping up some of Jessi's old toys or stuffed animals, just to give Jessi the feeling that it was a special time of year. Stephanie thought that Jessi would enjoy ripping open the wrapping paper.

I understood what Stephanie meant. Money played a very small part in gift giving when I was a child. My parents had always encouraged us to make each other's gifts instead of buying them. My sisters Pam and Sue would give us younger kids lessons in crafts, while Jerry and Tom taught us how to use the tools on the workbench. They would help us if we needed assistance sanding a breadboard or inscribing a name with a wood-burning tool.

We bought the Christmas tree as Stephanie had suggested, and once the lights were on we saw how right she had been. Pooh loved gazing at the lights. "Ight" had been Jessi's first word, and she was mesmerized by these. One night Jan got out his guitar and played some wonderful Dutch songs from his childhood. Jessi loved the songs, wiggling and dancing as Jan sang. We were finally in the holiday mood.

Jan wanted Jessi and me to come to the Christmas party at the print shop a few days later. The party was in the middle of the afternoon, so I had to wake her up early from her nap. I snuggled her up in her little snowsuit and headed out to the car, trying to hurry to get there on time. When we arrived at Jan's building, he dashed out the door to greet us. He slipped, fell down a few steps, and landed hard on his ankle. "I'm fine," he insisted. "Let's go in and enjoy the party." But it swelled badly, and later that night I took him to a doctor. He had broken his ankle in several places and would have to wear a cast for a couple of months. Jessi had no idea why Dad had to wear a cast, but she enjoyed crawling up to his feet and tickling his toes, just the way we tickled hers.

Jan and I really enjoyed our time preparing for Christmas together. Using the newspaper that Joan had hand-decorated with sponged-on Christmas trees, we wrapped up Gramps, the teddy bear that I'd had for years, and Dutchy, a doll that had belonged to Oma when she was young. Dutchy had little wooden shoes and a bonnet that she wore with her traditional dress from the province of Groningen, where Jan and his mother were born. Gramps and Dutchy were Jessi's favorite toys, and we knew she would love opening them up.

The whole family went to mass at St. Patrick's Church on Christmas Eve. Jessi just loved the poinsettia plants and the decorated Christmas trees. She listened so attentively to the choir, swaying and smiling in my lap. When the music got a little faster at one point, I was afraid she would start to clap and screech!

Jan and I had prepared our house for a family gathering after mass. The aroma from the holiday candles filled the air with the warmth of the holiday season as we sat around listening to Christmas music and telling stories. A few presents sat underneath the table that held the Christmas tree. We had set up an old Fisher-Price train set under the tree, with two trains, and lots of brightly colored animals and people. Jessi was able to pull herself to a standing position to grasp the train and bring it down to her level. It seemed to come alive as Scott and Jessi moved the train around and gave the animals voices. The conductor sat patiently waiting for Scott or Jessi to pull him so that he could twirl around as he scooted along the floor. Jessi would occasionally crawl across the room to visit with me or Jan, and Scott would try to carry her back in his arms. Although her weight was still too much for Scott's little hands, Jessi looked up at him and said, "Up! Uppa!" The simple pleasures of watching Scott and Jessi play brought back the true meaning of Christmas.

Barry provided the evening's entertainment by serenading Pooh with his famous whistling. His gift to Jessi was a crisp dollar bill in an envelope with a drawing of Jessi's Grove at the North Forty. It would go in Jessi's baby book next to the other one. Barry had also made us a special family gift out of the finest red oak from the crate wood, a sign that said "Home, Sweet Home," varnished in a special way to make the lettering stand out.

Grandma Jo gave Jessi a wonderful little dish set, decorated with farm animals. Even the spoon and fork had little cows and chickens on them. The bib caught Jessi's eye, and she wanted to put it on right away. She enjoyed Grandma holding her and rocking her back and forth to the tune of "Here Comes Santa Claus" coming from the music box that she had received from Jan's sister Nelli. Jessi loved the Santa climbing out of the chimney. Joan, Chuck, and Scott gave Jessi a red velvet Peter Rabbit outfit and some toys. I had collected some of Graham's old toys that Randy had brought to the garage sale and wrapped them up so that Jessi could have new toys to play with. As Jessi tore off the paper, she squealed with delight, especially when she opened the fire truck with little tools on it. As Jessi held up the tools to show to Jan, he said, "Great, Jessi! Now you can help me fix things, honey!" Jessi beamed.

Our special gift to Jessi that Christmas was inspired by Randy's gift to her boys for Chanukah, a set of glow-in-the-dark stars that stick on the ceiling. When Jessi had helped us put the stars up in the boys' bedroom, she was especially fascinated with the moon, since it was the biggest sticker. Before putting Jessi to bed that night, we placed the stars and moon above her crib, and we all lay in bed together and read *Goodnight Moon.* We told Pooh that now she would have her own moon watching over her. We held her up high so she could reach the stars and touch the moon.

At the end of the evening Jan held his little Sweet Pea and asked God for a special present this year. "Please, God," he said, "watch over my little daughter and place a guardian angel at her side to help her through the hard times ahead. And please, God," he added as he tucked Jessi into bed and gave her one last kiss, "let my daughter stay with her family."

Two days later, Patti, my college roommate, came to Ann Arbor to visit with us and to meet Jessi. She lived in New York and had come to visit her family in Kalamazoo, and on her way back to New York, she took the train to Ann Arbor. Jessi and I picked her up at the station and took her across the street to Casey's for lunch. Jessi loved going to Casey's, where she could sit in a booth and look out the window to see the trains coming in and listen for the whistle. Patti and I spent most of the time reminiscing about our old carefree days in college. Then she wanted to know all about Jessi. My account of Jessi's life reflected the two sides of things that were always there for our family: the unending joy of having Jessi and loving her beyond measure, and the devastating anguish we felt because we might lose her. It felt so good to just let go, and not feel as if I had to put on a happy face.

Patti spent the night with us. I was so pleased that she was able to get reacquainted with Jan and spend some time with Jessi.

I had hoped in vain that we would get some kind of news from Gary about either case while Patti was with us; she would have been such a comfort. We were incredibly tense as we waited for the call. The fear of losing Jessica was tearing at our insides.

On the morning of December 30, Gary called. Jan answered the phone. "Basically the judge had two findings," Gary told him. "One, that Schmidt is the father, and two, we haven't been able to show a present intent to abandon, so we lose." Gary went on to explain that because the court had ruled that Dan had a poor performance record as a father, the judge would send the file to the County Attorney's Office and the Juvenile Court, seeking a ruling on whether Jessi would need assistance living with a single father. "We can appeal and try to go to the Supreme Court. I believe January 12 is the date . . . to turn the child back over."

Jan asked slowly, "What would happen if we got the Supreme Court to hear the case?"

"The situation would remain the way it is until the Supreme Court decided. Kim tells me Cara's case will come down tomorrow. If we lose there, too, there's no sense in appealing this case."

Jan looked pale and lost. It took him a moment to gather the strength to go on talking to Gary. Finally he said, "I agree. Well, do you think that if we win tomorrow in Cara's case, there's a worthwhile opportunity to appeal?"

Gary answered tersely. "The way Kilburg wrote the decision, it's really an uphill battle. Basically what the judge says is that it's a tragic situation, but we can't prove today that Schmidt is going to abandon the child tomorrow. I wish the news was better. We'll talk to you later."

Gary faxed us Judge Kilburg's order. As we read it, Jan and I became furious with his lack of concern for Jessica's welfare. He was more concerned with Dan's rights as the biological link. He stated: "The best interests of the child analysis does not become material in this proceeding until abandonment has been established. It is obvious from this record that Mr. and Mrs. DeBoer have provided exemplary care for this child. They view themselves as the parents of this child in every respect . . . This Court is under no illusion that this tragic case is other than an unbelievably traumatic event. Absent such legal principles any court would be engaged in uncontrolled social engineering. The law is clear that there is a general presumption in favor of parental custody which is not overcome by a showing that others would provide the children with a better home. *'Courts are not free to take children from parents simply by deciding another home appears more advantageous.'* Roberta and Jan DeBoer shall return the child to the physical custody of her father, Daniel Schmidt, no later than 6 P.M., January 12, 1992."

Kilburg took no steps to protect Jessica, but Jan and I had to. There was no way that Jan and I would simply turn Jessi over in thirteen days like a piece of luggage. Dan had never even met Jessi. The court recognized that he had a "poor performance record" as a father. The judge even made reference to the fact "that Mr. Schmidt is the father of two other children and has abandoned these children in the past."

We were more frustrated than ever before. Jan looked ready to explode as he said, "I cannot believe the incompetence of the law!" My family could hardly speak when they read the order. The court spoke of how they could not simply take a child from her parents because we appeared more advantageous; that would be "social engineering." But wasn't social engineering coming into play when a judge moved to take Jessi from the only parents she had ever known? Parenting is an action, not a title just given out freely to anyone who donates sperm to the process of conception. I thought: Why don't they ask this child who her parents are?

Now, everything seemed to rest on Cara's case, as we waited for news. Jan and I were up all night, hoping against hope that news would come soon—and be good. The next morning, the phone rang. It was Kim.

"Hi," Kim said. "The Court of Appeals is saying that the Juvenile Court did have jurisdiction, and the judge should have ruled on Cara's request to set aside the termination of her rights on the grounds that the seventy-two-hours requirement had not been met. The question that they don't answer is whether or not she waived her right to that seventy-two hours by not appearing for the termination hearing. They have remanded it back to the Juvenile Court. One possibility is asking for a rehearing . . . It would do no good to ask for a rehearing unless we also appealed Judge Kilburg's decision. Those two would have to go hand in hand. If we're going to do something, we have to do both . . . or comply with Judge Kilburg's order."

I asked, "If we do not appeal the decision in Cara's case, would the court reinstate her parental rights? Or if we just dropped everything now, could they reinstate her rights?" It was important to me that Cara's rights be reinstated, so that Dan wouldn't have sole custody of Jessica.

Kim replied, "At this point, the case has been remanded, so the judge has to decide. The Juvenile Court judge could decide that she is still terminated."

We hung up the phone and just stared at each other. Tears fell down our cheeks and onto one another's shoulders as we grasped at each other for support to stay standing.

Six

ON NEW YEAR'S EVE I sat in a chair crying for hours on end. We had lost. Cara's rights had not been reinstated, and Jessi was to be dropped off at Dan's apartment by 6 P.M., Sunday, January 12. The thought of Jessi leaving our home in two weeks was unbearable. The questions which had surfaced in my mind so many times in the past year came rushing back. I couldn't believe that this was how Cara wanted it to turn out.

Jan kept functioning, as usual, going through the motions. He maintained his calm demeanor, but inside he was consumed with grief and anger. His way of coping was to take care of everyone else, make sure everything was in place, and then react in private. I would sometimes hear him sobbing in the garage, then pounding on something. When it was silent, I knew he was having a cigarette and trying to regroup.

Jan knew that I'd want my mom and Joan to come over to comfort me, so he called them before he went to the copy shop around the corner to pick up the fax Gary had sent with the appeals court's decision. Joan came over and collapsed in my arms in the rocking chair. She pulled herself together quickly, though, so that she could take care of Jessi. A few minutes later Mom walked in, tears running down her face. She fought so hard to hold it in, but that was impossible. Joan tried to comfort her, but my mother was unable to gain her composure. Watching this scene, Jessi began crying, too. Grabbing her toy Gramps for comfort, she came and positioned herself next to me on the floor. I drew Jessi into my arms, and we sat motionless, hugging Gramps.

Mom suggested that we come over to her house, just to have a change of scene. While I prepared a diaper bag and change of clothes for Jessi, Joan gave her dinner and a bath. Jan went upstairs to call his parents to let them know what had happened. I could hear him sobbing as he spoke on the phone. Having to convey this information to our families was very difficult for us. So many times they had called to offer their support and love. Today we would not be able to find comfort in their words nor they in ours. Jan came downstairs and nodded silently to me, as if to say, "They know now. They are so sorry." Jessi, dressed in her pink sleeper, was ready to go to Grandma's house.

When we got there, Joan and Uncle Barry went into the back room to play with Jessi. From the living room I could hear Barry's whistle, Joan's laugh, and little Pooh's clapping. Jan and I sat on the couch talking with Mom, trying to make sense out of things. Jan told Mom about his conversation with his parents, during which they had suggested appealing the lower court's decision. Mom didn't offer her opinion on the appeal. She was visibly shaken and distraught. As she got up to go into the other room, she gave me a hug and said, "I don't know what hurts me more, seeing you in so much pain or losing Jessi. I love you and wish I could do something to make this all go away."

Barry came into the living room, gave me a big bear hug, and told me, "You cannot give up on life. You have got to hang in there; you can't let this run you down. We all need you, we need you to be here a hundred percent. Jessi needs you! You've got to be strong for her. We all knew this could happen, and now we will have to deal with it as best as we can."

We decided to stay overnight at my mom's. Jessi had fallen asleep in her arms and was content to sleep in the crib we kept there. Standing there watching her, holding each other, Jan and I knew that we were incapable of turning Jessi over to a perfect stranger. The only images we had of Dan had been portrayed to us by people who were once close to him, women with whom he had conceived his other children. Looking at Jessi, we were reminded of those children, imagining the pain which they had suffered without the presence of their father in their lives. Jessi loved Jan so much! When he arrived home after work every day,

Jessi was glued to him. How could we be separated? We were all so much a part of each other now.

The joy of waking up to Jessi's bright smile made us forget for the moment the news from the day before. "Good morning!" came a deep voice from behind the pillow. It was Gramps sticking his head out and talking to Jessi in a voice I had given to him long ago. Jessi grinned at Gramps and at me as I carried on a Gramps kind of conversation. "Hi, Jessi, I love you! Will you come give me a hug, and how about throwing me way up high?" said Gramps. As we romped around on the bed, Gramps would fly through the air and come in for a special kiss from Jessi. She would grab hold of him and roll around the bed giving him big hugs and kisses. Jan stood by capturing these priceless moments together on video. We knew these might be among our last moments together as a family. Pooh had learned to pull herself to the edge of the bed and get down by herself, quickly crawling across the floor to play with the TV. She had already mastered turning on the TV and was now learning how to play with the buttons on the VCR!

The morning was quiet, allowing us time to collect ourselves and focus on the most important person in our lives—Jessi. We pulled out some of our old dress-up clothes: high heels, silk scarves, handmade skirts sewn by my dad for my mom, and outlandish hats. Jessi became absorbed in playing with a top hat which was filled with streamers, noisemakers, and tin rattles from a past New Year's Eve. She initiated a game of peekaboo with Jan, using the hat to hide behind. Jan started shaking the rattles, and Jessi had to have one. The two of them had their own little New Year's party, shaking the rattles and throwing streamers everywhere.

Looking for some quieter activity, Grandma Jo asked Jessi if she wanted to read a book. Jessi climbed up into Grandma's lap as she started to read the story of Frosty the Snowman and his friends, Nick and Graham, whose names we had inserted in the story long ago. Jessi kept turning the pages back to Frosty and screeching. Jan had made a snowman outside the window and she loved seeing Frosty in the book and then pointing to the snowman outside.

While Mom read to Jessi and then gave her lunch, Jan and I had time to talk. After debating the question of whether to appeal or not, we decided to address a different issue altogether. We would call Gary and ask him if he could submit a motion to have Cara's rights reinstated. If Jessi had to be taken away from us, we wanted to protect her as much as we could. Jan and I had nothing to gain personally by requesting that the judge consider Cara's request for reinstatement of her rights. Our sole objective was to try to minimize the harmful effects that a transfer might have on Jessi and to try to ensure that she be placed with someone who was committed to her care. We were exhausted; we had struggled to understand and work within the system and now after all this time the system had failed. There was no justice, not for Cara, not for us, and least of all for Jessica.

I decided to call Glenna for advice before calling Gary with our request. It was part of my routine now to call certain people whom I trusted to talk about the case. Glenna was one of those people and today I needed her insight. She told me that she was not sure if a judge would consider our request to have Cara's rights reinstated. In the interim she did feel that Jessi would be placed in Dan's care. Glenna's tone was soft and full of compassion; I could tell that she was deeply concerned for us and for Jessi.

Later that afternoon I called Gary. "Jan and I have talked, and made up our minds, Gary. I have also spoken with Glenna. It seems as if we have definitely lost . . . They seem to be looking out for the biological parents' rights and ignoring everyone else's. That bothers me. But what bothers me the most is to actually give Jessi to Dan. Because of that I think that it would be a good idea to appeal. Kim said that we would have to appeal both orders [Dan's and Cara's] . . . I know we have lost. I know we are going to lose Jessi, but I would like to do whatever I can to get Jessi to Cara, to see if the courts would somehow reinstate her rights . . . I feel that if we just keep going through this process, whether we give Jessi to Dan on the twelfth or not, that if we keep appealing just to see what happens, all of this will be pushed under the rug. Then this could happen to someone else. I just can't let that happen . . . This system is so unjust to adoptive parents and it is definitely unjust to the child, and if there is some way of getting that out to help other people, I would like to try."

Gary responded, "Well, Robby, we can do the appeals . . . but the other part of it we really can't do. That is, go to the media or whatever."

"But can I?"

"You really jeopardize your case, I think."

I wondered how we could "jeopardize our case" any further at this point. I said to Gary, "But we've lost our case. It seems inevitable. I think the system is just not working. It won't help us at all, but it will help other people . . . And if there is anything I can do to try to get Cara's rights reinstated, that will make a load of difference to me."

We wanted Gary to appeal Dan's case, and at the same time try to have Cara's rights reinstated in case we lost. That way Cara could be reunited with Jessica. Gary thought that was impossible; he said we'd have to appeal both cases in order to have any chance of getting Jessica back to Cara.

I said, "Okay. But in all of this, Gary, you still think we're going to lose, right?"

"I think your chances are no better than one in ten."

I swallowed hard. "What if we do all these appeals? . . . Is there a point where we can just stop and go to the Juvenile Court judge and say, 'Please give Cara her rights back'?"

Gary's answer came quickly: "No. I mean . . . a child has no rights." I thought that if any judge's opinion had ever proven that statement, it was Kilburg's decision about Jessi.

I pressed Gary further, looking for an angle that could protect Jessi's future. "Not Jessi's rights, Cara's rights."

Gary responded, "No, we are not even in a position to do that. Why should we spin our wheels trying to get Cara's rights back?"

We felt that Cara should not have to marry Dan to have her rights reinstated. We believed that she was still engaged to Scott. I thought that if I were Cara, I would be frustrated by a system which was trying to impose marriage upon me in order to regain custody of my child.

After I finished the disconcerting talk with Gary, the phone rang again. It was my mom, wanting to know how I felt and what we'd decided. I told her a bit about my conversation with Gary. "He informed us that we are in a legal quagmire, and suggested that in order to resolve it we would have to appeal both cases and see if the Supreme Court would consider combining the cases."

Mom wondered aloud about our chances for success.

"Robby, does he think the case is strong enough to justify proceeding?"

"He said that our legal arguments would have to be very strong in order for the Iowa Supreme Court to consider taking the case. If they did accept the appeal, he thought they would do so because the arguments had merit. We want the court to address the mistakes that were made in the beginning of the process of the adoption."

"But, Robby, if you turn Jessi over on January 12, will you have the strength to keep going in the courts?"

"We might not have to turn her over then. We would apply for a stay which would allow us to keep Jessi in our care until a decision could be made. If a stay was not issued, Gary agreed to approach the Juvenile Court judge to see if anything could be done about reinstating Cara's rights."

My mother seemed encouraged by the thought of the stay. "Robby, I pray that things work out. I want the best for all of you. I love you."

Jan and I sat and talked that night about our feelings and our perceptions of where things stood. We felt so much anger toward the CUB group that Cara had gone to on that fateful night long ago. We went over and over the events of the past eleven months. Were things done the wrong way? Yes, starting with Cara naming the wrong birth father. Like dominoes falling one after another, one thing led to the next in this adoption process. John Monroe thought he had interpreted the seventy-two-hour statute correctly. If he had not, his mistake should have been addressed and reconciled by at least one of the judges who examined the paperwork. Juvenile Court and District Court judges had reviewed all the documents, and all of them could see from Cara's custody release that she had signed it less than seventy-two hours after Jessi's birth. None of them mentioned any problem with the waiver, thereby allowing the adoption petition to be filed, and the adoption process to continue.

I wished that when Cara found an attorney, she had been advised to seek mediation instead of moving right into litigation. Then we all could have talked right from the start. Instead, Jan and I received notice of litigation out of the clear blue. We responded to the litigation instead of asking our new attorney about mediation. Perhaps we should have pressed for mediation.

We could not turn back the clock, but Jan and I wanted to stop Jessica from having to be the victim of all this, and by the time we tried to pull back it seemed as if it was too late.

That night I rocked in our favorite rocking chair for hours as Jessi slept peacefully in my arms. I liked to study the texture of her skin, so smooth and flawless; and her hair, so fine and delicate. I lifted her to my face to smell the wonderful fragrance of her face and hair, feeling myself breathing slowly and deeply, as if I could breathe in enough of her to last a lifetime. Images of our year together flashed through my mind like a newsreel at high speed. Waves of the deepest love I've ever felt washed over me as I drifted in and out of sleep.

The next morning I got up very early and started reading some of the court documents that I'd not seen before. One of the affidavits that I found to be extremely disconcerting was by Annette Baran, M.S.W. I found her reasoning to be quite disturbing:

> *Many experts perceive that this period [one to two months after birth] provides the child with a first most important sense of self. When a child is removed from the birth mother directly after birth, both child and birth mother suffer feelings similar to amputation. No matter how much the adoptive mother may desire to mother a child, she does not have the same aura as the birth mother and cannot replace the role of the birth mother in that first most significant and sensitive period . . . The adoptive parents experience great anxiety and fear which inhibits their ability to form a close trust-inspiring relationship with the child.*
>
> *The resulting pain they believe they would feel appears so great [if the adoption process isn't complete] that they keep distance to protect themselves. It can be assumed with some certainty that attachment is delayed and/or lessened when adoptions are contested.*

I didn't know anything about Ms. Baran, except that she had written a book called *The Adoption Triangle*, so I called Mary Beth Seader, a trusted adviser and vice president of the National Council for Adoption. She told me that Ms. Baran was deeply committed to the CUB philosophy.

I told Mary Beth that we needed an expert in the field of bonding; I wanted another affidavit submitted to the court. Mary

Beth advised me to contact Dr. Jerome Smith, M.S.W., in Indiana. I decided to call him immediately, not knowing how long it might take to get an appointment with him. He kindly offered to fly to Ann Arbor to observe Jessi, Jan, and me in our home, but we did not have the money for his plane fare. We'd have to drive to Indianapolis to visit with him there.

We liked Dr. Smith right away, because of the way he interacted with Jessi. We could see that he really understood children. He got down on the floor with her to play, and let her lead him in their games. Jessi had fun with him, at one point picking up the remote control for his television and dazzling him with her understanding of how it worked. He would clap for her, and Jessi would smile at him and clap for herself. Jessi responded to Dr. Smith with confidence. It was a day well spent.

In his affidavit to the court, Dr. Smith wrote:

> *When a parental role is well carried out, whether biological or adoptive, the state of psychological parenthood is reached. It is developed theoretically in the best-seller* Beyond the Best Interests of the Child, *by Goldstein, Freud, and Solnit. It states, "The physical realities of his conception and birth are not the direct cause of his emotional attachment. This attachment results from day-to-day attention to his needs of physical care, nourishment, comfort, affection, and stimulation. Only a parent who provides for these needs will build a psychological relationship to the child on the basis of the biological one and will become his psychological parent in whose care the child can feel valued and wanted. An absent biological parent will remain, or tend to become, a stranger."*

His affidavit continued:

> *Out of my need to assess this phenomenon, I conducted a clinical interview with the DeBoers, where I could observe firsthand the nature of the relationship between these adults and the infant in question. The result . . . indicates the unequivocal existence of such a parental bond . . . It is quite obvious that Jessica had developed trust and a willingness to engage with people . . . Jan and Robby feel this is their child, and their anxiety over the tenuousness of their situation has not diminished the quality of this bond with Jessica.*

Dr. Smith went on to explain in his affidavit about emotional disturbance among adoptees:

> *These assertions are (virtually exclusively) made by clinicians who see disturbed families all day long and do not appreciate or value the methodological research issues involved. (*The Adoption Triangle, *for example, is not a book about adoption, but about a group of individuals who sought out their birth families. It is, by most accounts, a biased sample, the findings of which do not, in any way, represent adoptive families across the board.)*

Sitting and watching Jessi interact with Dr. Smith had been a great learning experience. It gave me a chance to look at Jessi from a distance, and I must say that I found her to be a wonderful little girl. I knew her so well that it was sometimes easy to forget how unique she was in so many ways.

I also noticed that it was time for a haircut! Pooh's hair had gotten so long in front, and it was still so fine that we couldn't pull it all back. I wanted Jessi to be able to have long beautiful hair. I thought it would fit her personality; but the bangs just did not work. Joan and I set out to investigate the best method for cutting her bangs. Our old friend Angel, a licensed beautician, advised us to attempt to cut Jessi's hair when she was asleep. That may have worked for Angel, but it sure didn't work for us! Joan and I couldn't stop laughing every time we tried to raise the scissors up to her little forehead. It seemed so sinister! After Jessi woke up, we invited her to come sit on Mom's lap. Our little spirited angel wanted to know what we were up to, so every time we raised the scissors, Jessi would tilt her head back to see what we were doing. All three of us were laughing now. Finally, with a swoop of the hands and the shears we grasped some hair and sliced it off. Of course, Jessi turned her head at precisely that moment. Her bangs ended up in a dramatic slant, with no way to repair them. Happily for all of us, Jessi grinned from ear to ear when examining her face in the hand mirror that we held for her. As long as she liked it, that was all that mattered!

A few days later I spoke with Gary. He mentioned that Frank Santiago, a reporter from the Des Moines *Register,* had called him to ask about something that had come over the wire about the Iowa Appellate Court order from Cara's case. They briefly discussed the Appeals Court decision, without mentioning any of the litigants' names. Gary gave me Frank Santiago's phone number and said he was waiting for our call, if we chose to comment. He instructed us to maintain our anonymity. Gary reiterated that he had not initiated the contact with the press; rather, Frank Santiago had called him.

I hung up and thought it over. I knew I'd have to discuss it with Jan before I placed a call to anyone in the media. Who could give us advice about this? I got out my diary and wrote:

> *The tears just won't stop coming. The pain is so deep. What has this system done to Jessica? She is so young, so fragile. How can they do this to her? How could a judge look at the damage that has been done to two children and subject another child to this kind of life? We must do something to help Jessi, maybe go to the press. I can only pray that I find the strength to carry out whatever it is we decide to do. Jessi may not be with us after all this is over, but she will always be a part of me, and I plan on protecting her to the best of my ability. I pray someone will listen and step out on a limb like we are about to, and fight this injustice. I hope this is the right step to take. I believe the court system in this country has failed this child. As adoptive parents we are considered second class. This is unjust, but worse yet, Jessi is not considered at all.*

Jan and I talked about it as soon as he got home from work. We felt that we had nothing to lose. It couldn't make things worse to talk with a reporter, and it might help other people who could end up in situations like ours. Jessi had been abandoned by the courts which we believe should have protected her. I called the newspaper and asked to speak with Frank Santiago. I liked the sound of his voice; he seemed open and compassionate, and he was very interested in getting the facts straight. We briefly discussed his conversation with Gary. Frank indicated that the newspaper was interested in doing a story. The case brought a variety of issues about adoption, parenting, and bonding to the surface. He told me that he thought the paper would want to have our names.

I said, "Let me say just one thing, Frank. Because of the context of all of this, the court will not allow us to disclose our last names."

"Who told you that?"

"My lawyer."

"I'm not so sure that's true."

I insisted, "The court has ordered that the child's name not be disclosed."

"Oh, the child's name would not be."

I told him he would have to call Gary regarding the use of our names.

I hung up the phone feeling as if I had accomplished nothing. I had no experience in dealing with reporters and was feeling very protective of the information which he had requested, not knowing where all of this would lead. Dan's ex-girlfriend Barbara called wanting to know about our reaction to the ruling and to inquire if there was anything else that she could do to help. Kim Ten Eick had told her about the decision from the court. I expressed my disbelief in and my anger toward the system. The ruling had been so heartless. I told Barbara about my conversation with the reporter and my hesitance to discuss the case with him, fearing legal repercussions. I never asked her to call Frank Santiago, but Barbara felt she had to call for her daughter Amanda's sake.

Frank called back after having spoken with Barbara, who gave him all the information he needed. He needed to know if he could use our names, as long as he didn't use Jessi's, and we gave him the green light. The article came out in the Des Moines *Register* on Sunday, January 12, 1992.

A Family Comes Undone by "Tragic" Adoption Case

With a stroke of the pen, a judge had ordered an end to "this tragic case" . . . The DeBoers were to have turned over the child to her birth father in Cedar Rapids today. But Friday the case took yet another turn. The Iowa Supreme Court said it wanted time to study Kilburg's order. Robby DeBoer said . . . "I feel like there has been a great injustice done. Whatever happens, no matter what, it's going to affect this child the rest of her life. If she stays with us, she'll still have a lot of pain because we'll have to tell her. It's a disaster. I didn't want her to grow up with this hatred."

I felt surprisingly comfortable reading Frank's article. It put us in a very vulnerable position to tell our story to the press, and deep inside I had been fearing what Frank might say. People had warned us that the press can be very exploitative, but somehow I felt that if we just told the truth, it would turn out well. Frank's article was very fair. He told the story and stuck to the facts. I was glad that we had trusted him.

This was the first of many articles published in Iowa about Jessica's case. Jessica's name was never mentioned, and we never disclosed Dan's or Cara's name. It was not our intent to publicly display the private lives of Dan and Cara, but rather to focus on Jessica's situation and the impact a move would have upon her at this time. The article articulately presented the travesty of a judicial system which was jeopardizing the life of a healthy, well-adjusted child, with no regard for her well-being. It highlighted the law's inability to ensure that children don't fall through the cracks, leaving them as victims of a system biased in favor of biological parents, regardless of their ability or commitment to parenting.

The public responded to the article with outrage. Many editorials were written. "What About the Child?" in the Des Moines *Register*, January 17, 1992, stood out:

Interest of Infant Is Paramount in Disputed Adoption Case

The laws are written to protect the rights of birth mothers and fathers . . . An effort was made to honor that principle. Those handling the legal matters made a technical error in having the mother sign papers early. Eighteen years ago, in a case involving child custody, the Iowa Supreme Court stated, "The status of the children should be quickly fixed and thereafter little disturbed." The "thereafter" in this case spans the 11 most critical months of the baby girl's life, during which the bonds of parenthood were firmly cemented. The overriding concern must be the best interest of the baby girl to whom the court, and the society on whose behalf it acts, owes the emotional security of a future with its adoptive parents. Let "thereafter" become "ever after."

By the time this editorial appeared, we were on our way to getting a temporary stay and hoping the Iowa Supreme Court would take the case. Through Gary's written appeal, Jan and I were asking the court to be responsible to Jessica, to treat her as a human being, not a piece of property. We were concerned because once again the Guardian ad Litem, the attorney assigned to represent Jessi's interests, had decided not to look out for Jessica. We questioned his role and his concern for Jessica's welfare. He had never been to see Jessi or her home. Was he aware of how the court intended the transfer to take place? Was he following up on the judge's suggestion of having an agency oversee the situation once Jessi was in Dan's care? It was our expectation that the Guardian would be responsible for the role which we were now playing, trying to protect our child's interests. We felt confident that no one in his right mind could just hand a child over to a perfect stranger, as Judge Kilburg had ordered.

I spoke with a cousin of mine who is a newspaper editor, and asked her how to get in touch with the press. She gave me a list of possible contacts and said she would make a few calls. She mentioned that the best way to talk to the press was to just be honest and tell our story from the heart. I told Jan what she had said, and we talked about making the big plunge into the media. We had just lost Jessi, so not much else mattered to us. With the help of our friend Mary Anne, we prepared a chronological list of the events which had transpired to date.

It didn't take long for the media to show interest in our story. Our local CBS affiliate called us and asked if they could send a reporter named Kathy to interview us. It was a very difficult time for us; since we had never been on television before, our anxiety level was very high. Joan had come over to take care of Jessi while we were talking to the reporter. Seeing these people in her house was of little interest to Jessi. She sat happily on the couch playing with her new Santa Claus music box. Kathy made us feel quite at ease, asking us about the case and our situation. We told her that any day the courts in Iowa could decide not to take the case, and we would lose Jessica. We felt compelled to share our story, hoping that it would somehow have an impact on the future sequence of events. Considering how nervous we were, the interview went very well. Kathy asked if it would be all right if someone from her station came back in a week or so and talked to us again. She felt that interest in the case would be high and people would want to know how we were doing and what had happened. We agreed to be interviewed again later.

Joan stopped by around noon on Friday, February 7, before

going out of town for the weekend. She called the Supreme Court and asked the clerk one last time if she had heard whether or not the court would hear the case. The clerk said that no one had come down with a decision, but the moment she heard anything, she would call our attorney. It was time for Jessi's nap, so I turned on the answering machine, grabbed a bottle, and headed upstairs. Feeling a need to hide away, to withdraw from it all, I lay down with Jessi on the bed. We snuggled under the comforter to take a quiet winter's nap.

Jessi fell asleep right away, but as tired as I was, I just couldn't sleep. For some reason, I'd been thinking about my father a lot recently. With the rhythmic sound of Jessi's breathing comforting me, I drifted into a deep sleep, dreaming of our family's long walks in the fall. We would trek across a nearby golf course. Papa walked with staff in hand; a limb of a tree snatched up along the way served as the staff. Jim would carry a bag of apples which we would munch on during the course of our journey. I thought of how much I enjoyed those simple days and the wonderful times we spent together as a family. Jan, Jessi, and I would soon be robbed of those simple pleasures. A decision was expected at any time which would dismiss the existence of our family. "I miss you, Dad," I whispered when I awoke. It had been six years since he'd died. I wished he could be here now to make things come out right.

Three hours elapsed before Jessi opened those beautiful eyes. The answering machine had several messages on it. Almost afraid to listen, I pushed the button. Gary had called and left a very short message: the Iowa Supreme Court had given us a stay until the case could be heard and a final ruling issued!

I was overwhelmed with joy! I swept Jessi off her feet and we danced around the living room laughing and singing. I called Jan at work, hoping to catch him before he left to come home. Jan sighed in relief, "Oh, thank God, thank you for listening to our prayers! Robby, hon, I'll be home soon. Call your mom and ask her if she wants to go out to dinner to celebrate!" I couldn't even think about what the dinner would cost. I was just happy and thankful to know that we had a chance.

Diary, February:

You're one year old! Hurray! Waking up this morning, you carried a grin that could have lit up the room. With your doll

Dutchy by your side, you thought you would try to conquer going down the stairs. Dutchy sat and watched as, one step down after another, you would say, "Epp, epp." After you accomplished your feat, we had a knock on the door. It was a deliveryman coming to bring you a present from Bridget, a cousin of Mom's! The cutest outfits, true California style, a white cotton dress, with purple and royal-blue seashells. Perfect for the pool! And with it was a yellow shorts outfit with green palm trees. They were a little big, but we'll get them to work. Your new words for the month are "yuk," "clock," "hot." Aunt Joan bought you a bouquet of brightly colored balloons and a tape recorder. Dad and I found a Winnie the Pooh in the Honey Tree *videotape that I've always loved. Along with the video you received a wonderful soft pink onesie outfit, with white sleeves and Peter Rabbit on the front.*

The local CBS affiliate showed up again to film Jessica taking her first bite of her birthday cake. Jan had decided to take the day off from work to spend some time with us. Miles could feel the air of celebration, and he was frisking around in his jolly way. Unfortunately, he just couldn't wait for the party to begin. As he watched us welcome reporter Micah Materre at the door, he seized his moment, rushing over and chomping into the cake. He had icing all over his nose! Jessi motioned for my attention as she pointed to Miles and kicked her little feet against my hips, trying to get me to stop him. By the time I could get over to him, Miles had already completed his attack on the cake. With the cameras rolling, Jessi took her own large handful of the birthday cake. It wasn't quite the pristine celebration I'd had in mind, but at least Jessi and Miles showed a lot of personality!

After the attacks on the cake we waved goodbye to our guests and took a little nap. I wasn't sure Jessi needed it at that point, but Jan and I sure did. In the late afternoon Randy and the boys came down to have some of what was salvageable from Jessi's cake. All the kids sat at the table digging their little fingers into the cake, sliding around the clowns and balloons that sat atop the icing. What a scene! Knowing how much Jessi loved her tubby time, the boys had gotten her a plastic bath book and a few other bath toys. She was delighted with the gifts, her guests, and the feeling of her birthday cake on her hands and face and in her hair.

A few weeks later, Justice David Harris issued an order concerning the consolidation of the cases to the Iowa Supreme Court. The order included a section of the adoption statute that the judge had wanted us to follow—600.16 section (2 and 4)—which indicated that the names of biological parents or child involved in a custody action should not be revealed. It went on to say: "Any person, other than the adoption parents or the adopted person, who discloses information in violation of the provisions of this section shall be, upon conviction, guilty of a simple misdemeanor."

The judge was trying to stop us from talking to the press. The truth was that we had only given our names. Gary advised us that this was a form of a gag order and we should stop talking to the press.

On the morning of February 15, Jessi and I were upstairs getting dressed when Joan arrived at the door. From the stairs I could hear Joan whispering to Jan. I knew something was wrong, so I scooped up Jessi and came down the stairs quickly. Joan's face was as white as a ghost. She explained slowly, as her voice began to quiver, that our brother Jerry had been in a car accident. "It was yesterday, on Valentine's Day. Jerry was driving through a pass in Idaho. He hit a patch of black ice and spun out into a ravine." Joan paused, almost unable to go on.

"Joan," I said in a near-whisper, "please tell us . . . Is Jerry okay?"

"I'm not sure. Let me tell you what happened. A man pulling over to put chains on his tires saw Jerry's truck and instantly motioned for other people to stop and help. A medical team arrived pretty quickly and flew him into Pocatello, where they put him in the intensive-care unit."

Joan looked as if she might faint. Jan was holding her arm, and he guided her to a chair. She went on: "We should start getting ready . . . for a funeral . . ." Her voice trailed off.

Jan asked, "Joan, listen, hon, have you called your mom yet?"

"Yes. I got hold of her in Virginia. I also called Tom and Pam. They'll be flying into Pocatello this morning."

I could hardly think. I needed to hear more specific details of Jerry's condition. "Joan, did they say exactly what injuries Jerry sustained?"

"As far as I know, all of Jerry's ribs were smashed, his liver was lacerated, and his lungs ruptured."

Petrified, we sat in the living room saying a prayer for Jerry. Joan and I had to decide if we should fly out to see Jerry to say goodbye. After much thought, Joan and I decided to stay home and see how he progressed. The thought of death does such strange things to a person's mind. It's as if you become suspended in time. Everything stops. I can still picture this moment in our living room as if it were a photo in an album that I've looked at through the years. Jan and I could see how lucky we really were. We were alive and had a beautiful daughter; our troubles seemed minuscule compared to Jerry's. My regrets started flowing: Jessi had never met her uncle; I had never told him so many things; I hadn't spent enough time with him. We spent hours calling the family and making arrangements for everyone to fly to Pocatello. Barry had come back from the North Forty and was devastated to hear the news. He and Jerry had been very close, and the pain in Barry's eyes tore at all our hearts. Barry arranged to meet Mom in Salt Lake City; then they would fly into Pocatello together on a commuter flight. As we drove Barry to the airport, I told Joan that I thought we should contact Jerry's son, Gabe, and tell him.

Jerry had been divorced from his ex-wife for over eighteen years. Gabe was two and half when they split up. Jerry agreed to have his son adopted by his ex-wife's new husband, and decided that he would let Gabe grow up without interference from him until he was an adult. The rest of the family had kept in contact with Gabe, and he became very close to my parents. Jerry and Gabe had only recently been reunited. When we called Gabe, he was shocked and confused. I think it was almost impossible for him to accept the idea that he'd just been getting to know Jerry and now he might lose him. He decided to wait for more news of his condition before going to see him.

As the days passed, we all sat on pins and needles waiting to hear Jerry's fate. The priest at the hospital seemed to be giving Jerry his last rites every day, as Jerry remained unconscious, under heavy sedation. After several operations, his doctors were somewhat encouraged, thinking that he might pull through and might possibly be able to exist on an iron lung. Only time would tell.

Meanwhile, Jessi was growing so quickly! This was another

stage during which she seemed to do new things every day. On February 23, Jessi took her first half-step at Aunt Joan's house. Jan and I missed it! Joan said it was an amazing thing; she couldn't believe how proud and pleased Jessi looked.

Jan's parents called and asked if they could fly us down to Florida for a week. They thought getting us out of the house would help ease the tension until we found out more about Jerry. Coincidentally, Jan had some vacation time from work coming to him. Joan encouraged us to get away. She thought that if anything did happen to Jerry, we could just fly directly to Idaho from Florida. She gave us some money to take Jessi to Disney World for a day.

Jessica was so excited as we boarded the plane for her first flight. She was interested in all the little things about airplanes that I hadn't thought about in years: the window shades, the panels of buttons, the seat-belt signs, the adjustable seat backs. She loved looking at all the people, and many of them smiled at her and waved. Mary Anne had given us a tip on how to help Jessi through the flight. We wrapped up some of Jessi's toys to keep her occupied. As she opened them, she would mutter that she was going to see "O-ma" and "O-pa."

Jan's father and his sister Nelli met us at the plane. Jessi laughed with delight as Opa held out his arms to scoop her up. It felt so good to be out of the cold; the sun seemed to melt our troubles away. When we got to Oma and Opa's house, Jessi was asking, "Oma? Oma?" She opened the door and Jessi smiled her widest smile. Oma said, "Jessi, look how big you've gotten!" Jessi made herself right at home, crawling at high speed from room to room.

The trip to Disney World was just what the doctor ordered. Pooh, dressed in her hot-pink polka-dot overalls and white bonnet, was ready for a long day of activities. Jan's first purchase was a rabbit-face balloon, which Jessi bounced on its string as Jan carried her in the backpack. As we strolled through the merry streets of Liberty Square, Jessi looked radiant. The Jungle Cruise was a perfect place for Opa and his granddaughter to take a snooze in the early afternoon.

The highlights of the trip were the parade of all the Disney characters and the carousel ride. Sitting high on my shoulders, Jessi had a front-row seat for the parade and was able to see all of her favorite characters. She hooted and kicked and waved with joy. The carousel had beautiful horses on it which captured Jessi's fancy. She chose a great white stallion to sit on, holding on to my shirt and Opa's arm. By the end of the day, we were all worn out, but full of the happiness we'd shared as a family all day long.

Jessi especially loved visiting Aunt Nelli's family. She romped around the yard with her cousin Corey, and, of course, loved the swimming pool! We took our first plunge into the water together. I swirled Jessi around as she exclaimed, "More!" Jan dove in and swam toward us, delighting Jessi no end as he suddenly emerged from under the water and splashed us. Nelli's husband, Mel, started up the grill to begin a barbecue. The tantalizing smell of the food was the only thing that could have gotten Jessi out of the water! After dinner, Corey and Jessi played as the adults talked of our time at Disney World. We tried not to spend too much time talking about our legal problems, opting instead to enjoy each other's company and the happy sounds of the children.

My cousin Greg, who lived near St. Augustine, came to see us one day at Oma and Opa's. He wanted to meet Jessi and show us some sights in and around the area. As an archaeologist, he knew a lot about the local museums. Greg was a great tour guide, and Jessi was so comfortable as we walked through the museums that she slept a good bit of the time in my front pack. By the time Jessi woke up, Greg had taken us to a park by the river, which caught her eye immediately. She started squirming and begged to be released to roam free. Pooh had never really played in the sand before, and it proved to be a delightful discovery. She played and explored with great gusto, sifting through the sand and making hills, only to flatten them and immediately rebuild them.

Jessi's first real steps took place several days later in Oma's kitchen. Oma was so proud to witness the event. She clapped with Jessi to rejoice in her achievement. Jan and I had missed it once again. Jessi was so cautious; I think she was trying to master her technique of walking before she paraded her efforts in front of Jan and me. We couldn't wait to see her do it!

As the time approached to leave Florida, Jan became very distressed, not knowing if his parents would ever see Jessi again. "Robby, I just don't know what to say to them. I want to tell them we'll all be together again soon, but I just can't seem to get the words out. They'll know I'm pretending. But I can't bear to force them to face the truth."

"Jan, you can see it in their eyes; they know the truth. They need to talk about it. You've got to discuss it with them."

Oma came into the room as we were talking. She reached up to Jan and gently cradled his face in her hands. "Jan, we'll be okay. You have to hope for the best, just as we do. You keep your chin up and enjoy your little sunshine. She's a miracle." None of us mentioned any of this again, but it pervaded everything we did during our last days in Florida. I could see that when Oma and Opa said goodbye to Jessi, they had to swallow extra hard to fight back the tears.

Jessi must have wanted to give us a welcome-home present, because the very day after we arrived back in Ann Arbor, she walked again! Jan was at work. Joan and I spent the day with Jessi, getting her all dressed up in her beautiful green velvet dress for our lunch with Grandma Jo. I felt so sorry for my mom. She had spent a long winter in Idaho trying to help nurse Jerry back to life, and the experience had taken a toll on her. Apparently she had provided just what Jerry needed in terms of general care, moral support, and loving attention, because he was recovering far more quickly than the doctors had predicted he would. Jerry would probably be well enough soon to begin an extensive therapy program which could completely rehabilitate him.

Just as Joan and I were about to leave for my mother's house, Jessi stood in the corner with a determined look on her face. I grabbed the video camera in anticipation, while Joan sat on the floor coaxing Pooh on with a gentle voice. My voice had more of the tone of a cheerleader, "Come on, Sweet Pea, you can do it!" Miles circled around Jessi to get into the action, almost urging Jessi on with Joan and me.

The moment came; Jessi took a half step into Joan's arms. We cheered and told Jessi what a big girl she was! Jessi stood ready to try once more. Miles grew impatient, wanting Jessi to do more than stand. He went up and wagged his bushy tail, turned about, and gave her a big licking kiss right on the cheek, throwing her off balance and landing Jessi on the floor. It didn't faze her in the least. She stood right back up, determined to walk again. She really did it this time! Three steps into Joan's arms! I was so proud and wished Jan could have seen his little girl accomplish such a

feat. When he came home from work, we were ready to demonstrate. As he held the camera, Jessi walked right into my arms.
What a marvelous feeling!

As soon as we were settled back at home, I decided to delve
into case histories again, trying to find anything that might help
us keep Jessi. Glenna had gotten me in touch with an attorney at
the American Academy of Adoption Attorneys in Washington,
D.C., who was kind enough to help me find relevant case histories
that had taken place in the last year; I'd been unable to find such
updated information at the University of Michigan law library. I
then faxed the information to Gary to see if any of it could apply
to our case. When Gary called back in response to the fax, he
mentioned the timeline of our appeal. He explained that in child
custody situations the court cuts the usual waiting time in half.
Kim and Gary had decided that they would ask the court to
consider Cara's and Dan's cases simultaneously. Gary said that he
needed a thousand dollars right away, to cover the court costs. I
told him I felt overwhelmed about the thousand dollars, and asked
him what he thought the financial picture would be in the future.

Gary reassured me. "As far as additional costs . . . In terms
of printing expenses, I think the thousand should cover both
appendix and brief. It's close enough that I don't think the printer
is going to get too bent out of shape with us. That should be
basically all we need. There's going to be some expense for driving
to Des Moines and all that stuff . . . After that there really isn't
any other out-of-pocket expense."

Joan somehow pulled together a thousand dollars to pay the
printing bill. That was the end of her money. The family's money
had to go to help Jerry. Right about this time, we got a call from
the local CBS television station. After airing the stories about us,
they had begun to get quite a few calls about our case. People
wanted to help Jessi, and many of them wanted to make contribu-
tions to help us with our legal bills! The station manager suggested
that we establish a legal fund; they would refer any inquiries to
our bank. Jan and I went to the bank the next day and set up the
Baby DeBoer Legal Fund.

All of us were thrilled when Jerry called to say that he would
be coming back to Michigan to receive intensive physical therapy
at a hospital near Ann Arbor. It had been five weeks since the
accident, and his doctors felt he was well enough to be released

from the intensive-care unit. My brother Tom's wife, Cathy, and their daughter, Kalise, would be flying in to visit him, and we wanted to see him as soon as possible, too.

One night Jan and I dressed Jessi up warmly in preparation to meet her Uncle Jerry. We headed out in the snowy afternoon to Chelsea, planning to meet Joan and Barry there. This was Jessi's first time in a hospital, and of course she wanted to go exploring. Joan took her for a walk as Jan and I went into Jerry's room. Seeing Jerry caught me off guard. No one had explained that the left side of his torso was paralyzed. Jerry reassured us that he hoped to get movement back after extensive physical therapy. It really upset me to see my brother in this utterly vulnerable position. I could hardly imagine what it had been like for my mother during all those weeks in Idaho when Jerry was near death.

The nurses had advised us to keep the visit short, so we went out in the hall to look for Joan and Jessi to bring them into Jerry's room for just a few moments before leaving. Jerry enjoyed seeing Jessi; it really seemed to lift his spirits. Pooh gave him a wonderful sloppy kiss, and we all bade him farewell. Joan offered to drive Jessi home so that we could stay just a few moments more. We bundled her up in her snowsuit and told her we'd see her at home after Aunt Joan read her some books and gave her a snack. Barry stayed on at the hospital, as he did every evening; Jerry had gotten used to having Barry stay with him during the evenings when they were in Pocatello, and it was hard for Jerry to fall asleep without his brother there.

As we started our drive home from the hospital, Jan and I decided to drive slowly, because the snow had turned to sleet and was freezing as it hit the highway. The roads were treacherous. As we approached the exit before ours, a car pulled out in front of us suddenly, and another car hit us broadside. Jan swerved into the other lane to avoid more of an impact, and several other cars crashed into each other as the drivers all put on their brakes. The impact to our car was on my side. My head whiplashed into the smashed door, but luckily I was not bleeding. Jan got out of the car to assess all the damage and see if anyone else needed help. Startled by the collision, I remained seated. All three lanes were full of cars smashed from all sides. Within minutes ambulances had arrived. The paramedics came right to our car and told me not to move. They lifted me onto the stretcher very gently, helping me stretch out my body very slowly. My head was swelling from the strike on the door.

Jan came into the ambulance for a moment before we left the scene and tried to comfort me. "Robby, don't you worry. I think our car is okay to drive as far as your mom's house. I'll go there as soon as I can and get her car, and come straight to the hospital."

"Jan, try not to upset my mom too much. Tell her I'll be okay. And please call our house and ask Joan to go ahead and put Jessi to bed . . ."

During the ambulance ride, all I could think about was Jessi. I was so grateful that Joan had taken her home. I calmed myself by picturing her and Joan reading and laughing together. When we got to the hospital, CAT scans were taken, and showed no significant injury. I was released several hours later, with a large bump on the back of my head. Jan took me straight home. Joan had dressed Jessica for bed and the two of them had fallen asleep in Jessi's big-girl bed.

Seven

I GRABBED THE MAIL as I headed out the door. I had an appointment with Stephanie, my therapist. Mom was going to babysit Jessi while I was gone. They were planning to spend some time outside in the bright April sunshine, perhaps walking to the park with Cathy and Kalise, who were still visiting. Arriving a few minutes early for my appointment, I decided to open the mail in the car to pass the time. There was a letter from Gary among the bills and personal letters.

> *Dear Robby and Jan:*
>
> *By the time you receive this letter a decision will have been made on whether or not to file a reply brief in connection with your case . . . I also enclose with this letter a copy of the bill for services in connection with our representation of you in this matter. As you can tell, the bill has reached significant proportions. I also realize that you are not in a position to pay the bill in full and in fact at the rate the fees continue to mount, probably never will be in a position to pay the total bill in full.*
>
> *What I am going to propose in this letter . . . would be to accept the sum of $12,000 if paid in one lump sum payment as a full and complete settlement of your bill up to April 1, 1992 . . . I realize that this is a large amount of money and that it will be difficult to raise, but with an office our size I cannot continue to carry this size of an account receivable. It has*

also taken a significant amount of persuasion to convince my partners to reduce the bill by over $8,000 in the hopes we can reach some middle ground and resolve it.

In total disbelief, I could hardly make it out of the car. Was this some sort of April fool joke? I had spoken to Gary no more than two or three weeks ago about the bill and asked him if he thought we would be expected to come up with any other large sums of money, after we had paid the thousand dollars to cover copying costs for the Iowa Supreme Court briefs. At that time he never mentioned that the bill would have to be paid in this fashion. We were not in a position to just write a check, and he knew that, as he indicated in his letter. How did he imagine that we would be able to come up with this money overnight?

Stephanie and I discussed the letter. I was scared that Gary was implying that if we were unable to pay the bill soon, our continued representation was in jeopardy. I felt so helpless. Stephanie could see how tense I was; my whole body was constricted and my voice strained. "Robby, you have to find a way to let go of this stress. It looks to me as if you're in desperate need of rest and relaxation. I know it sounds difficult, if not impossible, but you must give your body some time off," she advised. I was painfully aware of the need to lessen my stress level. I tried to breathe deeply as Stephanie and I talked. Just verbalizing everything really helped.

I called my mom to see how Jessi was doing, and she said that Kalise and Cathy were there playing with her, having a great time. She was about to put Jessi down for her nap, and they all wanted to spend more time with her after that. I was so grateful. I wanted to find a way to follow Stephanie's advice and get a bit of rest before picking up Jessi so that I could be in good shape for her sake. I went home hoping to take a nap, but as I lay there, I couldn't put Gary's letter out of my mind.

I was in a state of half-dreaming, half-worrying when I came up with an idea. Our next hearing was in the Iowa Supreme Court. At that time oral arguments would be heard; all the required briefs had already been filed. I thought that if we could not afford legal counsel, I might argue the case myself in front of the judges with Glenna's guidance. I got up and called her, hoping she could advise me about protocol. I was desperate. I knew I didn't have the qualifications to present the legal arguments, but if the day of the hearing came and we were without representation, I did not want to miss the opportunity to go before the judge and plead our case. Someone had to be there to represent Jessica's interest.

Glenna told me that it was impossible. She knew how desperate I was, yet there was nothing she could do at this point to help me. Then I called Betsy, our personal attorney. She advised me to write Gary and outline the previous arrangement we had made, paying a hundred dollars per month, and make inquiry as to what had transpired to nullify that. We had been meeting that obligation as agreed.

I could hardly bear to show Gary's letter to Jan that night. "Robby, I just don't get it," he said. "Every time we turn around, someone else changes the rules on us. We try to follow the rules, don't we?" He was more frustrated than angry. "I don't know what we're going to do, Robby, but I know I just want to concentrate on Jessi."

It was hard for me to concentrate on anything. At times it was difficult even to perform the most insignificant tasks. Pooh was getting frustrated with my lack of focus. By the end of the week I forced myself to snap out of it, and Jessi and I went to an outdoor mall. We had a few favorite stores, including one that most people would never take a young child to visit; it was full of all kinds of breakable merchandise like fine china, clocks, and crystal vases. Jessi loved to look around, and understood that she had to be gentle and careful if she touched anything. The employees loved it when we came. They would talk to Jessi and show her new things that had arrived in the store, kneeling down in front of her so that she could see them up close. Jessi's favorite things in the store were three porcelain dolls in a big wooden cradle. They had lovely receiving blankets in their crib. Jessi would pick up one of the dolls and wrap it in a blanket, holding it very tightly to her. The dolls weighed five or six pounds, quite a load for Jessi! "Heavy, Momma!" she would say as she picked them up. We spent quite a while with the dolls this time, wrapping each one tenderly in a blanket before leaving the store.

Back outside, Jessi scurried to the stairs; she was always strengthening those little legs. She led me to another favorite spot, the ice cream parlor. We leisurely shared a vanilla ice cream cone at an outdoor table, with the sun warming our faces. Jessi remarked about all the passersby: "Dog, Momma! Man! Bird, Momma!" As I looked at Jessi's carefree smile and heard her gentle voice, I said a silent prayer of thanks for this time with the most wonderful little girl I've ever known.

Jan and I learned to hold our fears inside during the daytime so that he could work and I could be an attentive and energetic companion for Jessi. At night we would talk through the fear and cry together. Just when Jan and I thought we would cave in from the stress, a very large contribution came in to the Baby DeBoer Legal Fund. We were able to pay Gary's bill! I cannot adequately describe the sense of relief and gratitude that Jan and I felt. I was shaking all over for hours that night, as if my muscles were all letting go at once. We now had enough money to go to the Iowa Supreme Court. Pain and fear of the unknown were a big part of our lives, but they always were overshadowed by the compassion, generosity, and love extended to us by the people who knew us or knew of our case. It would be months before our case was heard in the Supreme Court of Iowa, and the emotional and financial support we received helped us immensely to cope with the situation.

One bright, sunny day, Randy called and suggested that Jessi and I come along on a trip to the Toledo Zoo. Randy and her boys were going along with a local day-care group that Graham sometimes attended. Doris, the day-care provider, was a kind woman who was very experienced with young children. "Come on, Robby," Randy said. "Jessi loves animals, and it's only an hour's drive. Jessi's ear infection is gone, isn't it?" Randy had supported us through many ear infections. Poor Jessi seemed to get them frequently. Luckily, she was a good patient and didn't mind going to the doctor. She seemed to understand on a very mature level that the doctor would help her.

"Yes, she is feeling much better. I think the zoo sounds great!" I said. I packed some snacks and cassette tapes for the ride, and told Jessi, "We're going to the zoo! We're going to see some animals!" She didn't know from firsthand experience what a zoo was, but she certainly knew animals. She was grinning from ear to ear, understanding that we were going to have an adventure.

We played tapes all the way there, singing, clapping, and laughing. As we entered the zoo, Jessi shrieked with delight, seeing the children running around and sensing the excitement. Our first visit was to the polar bears, who were frolicking in the water and rolling around on the cement in the sun. They were so playful and funny! When they shook off the excess water from their bodies, Jessi remarked that they looked like Miles. "Myse! Myse! Momma, Myse!" she said over and over.

When we saw the monkeys and heard their sounds, Jessi looked at me with great excitement and recognition. She had heard Uncle Jerry imitate monkey sounds quite accurately when they played together; I wondered if she might think that these monkeys were imitating her uncle!

"Dots!" Jessi shrieked when we saw the giraffes. I always pointed out polka dots to her; she loved them so! Now she saw the biggest polka dots ever! Our last stop was the petting zoo, a delightful area with sheep, goats, and birds. Jessi wasn't afraid of the animals at all. She walked right up to them and petted them, perhaps expecting them to lick her the way that Miles did. She especially liked the sheep. She patted one of them over and over, telling me all about it. "Momma, look! Momma, look!" For weeks afterward she told Jan about her experience with the sheep.

When we got home, there was a message from Joan on the answering machine. "Hey, Robby! We'd better get to work on my wedding dress! I'll pick up Jerry tomorrow after I'm done working and we'll come to your house so we can get started." Jerry had gotten a weekend pass from the hospital. The therapy seemed to be working, and he was gaining mobility on the left side of his body.

When they arrived, Jessi looked at Jerry and made her own little monkey noises. That was it, Jerry's cue. The two little monkeys spent the whole evening playing while Joan and I worked on her gown. My father had helped me design my wedding dress, and together we had selected the silk fabric and organza for the inlay. My father had been sewing since he was a child. He had made outfits for his sisters, and later dressed his wife in stylish maternity clothing. I would now take Papa's place in creating Joan's gown. Joan is petite; something very simple and elegant would fit her best. We pulled out our old dress-up clothes, finding among them our favorite gown, one of royal-blue satin acetate. The pattern was perfect for a wedding gown. With a few alterations to the design, it would suit Joan perfectly. We purchased seventeen yards of champagne satin, and one-quarter yard of handmade lace, and set up production. Jessi enjoyed playing peekaboo under the scraps of fabric.

Diary, April:

> *Jessica, you're getting so big, I can't believe you're growing up so quickly! You're fourteen months old. You can climb up on Grandma's chair all by yourself. You always clap with delight after every new thing you achieve. Mom and Dad give you so much praise for attaining each new goal. Randy has taught you how to throw kisses. The trips to the park down on the corner are your favorite pastime. You make sure we attend every day, rain or shine. You often ask if the boys can come along.*
>
> *You have been Mother's little helper this month. We went to Toys "R" Us to pick up a mop. You want to have one of your own so that you can work alongside Mom. Susan held a shower for Joan, and you were very involved in helping Aunt Joan open the presents. You have become so independent; walking has set you free. Miles, you, and I frolic around in the backyard, singing our favorite songs. Your favorite song is "Do Your Ears Hang Low?" It would really help if I'd learn all the words!*
>
> *You love your swing set that our cousins gave us. Many of your little cousins used it for years. Now it's yours! You especially love the swing. You could swing all day! Miles loves you so much, Pooh. He follows you everywhere, even back and forth, and back and forth, as you swing!*
>
> *You love to throw sticks for Miles to run after and retrieve. The problem is that you can't throw them very far yet, but Miles has adapted. As you throw it, he leaps through the air and comes running in for the stick as if it's been thrown fifty feet. He always gives it back to you and waits for the next throw.*

The sun was shining and the earthy smells of spring were all around us. Easter had arrived. Jessi, much older and more developed this year, was able to participate in many of the activities. Randy invited us over to paint Easter eggs. Demonstrating his artistic flair, Ben showed the younger ones how it was done. Jessi sat patiently watching, not sure what the whole process was all about. She enjoyed sticking her fingers in the dye and wiping it on her clothes to see the change in the colors of the fabric. Dye was everywhere. That was Randy's house; the kids were always welcome and free to explore, to create, to play.

My family gathered together for the Easter holiday. We hid all the eggs we'd dyed at Randy's house. This year Scott and my nephew Jordon wanted to hide the eggs. They claimed that it had been too difficult to find the ones I had hidden the year before. Scott and Jordan counseled Jessi on the object of the hunt. "See, Jessi, you look for these eggs, in the grass, under the bushes, in the mailbox, behind a rock. Do you get it? Do you get it?" Jessi smiled. She got it. She stumbled down the hill and searched for the eggs, finding a few of them and holding them up triumphantly. Jan had put an extra egg in her basket to let her know what she was looking for. Uncle Barry stayed by Jessi's side, further explaining the object of the hunt. Scott dashed in and out from behind the trees, running by Jessi to show her how many eggs he had found. Jessi decided to sit down and crack one of her eggs, hoping finally to see what was inside. Jan rushed to her aid and gave her a chocolate egg in its place. The boys tied in their competition to get the most eggs. Jessi's reward waited inside; the family had bought Pooh a talking telephone. After watching her play with an old phone, Grandma Jo had recognized that Jessi needed a voice on the other end of the receiver. She wanted to have a conversation. The new phone had many buttons to push and she was now able to talk to a variety of callers, such as the doctor and the teacher. The phone also had a piano keyboard on it. Cara had said that Jessi would have the fingers to play; she was right.

"Momma, edding? Momma, edding?" Jessi chanted as I fixed her breakfast on Joan's wedding day. We had all been working on the wedding so much; now Jessi was ready! Coincidentally, Jan and I were celebrating our ten-year wedding anniversary on the same day, so it was a double celebration. The wedding was a regular family reunion. Jessi wore a purple velvet dress with an organza collar that had tiny white roses outlined on it. The day was gorgeous, perfect for an outdoor wedding. Bridget sang beautifully, as she had done on our wedding day, and I stood up as Joan's maid of honor.

We continued the family reunion the following day with a

picnic at Gallup Park. All of Mom's brothers and sisters were there. Family gatherings were standard in our family; the clan would assemble for barbecues, trips to the lake, whatever reason Mom could think of! She was at her happiest this weekend, having her family together for the best occasion, a wedding. The year had been tough on several extended-family members; we all now realized how important it was to live for the day, cherish and support one another, and get the most out of life.

Knowing that Jan and I had been going through a trying time, my family made a point of celebrating our anniversary at the picnic with as much merriment as possible. Joan and Jerry brought all kinds of gag gifts for us, including a pair of water pistols, already loaded and ready to go, and a dart game, perfect for relieving stress. They even brought a teddy bear and a candy necklace for Jessi. After thoroughly soaking each other in a spirited water-pistol fight, Jan and I brought Jessi to Mom's to watch Joan and Chuck open their wedding gifts before leaving on their honeymoon.

In Iowa, Cara and Dan were to have wed sometime in April.

Diary, June:

Jessi, you had a wonderful time playing with your cousins at the wedding, and you were sad when you had to leave. Ashley and Daddy played with you by the outdoor fountain. You were attracted to it immediately, just like the fountains at the mall. We've started to use our craft closet and you enjoy coloring with markers, mostly on yourself rather than on paper, but that's okay! The other day you took a red crayon and while I was in the kitchen you drew all over the panes of the French doors and on the wallpaper. You ran in to get me to show me your artwork. When I saw it, I almost lost my temper, but I remembered that we had not yet told you that you needed to use paper. I explained that it was a "no-no." You proceeded to show Dad that it was a "no-no" when he came home. Grandma Jo humored us with a story about Aunt Pam. She had left Pam in her crib and Mom's lipstick had fallen out of her pocket into the crib. When she returned later, the wall next to the crib had all been colored. Oh well, that's parenthood! Purse scrounging has become a favorite pastime. Jessi pulls out all Mom's papers and then proceeds to write checks to Mom. The phone remains your main love and you pick it up whenever you can, to talk. Your vocabulary is amazing! You are able to say over thirty-two words now. Dad has become your favorite friend; when he is around, you never notice anyone else. It makes me feel so good to see how much you love him.

The oral arguments for the Iowa Supreme Court were heard on June 8. Having filed a statement earlier, Rick Boresi, Jessi's Guardian ad Litem, didn't show up for the hearing. His written statement focused exclusively on the legal aspects of the case, citing biological parents' rights, while failing to look at the immediate and long-term effects which the transfer might have upon Jessica. The following is an excerpt from his statement asking the court for further orders:

> *During all the phases of this case, [I have tried] faithfully and conscientiously to represent the interests of the child who is the subject of this matter . . . I have supported the position of the putative father in regard to the issues of paternity and the termination of his parental rights . . . If [I] were appointed to represent the minor child before this high court, I would continue to support the position of the putative father.*

Rick had asked the court to determine who would be responsible for the payment of his fees; he also asked to be relieved of his duties. The Supreme Court responded by directing him to the District Court to resolve the issues of payment and relief. To my knowledge, he never followed through in these proceedings with the District Court. Jessi had been abandoned by her lawyer.

Kathy Miller and Onita Mohr, attorneys from the Youth Law Center in Des Moines, Iowa, contacted Gary to say that they were outraged about the rulings issued in our case, and they wanted to file an amicus brief on Jessica's behalf. They explained to me that any interested party can file a brief on behalf of a person involved in a court action, to support a certain aspect of the case which should be considered. For instance, a lawyer who is not representing any parties in a case might write on behalf of one party, citing constitutional standards or case precedents; a therapist might submit an amicus brief citing psychological theory as it relates to one of the parties.

When Gary petitioned the court to see if the amicus brief could be entered into court records, the Iowa Supreme Court authorized the filing. The arguments in the brief focused on the trial court's errors in judgment:

    1. The Trial Court did not properly construe the impact of the United States Supreme Court cases dealing with the rights of unwed fathers.

    2. The Trial Court erred in finding that evidence of the past behavior of the putative father was not admissible in determining his present intention to abandon the child.

    3. The Trial Court erred in finding that the putative father had not abandoned the child.

    4. The Trial Court erred in failing to give any consideration to the welfare or the best interest of the child, in determining if D.S. parental rights should be terminated.

Finally someone had written a legal document that treated Jessi as a person who would suffer the consequences of court decisions. The brief developed the issues which we felt were central to this case, and it highlighted the inconsistencies within Dan's and Cara's cases. It suggested that Dan should have participated in Cara's care before the child was born. If he questioned whether or not the child was his, acting as a responsible sexual partner, he should have discussed the possibility with Cara. Oregon law was cited regarding a putative father's rights; to insure such rights a man should support the birth mother financially during the pregnancy, taking responsibility from the beginning of conception. Otherwise the father's rights would be terminated on the grounds of abandonment.

Iowa itself had case history stating that blood lineage alone was not enough to separate a child from the nonbiological parents she had come to love—*Painter* v. *Bannister,* Iowa Supreme Court. Over a long period of time, Dan had not financially supported his other children. Payment was finally received through wage garnishments. In the consideration of abandonment in Jessica's case, Dan had not supported Cara financially or emotionally through her pregnancy and delivery. Since the day that his case was filed in court, he had never initiated any contact with Jessica, Jan, or me. He had never requested visitation. It bothered me terribly that he didn't send a card or some memento which we could share with Jessi. We read Cara's letters to Jessi quite frequently. Cara and her letters were a part of Jessi's life. We wanted her to know about and to see the love that Cara felt for her.

Jessi loved all the activities of summer. Of course, swimming was her favorite! But she was happy doing almost anything outdoors. When Kalise and her husband, Dave, sent Jessica some money for a special "summer present," we bought her a bike seat and a riding helmet. She loved to ride that bike with Mom and Dad! The helmet was a chore in the beginning, but she got used to it and insisted Mom wear hers while we were riding. We spent many hot summer evenings riding around the neighborhood with Randy and the boys. Jessi and Graham sat in their special seats directing the group from the rear.

Jan and Barry had taken on some summer painting jobs. A neighbor owned a home on Lake Charlevoix and asked them if they would consider painting it. Jessi and I, always ready for an adventure, tagged along to spend time on the beach. The house was very comfortable and included a hot tub which overlooked the lake. Jessi enjoyed playing with the rocks down by the beach in her pink polka-dotted swimsuit. When she grew tired of that, she would walk back up to the house and offer to help her dad. Jan gave Jessi her own paintbrush, and together they would work. In the evenings we would all settle back in the hot tub, gazing at the stars and the moon. "Big ball moon, Dad! Big ball moon, Momma!" Jessi would say, her face animated. "See the big ball moon?"

The stress of waiting to hear about Jessica's future built daily; the ruling could come down in a couple of weeks. Fearing we might lose, friends and relatives called every day, anxious to hear any bit of news. We had begun preparation for an appeal to the U.S. Supreme Court, to be filed in the event of a ruling against us in Iowa. Glenna was continuing to research case histories and rulings. While in New Orleans at a convention of the American Academy of Adoption Attorneys, she met Larry Ivers, a new member of the Academy from Iowa. She spoke to him briefly about the case and he indicated he might be interested in helping out.

Joan called one day from work. "Robby, I have an idea. You need a break from this waiting for the court ruling. I've got some vacation time coming, and Chuck can't get any time off. How about going to California with me for a week?"

"Thanks for asking, Joan, but it's just out of the question! I can't possibly go. I can't leave Jessi and Jan. Can't you get someone else to go?"

"Look, Robby, just think about it. Don't say no now. Talk it over with Jan." I hung up and forgot about it for the rest of the day.

Later that night Jan mentioned that he'd love to have some extra time with Jessi. He had been thinking of taking a week off from work just to be with her. "Jan, would you like some time alone with Jessi?" I told him about Joan's idea, and how I hadn't even taken it seriously. Jan was so enthusiastic about the idea that I finally agreed to do it. I thought it would be good for Jessi to have a whole week of special time with her dad. This would be the first time Jan had ever taken care of Jessi by himself for any extended period of time. I wrote out Jessi's daily schedule for him.

> *Dear Jan,*
>
> *I wish you the best. Stay calm, enjoy, and get out and see people. You will do a great job! I have faith in you. Be patient with Jessi; she will be going through a bit of a change without me at home.*
>
> > *Love, Robby*
> > *July 3, 1992*

Note to Dad from Jessi (transcribed by Momma!):

> *Dear Daddy,*
>
> *Mommy says she's going to go away for a few days, and that if we make a calendar and stick it on the refrigerator I can look at it every day. We can mark off the days so we will know when Momma comes home. She also thought I should let you know what I enjoy doing with my days and what I like to eat. Remember, my favorite thing is "go to the park." I sleep best with my buddies by my side, Gramps, Jo, Tinker Bell, and Baby.*
>
> *Dadda, I like to get up right away in the morning to greet the day. Teatime is for both of us. I get to play with my toys and sit and have tea. I use my little teapot that Randy bought me. At nap time if I wake up Momma sits on my bed and holds me tight and tells me it will be okay. I rest my head on her*

shoulder and sometimes I go back to sleep. That's a great day for Mom if I take a full nap. In the evening, I like to take a bike ride over to see Grandma or take a ride in my stroller. As you know, tubby time is a must. I like to bring my toys in the tub to play with. This is a special time for Daddy and me to talk.

The trip to California was just what I needed to relax and reenergize my body, but it was almost unbearable being without Jessi, right from the start. When we boarded the plane, I thought how much Jessi had loved the plane flight to Florida. I thought about her constantly. What was she doing? Would Jan be able to get her to sleep? Would he be able to keep up with her? She was so active! I couldn't stand being away from either one of them.

"Joan, I think this is a big mistake," I said as the plane prepared for takeoff. I was considering asking the flight attendant to stop the plane and let me off.

"Robby, it's okay," Joan said. "Jan and Jessi are going to be fine! Jessi will see that her daddy can take care of her, and she can help him learn to do the things he can't do! She'll lean on Jan in ways that will make their bond stronger than ever. Jan will see what it takes to keep an energetic child satisfied, see to Miles's needs, and take care of the house!"

I finally took a deep breath and sat back in my seat. Jan and Jessi deserve this special time together, I thought. Jan will come to realize that being at home with a child is probably the most demanding job in the world, but unlike any job that I've ever had, the rewards are far greater.

On the Fourth of July, Joan and I went to visit some friends of Joan's in Pleasanton, California. They had invited a gathering of friends over to celebrate the holiday, many of whom were originally from Michigan. Their friends could not believe that we had just flown there and rented a car, and were heading off the next morning to go camping without any idea of where we were going. One couple even stopped the next morning as we were leaving to see if we had really packed a tent and sleeping bags. There in the back of our Tempo was a Wilson golf bag complete with a canvas tent and two sleeping bags. All we needed to do was borrow a couple of lawn chairs and some cassette tapes and we were set.

No matter how hard we tried to talk about other things as

we drove, the conversation kept coming back to my concerns about Jessi and Jan. Joan was a perfect companion; she let me worry out loud, and then guided the conversation to happy stories about things that Jessi and Jan had done together before. "Remember when Jessi and Jan went to the park just after the heavy rainstorm, and the whole park was mud? Jessi wanted to take her shoes off and feel the mud between her toes. You or I might have insisted that she not do it, but Jan thought it would be a good experience for her. Remember, Robby? He finally took off his shoes, too, and marched through the mud with her. Then they came home and spent an hour sitting on the side of the tub, dangling their feet in bubble bath." I remembered the joyous looks on their faces as they sat on the side of the tub, with their pant legs rolled up and their feet soaking. I felt a surge of confidence that things at home would be fine.

We soon ended up in Humboldt Park. The sites were spacious and secluded, just what we'd wanted. Arriving at dusk, we started to unpack the tent right away, knowing we didn't have much time to set it up before dark. Sorting through the pieces, Joan tried to figure out how the tent fitted together. She was telling me about problems she and Chuck had had with it in the past. After a few futile attempts we realized that a main connector was missing from the set. The harder we tried to figure out a solution, the more annoyed Joan and I became with each other. Finally, in complete darkness, we managed to tie the tent to a tree with some twine. When we finally got into our sleeping bags, we were exhausted! Just before I drifted off to sleep, I saw Jan and Jessi in my mind's eye, enjoying each other's company and getting along fine. "I love you both so much," I whispered.

I woke up with a start in the early morning, almost jerking awake as I listened for Jessi to call me. I knew I'd need to call Jan and Jessi early in the day. Joan and I decided to take a morning hike, and we happened upon a phone in a store at the end of the trail. "Hello, Jan! How are you?" I said, sounding anxious. "Hey Robby, we're great; how are *you?*" Jan answered. "Jessi and I are just fine. Here she is!" I heard the sweetest voice saying, "Momma! Myes here. Dadda here. Momma here?"

"Momma will be home soon, Pooh! I love you!" Jan got back on the phone. "Rob, don't you worry. You and Joan have fun and relax. We're going to the park in a few minutes. We'll be fine! I love you." They did sound good, and very happy. I felt so much better!

Joan and I headed for the coast at Mendocino. We camped on a bluff overlooking the ocean. It was truly a heavenly place, breathtakingly beautiful. We stopped at a little shop and picked out a card to send home to my little Jessica. The black-and-white photo on the card was of a mother laughing as she held her bright-eyed smiling child with extended arms. I wrote:

My dear little Sweet Pea,

Momma misses you so very much. Happy 17-month birth-day. Wish I could have brought you on our camping trip. You wouldn't have been very happy with Momma taking you across the country to sit in some tent, though. Momma will be home soon to hug and kiss you, and I won't go away without you ever again.

Love always, Momma

The flight home seemed to take forever. Jan and Pooh met us at the gate. It felt good to be home! Jessi reached out and said "Momma!" when she saw me. We smothered each other with kisses. Joan swirled her around in her arms and gave her a great big hug and kiss. Jan looked so happy, beaming with love and pride. "We did fine, didn't we, Jessi?" he said, smiling. "And, Robby, I get the picture now. *Mothers work so hard every day!*"

"Oh, Jan, I love you so much!" I said as I hugged him. "I'm so grateful to have you! You're such a wonderful father to Jessi and a wonderful husband to me!"

Tucking Jessi in bed that night, I could hardly let go of her. I had told Jan I would be right down, but with Sweet Pea's head on my chest I couldn't bear to move. Our love was so deep, it was as if we were one. Jan came in and put his arms around both of us. The look in his eyes said it all. We all loved each other beyond measure.

In the morning Jessi rose early. She sprang up and smiled and chirped, so happy to see that I was home. Cheerfully she took me down the stairs and into the kitchen, to the little calendar that she and Jan had drawn on. Jan had proudly filled in most of the spaces, telling of his time spent with Jessi. They had made trips to the farmers' market, the mall, and a fireworks display. Jan even mentioned that "Jessi misses Momma, wants to hear her voice, and wonders when she will be coming home." At the bottom of the calendar was a large note saying "WELCOME HOME!!!!"

This had been a good week for all of us. Even though we had all missed each other, we'd grown from the experience. Jessi loved her daddy so much; it was hard for her when the weekends were over and she only got to see him after work or for an occasional lunch. This week they'd finally had the time together that they deserved. For the first few days after I returned, Jessi seemed a little distant from me, almost as if she were mad at me. I was prepared for that possibility, and took it in stride, hoping that once we were back in our regular routine, she would be fine. I made sure that I gave her my full attention all the time, and soon she seemed to have recovered from any misgivings she might have had.

Kim sent a letter dated July 28. She told us that a decision was expected from the Iowa Supreme Court on September 23, 1992. She indicated that a motion had been filed by the Schmidts' attorney and in response our counsel had issued a motion of resistance. Jacqueline Miller's motion stated:

> *This court has the duty under Supreme Court Rule 15 to provide for the custody of a child in a manner which is in the child's best interest in appeals of this nature . . . D.S. [Dan] and C.S. [Cara] suggest that this court order every other week visitation to take place at least initially in Michigan. However, they will be agreeable to any visitation this court orders. The relationship of appellees to their child will suffer great impairment if this motion is not ruled on immediately by this court.*

Litigation has a life of its own, often having little to do with the parties involved. Attorneys take the initiative and make decisions on their own, without asking their clients for their opinion. We did not even know that Gary filed a resistance on our behalf, stating that the interjection of "complete and total strangers" into Jessica's life would only serve to confuse and upset her.

The court rejected Dan and Cara's motion for visitation. This was to be the first and last request for visitation filed in the courts. When we heard the news about the court not authorizing visitation, we began to speculate on the outcome of the case. If they were going to rule in Dan and Cara's favor, they would have allowed visitation to give Jessica the opportunity to get to know them before being placed in their care. This was one of the central issues of the case for us: How could they turn a child over to complete strangers without allowing for the establishment of some type of relationship? Kim felt this was a good sign. Our hopes were lifted.

Diary, July:

Dear Jessi,

I wish I could keep a part of you as you are now. I cannot fully express in words what it is you mean to us. Your personality is developing, and we love the person you've become. Your father continues to mean the world to you. He's been working a lot of hours and he's not around all the time but every day around 4 A.M. you wake up, come in our bed, and get your very own hug from your very own special dad.

Jessica's trips to the pool at Joan's apartment complex were the highlight of her summer. No longer content to bask in the sun under her umbrella, she had become active and wanted to be in the pool all the time. Scott loved to play with Jessi in the baby pool. Jessi would throw her toys into the pool and call for Scott to retrieve them. They would end up splashing each other gently and laughing together for hours. Randy and the boys were among the regular guests at the pool; Randy's mother lived in the same complex, and the boys would spend many hours visiting their Grandma Ann. Ben and Nick could swim, leaving Jessi and Graham on the steps learning to dive into their mothers' arms. Graham would boast that he could dive better than Jessi, and would attempt to prove it. My cousin Ann would bring Will over to the pool. He was two and was able to show Jessi all kinds of new things (everything that a two-year-old knew). Jessi loved the boys. Whether they were roughhousing or giving her instructions, she was glued to them. Jan and I enjoyed watching Jessi interact with other children. Like Scott, she was so generous and patient, a very considerate child.

Jerry, almost fully recovered, was going out of town for a while. Jessi and I took Jerry to the train station. They had become extremely close, and seeing him go was hard on her. Jessi loved the way he played; they had special games which only they played together. Jessi loved it when he would squirt her in the face with water from her bottle. We have great pictures of the two of them in action. Aside from when I went to California, Jessica had said goodbye to very few people. We waved goodbye as the train pulled away from the station and Jessi began to cry, not knowing what was happening to him. He had said he would return, but she didn't really understand.

The summer was dwindling, and we knew that the decision would come down any week now. Jan's parents decided that they would fly to Ann Arbor and be our support system while we waited to hear the news. We knew how much it would mean to them to have another visit with their granddaughter. Jessi's eyes sparkled when her grandparents arrived. Oma was quite surprised at how well Jessi was getting around; she had grown so much since February! Pooh, anxious to show them to their room, motioned with her hand to follow her upstairs. Oma put Jessi on the big bed and Pooh pointed to the pillows and stated quite clearly, "Mine." Moving on to her room, she initiated the same type of conversation. Everything was suddenly "mine, mine, mine" as she went about showing Oma her territory.

Mornings were Jessi's best time of the day. She would crawl out of bed and head for the stairs to go see her Opa. As she proceeded up the stairs, you could hear her little voice say, "Opa, O-pa!" He would answer in a mock gruff voice, "Who's that? Who's coming up those stairs?" Pooh had such a teasing smile on her little face. "Mine," she would say, pointing to the bed as she approached them in the bedroom. Opa lowered his hands to pick up his little granddaughter, giving her a great big smooch on her cheeks. Opa and Oma brought a lot of happiness into our lives that week. Opa even took his little sweetheart on several bike rides, circling the block several times in the evening. Oma loved to push Jessi in her stroller through the park.

September 23 was right around the corner. Oma and I had been talking about how Wednesday could bring very bad news. Jan's parents never believed that such a thing could happen in the United States. They had come from Holland to bring their children up in a country which they believed to be very just. Their image of the legal system was of fairness, and protection against trage-dies such as this. They could never understand us when we told them that we could lose. It was too far to stretch their imaginations; they could not comprehend such an injustice. After dinner one evening, Jan decided to tell his parents that they should leave before things got worse. Jan was concerned about his mother's health. He feared that hearing the bad news in our presence and seeing our pain could cause his mother to suffer another heart attack, and he wanted to protect her.

Jessica was devastated when Opa and Oma left. The night they left Jessi had a terrible time sleeping. She was developing another ear infection, and in her dazed state she would call out, "Opa." In the morning Jessi searched all over the house trying to find her Opa and Oma; she looked in every room and every closet. It was so hard seeing Jessi go through this separation. She missed them more than I ever thought she would.

Jan had planned to stay home on September 23. He knew that we would all need to be together if things went wrong. Jessi and I got up and had our teatime early that morning. The phone rang; it was Kim. Jan was outside working on his car when the call came in. As I stood in the kitchen holding Jessi, Kim's voice sounded so distant. I could hardly hear her. She was talking in generalities, not getting to the point, until she finally said it: "You have lost. The judges did not reinstate Cara's rights." I looked out the window and saw Jan looking at me. He ran in as he saw my eyes starting to fill with tears.

Trembling, in a state of disbelief, Jan grabbed the phone: "We will call you back, Kim." She said, "Try to call soon. We have a lot of things we must work out."

"*Why*? Why? Why? . . . Why is this happening, Jan, why don't the judges care about Jessi? What are we going to do?" I cried. Jan paced the floor; Jessi followed right behind him. "We'll call Kim back and see what they have decided. Maybe we should put in a call to Glenna. We are going to appeal, Robby, that is all there is to it. Kim told us we can appeal. The U.S. Supreme Court will never let this happen to Jessica. Never."

We called Kim back, hoping that she could guide us, hoping she would say the things we wanted to hear. Instead she said, "Robby, you have lost. Eight out of the nine judges ruled against you. Judge Snell was the only dissenting judge." Kim read from his opinion:

> *The evidence is sufficient to show abandonment of the baby by Daniel. The record shows he has previously failed to*

raise or support his other two children. He quit supporting his son, born in 1976, after two years. From 1978 to 1990 he saw him three times. He has another daughter whom he has never seen and has failed to support. He stated he just never took any interest in her. In every meaningful way, he abandoned them.

Daniel knew that Cara was pregnant in December 1990. He saw her in the building where they worked for the same employer. The child was born February 1991. Having knowledge of the facts that supported the likelihood that he was the biological father, nevertheless he did nothing to protect his rights. The mother, Cara, who knew better than anyone who the father was, named Scott as the father. The legal proceedings logically and reasonably were based on these representations. The termination of parental rights as known to exist at the time was legally completed and an adoption process was commenced. Daniel's sudden desire to assume parental responsibilities is a late claim to assumed rights that he forfeited by his indifferent conduct to the fate of Cara and her child. The specter of newly named genetic fathers upsetting adoptions, perhaps years later, is an unconscionable result. Such a consequence is not driven by the language of our statutes, due process concerns or the facts of this case.

The order from the eight other judges said just the opposite. Dan's right had come before everyone's, including Cara's.

As tempting as it is to resolve this highly emotional issue with one's heart, we do not have the unbridled discretion of a Solomon. Ours is a system of law, and adoptions are solely creatures of statute. As the District Court noted, without established procedures to aid courts in such matters, they would be engaged in uncontrolled social engineering. This is not permitted under our law. Courts are not free to take children from parents simply by deciding another home appears more advantageous.

This had nothing to do with a more "advantageous" home. The judges did not recognize the definition of "parents." Parenting is an action, something that develops over time; blood alone does not make a parent. The social engineering came into play when the judges chose not to acknowledge Jessica as a person, instead treating her like a piece of property. The judges said it themselves: "Courts are not free to take children from parents simply by deciding another home appears more advantageous." We were Jessica's parents, her only parents at that point. Dan and Cara were biologically related, but they were perfect strangers to Jessica. The bias of the court in favor of biology had put Jessica's psychological well-being in jeopardy.

Kim advised us to lie low. The press had already started calling, and it would only be a matter of hours before they would show up at the house. I began begging: "Kim, please, please get us a stay. What will happen to Jessi, Kim? Will they come and try to get her?"

Kim replied, "Robby, Jackie has already started calling. She wants to know when Dan and Cara can come and get Jessi."

"*What?* What are you talking about? Can they do that, Kim?"

"Well, I told Jackie to just sit back, because we were appealing to the U.S. Supreme Court," replied Kim. "She was not happy with that idea. She plans on going to the District Court to get an order to have you bring Jessica back right away."

"Kim, please, *please* get a stay!"

"Robby, I will do everything I can, but we're not sure who to file the stay with at this point. As soon as we find out, I will file the stay. Now don't forget what I said. Lie low, and I will call you and leave messages to let you know what is happening."

Eight

JESSI WOULD BE GOING to live with Dan. There was very little else we could do. We had lost, and our chances for success in the U.S. Supreme Court did not seem promising. Jan and I knew that Jessica would be taken at any minute. Kim's recommendation to lie low was distressing. We had not discussed this scenario with Gary or Kim in the past, so we were totally uninformed as to what might transpire. We had always hoped we would prevail and that justice would be served after all this time. We were wrong; there was no such thing as justice for children. The callousness of the courts' decision devastated us.

Jan and I were panicked, scared, and bewildered. We looked into each other's eyes for comfort, but none was there. Both of us were too shell-shocked to rally and take charge. Jerry stopped by after Jan called to tell him what had happened. He had only recently returned from California. "I'm so sorry, Robby," he said gently. "I wish Mom was in town. I bet you'd like to talk to her right now."

I nodded, unable to talk. Jan told Jerry about Kim's advice, not really knowing what she meant. "We're leaving. Get some things packed," Jan said as he picked up some of Jessi's clothes and started putting them into a bag. His voice was hurried, almost frenzied. "Robby, I'm not letting this happen to Jessi. She deserves better. Kim will work on the stay, but we're going into hiding. Are you with me? I think we should call my family. They've said they

will help us. No one would be able to get Jessi in Holland." Jan
was serious. He was not going to let anyone take Jessi away
from us.

Dreading the reality of Jan's statement, I responded, "No,
Jan! I am not going to Holland. What kind of life would Jessi
have there? We would always be on the run. No one should have
to live like that. I am *not* going to leave this country. I believe the
courts are responsible for this child's future and I am damn well
going to hold them accountable for it."

Jerry interjected, "You guys have to pull together. If Kim said
to lie low, she means it. You can talk all you want on the road,
but right now we have to come up with a plan. Get your things
and we'll load them in the car."

I said, "I'll go for now, but I'm not leaving the country. Jan,
do you understand?" Jan knew I would not budge, and deep
inside he knew I was right. He just wanted to protect Jessi with
all his heart.

"Look, Robby, let's just get you ready for this trip," said
Jerry. "Let's pack now so you can leave."

"I'm afraid that the neighbors might see us, and if the press
comes by they might stop and ask them where we are," I said.
"They might tell them that we packed up all our things and we're
on the run. The FBI could get involved. We've got to be careful.
We have no idea what our legal authority is at this point. The last
thing we need right now is getting picked up for kidnapping."

"Let's *go*, Robby. We'll go out the back," said Jan. I got out
some plastic garbage bags and began throwing clothes in them. I
was not conscious of what I was packing; I was frantic. We had
no idea what we were about to do. Jerry and Jan pulled the car
around to the back so that no one could see us pack the car. I
threw the bags of clothes out the window, then ran downstairs
and grabbed the binders containing the case history, in case I
would need them at some point. We had all the paperwork stating
that we were Jessica's legal custodians; I thought we should bring
it along for documentation purposes in the event of a problem.
Jerry, wondering what was delaying me, came in the house and
said, "Robby, you've got to stop! You don't need all these things.
Just bring the clothes you need. It is not as if you're leaving
forever."

Jerry was right. I was so afraid of losing Jessi that I could not think rationally. I felt driven to do whatever it took to protect Jessi. She was tired; she had no idea what was causing the commotion around her. She just wanted to take her nap. I got her a bottle and told her that we were going away on a little trip, letting her know that she could sleep in the car. Jessi, inquisitive by nature, wanted to know if we were going to get "Gamma" and bring her home; she missed her and wanted her back.

We decided that rather than take our Taurus, we would go in Mom's car. If the police were to look for us, they would not be looking for Mom's car. Jerry gave us some money as we transferred our baggage into the car. We had decided to keep completely to ourselves, not use the credit cards, and not call home, in case someone was tapping the phone. Barry came over as we were about to leave. He was very concerned about us running away. He suggested that we just go hang out at the property up north and come back when things calmed down. We thought this was a terrific solution.

We never made it to the property. Jan and I could hardly drive. The pain of losing Jessi had begun to stab into us deeply, and our depression level was at an all-time high. The farther we went, the harder it got to run away from the nightmare. We pulled off in Cadillac and stayed for the night at a hotel, under assumed names. Jessi slept next to me the whole night. Jan was silent.

In the morning when I looked into Jan's eyes I saw something totally different from the night before. Gone were the fear and panic. Now I saw determination and energy. He was the "old Jan," rested and ready to fight. "Robby, we're gonna fight this. We can't give up. The courts have ignored the basic human rights of Jessica. I think that if more people knew about this, they would want to help us. They would be outraged."

We knew we couldn't survive cut off from our families, our support system. This was no way to live. We were going through the motions, knowing absolutely nothing about being on the run. It was as if we were actors in a television show. Who were we kidding? I agreed with Jan completely: we had to fight this.

Later that morning, Jan disguised himself with a hat and glasses so that he could go out to get a newspaper. We were not on the front page, thank God! We had time to work on the case without feeling that people were watching our every move.

I called Glenna, anxious to get her advice. She felt that it would be better to appeal the Iowa Supreme Court's decision, asking for a rehearing, rather than to go right to the U.S. Supreme Court. I faxed her the court order, and she promised to get in touch with a few attorneys in Washington, D.C., to seek advice. She also contacted Kathy Miller at the Youth Law Center to see if they could determine a course of action regarding the rehearing. Since I was afraid that our phone was being tapped, I called Mary Anne and asked her to call our answering machine and listen to the messages. She called back to say that Kim had phoned and wanted us to get in touch with her immediately. Mary Anne volunteered to work out a plan with Joan to ensure that our house looked lived in for as long as we were gone; they would go in at different hours and check to make sure everything was okay.

I hung up and called Kim right away, anxious for word on the motion for a stay. To my complete surprise, Kim said that Gary was in Des Moines trying another case; in his absence, she had been unable to figure out what steps to follow to proceed with the stay. Surely Gary must have considered all possible outcomes for our case. Why hadn't he left Kim with instructions? I asked Kim to keep working on it.

As I hung up the phone, I looked at Jessi, who was engrossed in the book Jan was reading to her. What a mature girl she was! Confident, caring, energetic, beautiful. I could think of a thousand words to describe who she was, but the courts didn't seem to think she was *anyone*. They didn't see her as an independent person who should be treated as a human being with needs and rights of her own. "It can't stop here!" I said aloud. "Jessi's rights have to be considered!" Jan looked up from the book with a look of determination and very deep love. I felt so blessed to have a husband I could love and rely on in this struggle. He was strong and unwavering in his commitment to Jessi and to me.

I wondered who else might be able to help us. My mind flashed to a conversation I'd had with my cousin Patrick at Joan's wedding. He was an attorney who worked for one of the top law firms in Washington, D.C. Jan and I had tried to keep our family out of direct involvement in the legal issues of our case, but now I felt I really needed Patrick's help. When we discussed the case, Patrick indicated that he failed to see how it could get to the U.S. Supreme Court; he felt it was lacking constitutional merit. All the constitutional issues were on Dan and Cara's side, since the law recognized only them as parents, not us. He said he'd give it thought, and to call him if I ever needed his help or advice.

I was lucky to reach Patrick in his office. I told him of our fear of kidnapping Jessi and begged him to tell us what would happen to us next. Pat said he would call back in a half hour, after he talked to a few associates in his office. Looking for a distraction while I awaited his call, I put one of Jessi's tapes in the recorder. There we were, the three of us, sitting in a hotel room, singing "Baby Beluga," as we had so many times in our own home. We were still a family, with our own family traditions.

After lunch Pooh was in the mood to play, and asked if we could go to the park. Jan said he would be happy to take her; he had seen a little park as we came into town. I told Jan that checkout time was around twelve and he should be back by then so we could start heading home.

I jumped when the phone rang. "Robby, don't worry. I have researched the process which you will need to go through in order to obtain a stay from the U.S. Supreme Court. First you should tell your lawyer to pull out his copy of Stern, Gressman, and Shapiro. This text deals with U.S. Supreme Court rules. It's like the bible for anyone who plans on going to the U.S. Supreme Court.

"Each state is assigned a Supreme Court Justice; Iowa's is Justice Blackmun. The request for a stay should be submitted through his office. However, your first action is to file a stay in the state of Iowa, letting them turn you down before moving into the U.S. courts. Take a deep breath and slow down a bit, Robby. You've got at least a couple of weeks before your custody of Jessica is in immediate jeopardy. I'll be in touch in a few days. Please call me right away if you have any other questions."

"Thank you, Pat. I'm so grateful . . ." My voice broke, and I could not continue. I felt such a sense of relief knowing we had a little time to work on our next step. I called Kim again and told her about my conversation with Pat. Kim thought we should still stay out of sight until the Iowa Supreme Court decided about the stay. I said we'd be home on Sunday and she could contact us then. Just as I hung up, Jessi and Jan came back. "Momma, swings! Doggie like Myse!" She was exuberant! I filled Jan in on the calls, and we decided to go ahead up to the property.

When we got there, we decided to stay in a motel. The

thought of staying on the property scared us; someone might be following us. I bent over in the car hoping the desk clerk would not see my face and recognize who we were. After we checked in, we knew we'd have to head back out to get some milk for Jessi, but I wanted to call Mary Anne to get our messages first.

Several reporters had called wanting to know our response to the court order. Frank Santiago had been one of the first callers. He wanted a few words from us, and asked us to give him a call before the paper went to press that night. "Some reporters called us, Jan, including Frank Santiago. The story has been in the papers. If we're going to the store, we'd better disguise ourselves. It looks as if we might have been on television today, too." I suddenly felt naked before the eyes of the world. It was scary.

"Robby, maybe we'd better call Frank back soon. He's always been fair and honest. If anyone is going to quote us at this point, it should be Frank."

I agreed: "I've got his number. But let's go to the store first, and I'll try to gather the strength to talk to him. I just don't think I can do it yet."

Covered with rain gear from head to toe, we marched into the store. Jessi kept asking why Momma was wearing glasses in the store. I could hardly wait to get out; I felt like a prisoner inside a cell. We had done nothing wrong, but we had to hide out as if we were wanted for a crime. Being on the run and living like fugitives was not our idea of an ideal life. Jessica deserved better.

Restless and scared, I sat up most of the night. I was afraid for Jessica; her life was surrounded by uncertainty. Jan and I had always provided a secure home for her, and now that was all in question. At 3:30 A.M. I finally felt ready to call Frank. I knew he'd want to hear from us at any time, so I went ahead and placed the call. I was unable to start the conversation; I couldn't stop crying. Finally, the words poured out of my mouth as I spoke into Frank's machine: "How can someone sentence Jessica to a life of psychological hell?" Just being able to say these few words helped me get through the rest of the night. That morning I asked Jan if we could go to the property before heading back home. I wanted Jessi to be able to run around and play for a while before we hit the road. Jessica was so happy to be outside; it was where she loved to be most. Having associated the property with her Uncle

Barry, she kept asking, "Where Unka Berr-rree? He come soon with Myse?"

"Pooh, we'll see Uncle Barry and Miles soon when we go home. Let's drive home."

"Myse! Myse! Go see Myse!"

Seeing what being on the run could be like, we had learned our lesson. Coming home felt very good to all of us. Running away just was not in us. We could not subject Jessica to that kind of life. I thought back to when we first got to Iowa, and the joy Jessica brought to our lives. I wished that the court battle had never happened. I could see clearly that Jessica's life would never be the same. All of us had to take responsibility for that. No one person stood alone in my mind as the one to blame.

It made no difference who was at fault. Jessi would always come first and we would do the best to protect her within our means. If we were to fail, it would not be without a passionate fight. Jessica would one day know that we put her needs before our own. We would fight for the injustice being done to her, and not give up until we felt that Jessica's voice was heard.

The Iowa Supreme Court had waited from December 31, 1991, until September 23, 1992, to come back with an order almost identical to that of the District Court and the Court of Appeals. Rumors had gone around that the Iowa Supreme Court simply didn't want to deal with this mess.

Dan's and Cara's names had not been mentioned up to this point by the media. The man that we described as abandoning his children was completely unidentified until the judges in the Iowa Supreme Court named Cara and Dan by their first names; this information was now part of the public record. The papers contacted Barbara Schlicht, Dan's ex-girlfriend, to verify if "Daniel" was indeed Dan Schmidt. Barbara felt free to acknowledge that it was the same man. From this point on, Dan and Cara were openly referred to by name in the media coverage.

KGAN, a CBS television station in Iowa, aired the following editorial on September 30, 1992:

> *About 2½ years ago, a woman who is not identified by court records, coupled with "Scott," "Daniel," and presumably a few other males. She became pregnant, had a child, named Scott as the father, and gave up the child for adoption . . . Now*

the biological mother—she's the one who couldn't remember who the father was—decides that Daniel is the father and wants the child back. And Daniel the father has two other children that he has literally abandoned.

We were distressed when we received the news that this comment had been aired. Jan and I never wanted Cara to be characterized in this way. We believed that Cara had been confused. Jan and I never thought the media coverage and exposure would go this far.

Donald Kaul, a columnist for the Des Moines *Register,* gave his opinion of how well the judges had fared in a column headlined "Iowa Supreme Court Had a Choice" on October 11, 1992:

When I first heard about the Iowa Supreme Court decision that took that 18-month-old girl from her adoptive parents and gave her to her biological father, naturally I was outraged. It seemed like a truly wacko decision, a sign that the justices had taken leave of their senses. Then I read the opinion, excerpted in these pages, and I changed my mind, it was not a wacko decision. Cowardly perhaps, even feckless, but not wacko. What it represented was a total failure of the imagination. It was law served up cold, without a heart and with precious little common sense. It was the sort of decision that makes you wonder what planet Iowa Supreme Court justices live on . . . The importance we attach to the rights of biological fathers is ludicrous. The distance between conceiving a child and being its father is vast: many men never bridge it . . . Too many biological fathers are all biology, no father . . .

As more facts were revealed to the public about our case, many people became outraged. Letters came pouring into the papers, and pages were filled with comments from angry Iowan readers: Why had the court not addressed Jessica's needs? Why was biology more important than a child's right to maintaining the only family she had ever known? Why didn't the courts ever deal with Jessi? They had done all they could to prevent bringing her into the picture. Why did the law consider children to be only an extension of the biological parents? Thanks to Mr. Kaul's column, the central issue was now on the table. The courts were the ones who had erred, who had failed to be responsible in this case. We prayed that the media would stick to the real issue and not get sidetracked.

"Ears hang low, wobble to and fro . . ." Jessi sang as she soared on her swing. It was a glorious sunny day, and I had decided to spend unlimited hours with Jessi outside, no matter who called, faxed, or came over. This was our day in the sun. "Momma sing it!" she said, looking at me with such a wide smile and such open eyes that my heart melted just to look at her.

"Okay, Pooh, I'll sing it! Do your ears hang low, do they wobble to and fro, can you dah dah dah dah dah . . . dah dah dah dah . . ." I continued the song in my usual manner. I knew all the tunes, but none of the words. Joan was the same way. Every song Jessi knew began with words and evolved into a chorus of "dah dah." Jessi beamed. It didn't matter to her if I messed up the words.

"Momma, lunch?" Jessi asked. We went inside, and as she opened the refrigerator, I turned on a new cassette I'd borrowed from Randy. The first song on it happened to be "Do Your Ears Hang Low?" Jessi sang along happily until she came to the part where I sang my "dah dah" chorus all the time. Of course, on the tape they sang the real words. Jessi looked up at me quizzically. "Dah dah dah dah . . ." she sang along, as if to say to the singers on the tape, "Now look, tape, Mommy sings it *this* way, and you sing it *wrong!*"

I felt renewed by our morning in the sun; I was ready to get as much work done during Jessi's nap as possible. I called Gary first. "Please, Gary, explain everything that you know at this point about our next steps. We need to understand all our options."

"Okay, Robby," he said. "Let us assume that the U.S. Supreme Court takes the case and issues a stay. If that happens, realistically you're looking at about another year before there would be a decision. And maybe even longer than that. But realistically, probably a year. If they decline to take the case, then I think we need to sit down in person, and it may be easier for us to come to Michigan, for a couple of reasons, than for you to come here, but we may sit down in Michigan and decide with your local counsel what we want to do."

"Gary, I know our chances are really slim in the U.S. Supreme Court. But as I've told Kim, I just can't hand Jessi over to Dan and Cara. It makes me sick to even think of it. The other thing is,

I can't hold back from the media anymore. I've done the best I can but they want to talk to us and I don't know if I need to keep putting them off."

"Robby, I don't have any problems with you [talking to the media] in Michigan. Because whatever gag order was in effect, it died with the decision . . . I think at this stage we don't have a whole lot to lose."

Gary went on to say that it would cost another fifty thousand dollars to start the process of going to the U.S. Supreme Court. He asked for half of the total amount before he could put in the stay to the court. There was a chance that the U.S. Supreme Court would not even look at the case. Jan and I questioned taking such a drastic step if it would not do any of us any good. Gary explained that in order to keep going with legal proceedings, we had to file with the U.S. Supreme Court.

We were all thrilled a few days later when Grandma Jo came back from her trip to Hawaii. She had been there visiting my sister Sue and Sue's son, Jerrod, for a few weeks. We'd really missed her! Jessi was so happy to see her; she dashed into her arms, wanting Grandma to hold her and kiss her. Mom and Jessi talked over macaroni and cheese. There they were, separated by some seventy years, talking like schoolgirls as they ate lunch. They were solid, trusting friends. Jessi told Mom about going to the "poppertee" and how we had to leave our house for a while; Miles stayed with Uncle Barry. They had so much to tell each other. Jessi asked "Gamma" not to go away again, and Grandma promised that she was going to be home now for a long time.

The next few weeks were hard on Jessi. She couldn't get used to my working so much, and neither could I. What I wanted to do was spend every precious moment with Jessi, but I had to keep putting time and energy into the case. I tried to schedule all my phone calls for the hours when Jessi took her nap, and all of my book work for the hours after she went to bed at night. Even so, I ended up doing some of the work during her waking hours. Jan and I tried to hold our heads high, thinking we would not lose Jessi; but we couldn't completely ignore the fact that we were getting so close to the end of our time with her. She had become more precious than ever. Her vocabulary was astounding! She could say half sentences and could communicate with almost anyone.

By the third week in October I had spoken with attorneys across the country, hoping to find some answers. By and large, they encouraged us to try one more time for a rehearing at the Iowa Supreme Court level. Glenna, who was working closely with Kathy Miller of the Youth Law Center, had spoken with Mark Smith, the director of the Drake Law School in Des Moines. Mr. Smith indicated that he was interested in the case and would consider taking the case up on a rehearing. Glenna advised us to go see him and give him a full copy of all the court documents. We had been feeling uncomfortable about how things were going with Gary, especially in terms of money.

Jan took the five binders of court documents to a photocopy store and requested six separate copies, in preparation for going to the U.S. Supreme Court. Since Jan could not get any more time off from work, my mom volunteered to drive with me to Iowa to meet Mark Smith. Mom was very concerned with our financial situation, knowing we could never pull ourselves out of the debt we were taking on. Fifty thousand dollars would be too much for anyone, but for us it meant two years of Jan's gross salary.

I called John Riccolo to let him know that we would be in town, and asked if he could come with me to see Gary. John said he would be more than happy to, and that he looked forward to seeing us again. After arriving in Des Moines, Mom and I went directly to Mark Smith's office. He had already received the copy of our case history, and had asked his students if they would like to take on the case. The legal clinic served as a training ground for the law students. If they accepted our case, their representation would be pro bono, meaning we would not have to pay attorney fees, with the exception of expenses incurred in the case.

I told Mark about our financial problems and how our communication with Gary had gotten off base. Mark felt that most likely it was the strain of the expenses that had hurt our relationship. He advised talking it over with Gary and coming to some kind of mutual agreement to move on. We thought that was good advice.

After looking at the documents, Mark concluded that the Iowa courts had erred. They had decided custody based solely on the rights of the biological father. He felt that there was enough of an argument to take it up on appeal. He would first ask the court for an extension; then he would file a brief in support of his argument.

While we were there Mom asked Mark how the clinic managed to underwrite the expenses of its services. He explained that many law schools run such clinics to help students get firsthand experience with real case histories, giving them a better idea of how the law really works. Mark mentioned that the University of Michigan had such a program and they might be able to help us if we went any further with the case.

Next we had an appointment to meet Kathy Miller and Onita Mohr at the Youth Law Center. It felt good to finally meet these two women who had come forward in support of Jessica's rights. I thanked them over and over again. In the course of our conversation, Kathy also mentioned getting in touch with the University of Michigan Child Advocacy Clinic. She thought they might be able to file a brief to the U.S. Supreme Court if we ever got that far.

We ended the day at the Riccolos, where we were able to relax and talk over all we had learned. Diane made a wonderful dinner. Being with the Riccolos made me think back to my unforgettable time in their home with Jessi, just after she was born. Cathy and Mark Gullickson stopped by with the kids to have some dessert. As we talked after dinner, John and I discussed my problems with Gary. I told him that after Gary sent us an unexpected letter asking for twelve thousand dollars, it had become harder to communicate with him.

"Gary is on your side, Robby," he said. "He probably is having a hard time with his partners about your bill, and for their sake he needed to know where you stood financially. We'll talk things over with him tomorrow and come up with a plan of action. Okay?"

The meeting with Gary proved to be very beneficial. The first thing on the agenda was the time constraints we were under in terms of our actions in the U.S. Supreme Court. We had ninety days left. The Iowa Supreme Court had turned down our request for a stay. Gary had already prepared the brief for a stay in the U.S. Supreme Court, and planned on filing it by the end of the week.

The conversation drifted to the mistakes that had taken place within the Iowa court system. It seemed that Judge Kilburg and Judge L. Vern Robinson erred in not having addressed Jessica's needs as submitted to them in the Adjudication of Law Points. Both judges had forgotten to address the issue of the custody of Jessica. Dan and Cara had not announced their engagement at the time when the case was being considered, leaving the issue of custody a very relevant point. The Supreme Court of Iowa failed by not looking at the custody issue and trying to rectify the oversights of the lower courts. Together we decided to let the Drake Law School take the case up on appeal; Gary would work on the stay to the U.S. Supreme Court.

Mom and I had done all we set out to do in Iowa, and it was time to get back home. The drive home felt better than the drive there because so much had been resolved. We were not in any way certain about Jessica's future, but we had reconfirmed our commitment to her and to move ahead, setting aside our personal losses.

While I was gone, Jessi had developed a severe ear infection. Jan took Jessi to an otolaryngologist, who recommended that Jessi have tubes put in both ears. She had suffered for a good year and a half with recurrent ear infections, and it was time to take care of the problem. We were relieved when the doctor decided to operate immediately; since we had friends whose children had the same problem, we figured it would only be a matter of time before Jessi needed the operation. We were concerned about what medical coverage she would have if she were transferred to Dan; now we were assured that her ear problem would be remedied. We made an appointment for the operation for November 9.

Before our next visit to the doctor, we had the pleasure of Halloween to look forward to! This year Jessi would be a bunny. A friend of Joan's had passed her daughter's outgrown costume (as well as many other beautiful outfits) on to Jessi, and it fit her perfectly. The costume included a floppy-eared hat and little mittens. It would be perfect for Halloween.

It was chilly this year, so we dressed her in white thermal underwear beneath the costume. Since Jan was up at the North Forty, Aunt Joan came to trick-or-treat with us. I got dressed in the makeshift bunny outfit that I had whipped up that day from old white flannel sheets. Jessi and I matched. After we put on the hats with the floppy ears, Joan and Jessi hopped into the bathroom to look at Jessi's outfit. I could hear the two of them laughing as

Joan positioned the hat on Jessi's head. I soon followed to arrange my ears. "Look, Aunt Joan!" said Jessi. "I can opp-opp."

Off we "opped" down the street. Randy greeted us at the door in her Bride of Frankenstein costume, which she had put together that afternoon. The boys were all dressed in black. Nick wore the Spider Man outfit from last year, Ben was a magician, and Graham was a black widow spider. Jessi was in a trance, mesmerized by the costumes, as the boys told her excitedly how to trick-or-treat. She clutched a little orange pumpkin basket in her hand. She was ready! Along with the other children we met along the way, Jessi waddled to the door holding out her basket. Curious as she was, Jessi tried to walk into everyone's living room!

Grandma Jo wanted to see her little granddaughter in costume, so we broke away early and headed up to her house. Jessi knocked on the door, waiting patiently for her grandma to come out with candy. Uncle Jerry met her at the door instead and invited the little rabbit in for a tasty treat. Once inside the house, Jessi gave Grandma Jo a great big hug and went off into the living room to play with her uncle. Jessi grabbed the "piwwows" off the couch and placed them on the floor, as her uncle had shown her many times in the past. Having forgotten the "banky" (afghan), she went back to the couch to get it so that they could play peekaboo. They brought each other so much happiness, rolling around on the floor, playing games and squealing.

On November 9 we took Jessi to St. Joseph Mercy Hospital in Ann Arbor to have the ear operation. We explained to Jessi that the doctor was going to put tubes in her ears. She trusted us, as always, and seemed confident and ready. When the nurses called us into the prep room, we dressed Jessi in the little nightgown which they had provided, and sang together as we often did when we changed her clothes. We had brought Jessi's soft fabric dolls Tinker Bell and Puff-a-Lump along to keep her company. The nurses said that Jan and I could have a seat in the lobby; they would let us know when the procedure was over. We were both very nervous, but we told each other that it would be okay; Jessi was in good hands.

Within minutes a nurse came in and told us that Jessi was fine and that the operation had gone well. I couldn't believe that they were finished so quickly. We had spent twenty-four hours worrying about the operation, and the whole thing took just a few minutes! The nurse told us that children usually don't even know what has happened, and she said there would be no pain involved. This was not the case with my little Pooh; she was screaming! I held her, trying to comfort my little Sweet Pea; her cries tore at my heart. By the time she'd had her nap at home, Jessi was fully recovered. It was such a relief to know that her ears were no longer full of fluid, that she could hear perfectly, and that the chances of further ear infections had been greatly reduced.

The following days were very stressful. I had a flare-up of severe bronchial asthma, which was exacerbated by the stress I was under. My doctor warned me that I had to find a way of getting more rest and lessening the stress in my life if I wanted to get better. She suggested that I enroll Jessi in a play group for a couple of hours a week, giving me time to shut down and rest.

I couldn't even consider it at first. Why would I ask someone else to take care of Jessi if I could have that time with her myself? I told Randy what the doctor had said.

"You know, Robby, I think it's a good idea," she said. "Why don't you try it for just a couple of hours a week?"

"Randy, I just can't bear the idea. I love my days with Pooh. We have our whole routine all worked out. I know just what she likes to do, and what she needs. She's my constant companion!"

"Look, Robby, we're only talking about a couple hours each week! It would be good for both of you. Jessi can play with other kids in a new setting, and you can take naps or get work done during that time, so you won't have to stay up at night. Why don't we stop over at Doris's house and see if she has room for Jessi? You know that Graham has been going there for years, and he loves it!"

I finally gave in. Randy was right; Jessi was ready for this. On the morning of her first day with the play group, Jessi and I put a picture of Momma, Daddy, and Miles, along with a photo of our house, in an envelope to take to Doris's; she had requested that we bring these to help Jessi make the adjustment. Jessi was excited as we walked over to Doris's house. We saw Mike, our next-door neighbor, there, as well as Graham, two little girls, and Doris's son. It was a great little day care, and Doris was well versed in child care, with her years of experience as a kindergarten teacher.

Jessi strolled right in and began playing with the toys in the living room. Graham immediately started explaining to her which toys she could touch and which ones were off-limits to her. Jessi, ignoring Graham, marched over to the little play kitchen and played with Mike there. I gave Jessi a big hug and kiss and said goodbye. She said "Bye, Momma" and went right back to playing.

Diary, November 16, 1992:

My Dearest Jessica,

Today is your first day at Doris's house. I have spent the whole morning in tears, trying to wipe them away, pretending that this is not happening. It has taken me twenty-one months to let you out of my arms, to let someone else watch over my precious little Pooh. Today that day has come. I feel you should be able to have friends and children your own age to play with now. I know that I cannot always be with you. I walked to the car holding back the tears, feeling so rejected, so tossed aside. The whole time I was wondering, "Why did I just leave Jessi there with a stranger? Why?" I could have taken care of her today. Was Jessi really going to be taken away from us? Was my baby Jessi gone forever? I realize that this has nothing to do with the day care. This is the ultimate question of my Sweet Pea's life, her destiny. I feel like I have no control over anything anymore.

When I picked Jessi up, she was in a great mood, full of stories about her morning. She had played with all the kids, had a great snack, lots of stories, and even a walk down to the park at the end of the block. Her happiness was very reassuring to me. I made a silent promise to myself: "When Jessi goes to Doris's the next time, I will not spend the morning crying."

Having followed up on Mark Smith and Kathy Miller's suggestion that we contact the University of Michigan Child Advocacy Clinic, I was thrilled when they returned my call and scheduled an appointment for me to meet with an attorney and a few students there. I dropped off all of our case documents for Suellyn Scarnecchia, an attorney and clinical professor of law, who worked at the Child Advocacy Clinic. The students were expected to look over the case history and see if they wanted to take on the case. They contacted me and asked if I would like to talk about the case. After that meeting I was to meet Suellyn the last week of November.

Suellyn's office was located at one end of the Law School reading room, overlooking the Law School courtyard. As I climbed the stairs I wondered what the meeting would be like. I had met Suellyn only briefly when I dropped off the legal documents. She appeared to be reserved, kind, and about my age, but for some reason I felt a bit intimidated. I was tired of dealing with attorneys. I was going in with the attitude that Jessica deserved justice, and justice was what I was going to get for her.

We shook hands and began to talk as we sat down. Suellyn asked if we were sure we wanted to continue our case. She couldn't predict what would happen. She explained: "What I am worried about is having the judge say way down the line, 'Okay, now I'm even going to find that it is in Jessica's best interest to stay with the DeBoers. What is their legal status going to be?' What we could end up with is a really bizarre legal status. You would be like legal custodians, which could potentially leave the issue of her custody open forever. My other concern is that I think our chances of success are extremely low. I just wanted to be sure that I said that straight out to you."

I liked her straightforward approach. I wanted to hear the truth without any sugarcoating. "That's fine," I said. "I'm glad you did. I already know that our chances of keeping Jessi are minimal. The reason that we're going ahead is that never in my life have I seen anything so unjust. If we were to give up now, we would fall to pieces. Why? Because all my life I grew up with the belief that right was right and wrong was wrong. I have lived my life that way. If Jessica were to be taken away without my attempting to get a Best Interest hearing, I'd fall apart, because none of this fits with the whole construction of my life. We have always been told that this system is here to work for us, that we have constitutional rights, and we believed that children had rights as well. We have gotten to the point where we feel like we have done everything we can to protect Jessica. I think it will make a tremendous amount of difference for Jessi to be able to speak clearly. She needs to be able to communicate her needs, her feelings to those whose care she is in. It will help her to be older if she has to be transferred. I already know the projected success rate. I know what we are up against . . . But we're not giving up, not now!"

Suellyn had listened closely to my words. "Okay," she said.

"That's all I needed to hear. I'm sorry to make you go through this."

"I understand this clearly, Suellyn. Jan and I know we have lost. It's got to become a public issue. This isn't about adoption, this is about a system which clearly states that we are parents and under their definition we have the right to protect this child. It is clearly identified in Iowa's statutes. Jessi should have rights above us all, and her best interest should be paramount. When are we going to face that law? Are we going to face it by walking away every time somebody says you have a very little, minute chance of success? Well, no wonder we haven't gotten anywhere, because no one is going to come forward and challenge this lousy system. We must bring the issue of children's rights to the table at least."

Suellyn said, "Okay, but you can see why people don't go forward. It's because they have to go through what you are going through right now. It isn't like you want your life to be like this. Okay, we are going to file a petition for modification of the Iowa order under the UCCJA as soon as we hear the Iowa District Court order has been issued."

As the conversation went on, she explained to me that the UCCJA stood for Uniform Child Custody Jurisdiction Act. She promised to explain more about it later, but suggested that now we should call Gary. She thought a conference call would be best, so that we could all openly converse about a strategy.

I placed the call. "Hi, Gary. It's Robby . . ."

Gary spoke immediately: "Dan has been in an accident; the other driver has been killed." I was paralyzed, I couldn't breathe. I tried hard to pull myself together, but I failed miserably. I needed to get out of the room. What was Gary talking about? Suellyn asked Gary for more details. He said that a woman had gone through a red light, and Dan, being unable to stop, had hit her broadside with his rig. The woman died instantly. Dan was ticketed for driving his truck in an area in which trucks of that size are prohibited. Gary went on to say that it was on the front page of the Cedar Rapids *Gazette,* with a half-page photo of the accident.

I couldn't take any more. I needed to be home with my little Sweet Pea. Nothing could take away the impact of the day's news like my little Jessi. I picked her up at Mom's house. When I told Mom about the accident, she left the room, trying to hide the tears which welled up behind her glasses. She was unable to compose herself or hide her sorrow. She told me that I shouldn't think badly of Dan, because it was an accident, something over which he had no control.

As I drove Jessi home, she talked on and on about what she and "Gamma" had done all morning. As we came in the door, the phone rang. Jan answered, and was talking to Kim when I got on the line."Hi, Kim, I just walked in the door. What is happening?"

"Robby, the Iowa Supreme Court denied our appeal on all grounds."

"Oh my God!" I cried. "The petition for rehearing, the stay, everything?" I couldn't believe what I was hearing.

"I was just telling Jan that Jackie called to see if you were willing to make arrangements to turn Jessi over. I told her I wasn't going to pretend to call to ask you that, because I could tell her right now that you were not going to do it. I informed her that you would pursue an appeal to the U.S. Supreme Court before taking any other action. Jackie responded that her clients are not willing to wait any longer."

Nine

"I LOVE YOU, JESSI, I love you . . ." I chanted softly to Jessi as she drifted off to sleep. Her face was totally relaxed, her mouth slightly open, and she breathed slowly and deeply. I consciously matched the rate of her breathing, slowing down from the frantic pace of the past day. Ever since the phone call had come from Kim, I couldn't slow my hectic pace; my thoughts, my fears, my breathing, my motions, were all going at breakneck speed. It was as if I thought I could change things if I only went fast enough. Now it was Jessi who managed to slow me down as we lay together on the bed. I wondered if I could take a nap for an hour or so with her; I hadn't slept at all the night before.

It was two hours later when I was awakened by Miles barking. Jessi stayed asleep as I crept out of the room feeling dizzy and sick to my stomach. "Come on, Miles, let's get you outside," I said as I walked him out to the backyard. The air was shockingly cold on my cheeks; it was not until I felt the cold that I realized I had been crying hot tears. I sat down on Jessi's swing and gently swayed, letting the tears fall into my lap. "Jessi, Jessi," I said aloud, "how will you ever be able to trust anyone? You don't deserve this, Jessi. The courts don't have the right to destroy your world. Why, God, why are you taking our child, our soul mate, away from us? Why are you tearing our hearts out piece by piece? What right did you have to bring her into our lives and then hurt all of us so deeply? What kind of loving God are you? How could this happen, God? How?"

I was sobbing uncontrollably. Miles sat close to me, moaning and looking deeply into my eyes. He started walking back toward the house, as if to say, "Come on, let's go inside and see Jessi." Miles went straight up to Jessi while I put some water on for tea. I crept slowly up the stairs, hoping Jessi would still be asleep, so I could just look at her for a while. Sweet Pea was beginning to wake up when I got there. "Momma . . . Myse . . ." she murmured, her face brightening. I felt a wave of thanks go through my body, a physical sensation from head to toe. God had been kind, not cruel. He had given us the greatest twenty-two months of our lives, a time of love and growth, a time that would be in our hearts forever. "Momma have tea now?" Jessi was ready for our afternoon tradition, and so was I. "Yes, Pooh, let's have tea together. I put the water on already."

The phone was ringing as we sat down in the kitchen. "Hello, Mrs. DeBoer, I'm calling from Channel 2. We'd like to come and interview you and Mr. DeBoer this evening, if possible, so we can air a segment on the eleven o'clock news about your reaction to the Iowa court's refusal to consider your appeal for a rehearing." I invited them to come by just after Jan would get home from work.

The central issue that Jan and I wanted to emphasize was that the courts had failed to consider Jessica's best interest. My fury was apparent. "This is not about us having a better home. This is not about us being better parents. Whether it is in an adoption or any other custody case, it is about the children. Children do not have rights. They cannot be the ones to suffer because the courts don't know how to deal with children."

Jan, with resentment in his voice, said, "There are no words to explain how angry I am. No matter what happens, she will always be our little girl."

Local interest in our case was increasing, and members of the media beyond Michigan and Iowa were beginning to be interested as well. Mary Beth Seader, my friend and adviser from the National Council for Adoption, put me in touch with columnist Mary McGrory of the Washington *Post*. I sent her information about the case and asked if she would consider doing a piece in her column. One morning I received a call from Mary McGrory's assistant, telling me Ms. McGrory would appear on *Meet the Press* the following Sunday and planned on mentioning the case. Jan and I tuned in eagerly that Sunday morning, hoping that Ms.

McGrory's words would help clarify what was going on with our case for millions of viewers. One of the central topics that morning was our country's children and the potential impact of the new administration on their status. Ms. McGrory commented: "If we are going to save this country, we have got to save our children. Hillary Clinton would help enormously. She's been an advocate for children for over twenty years. We have these ridiculous laws which give total preference to biological parents. There is a case before the Iowa Supreme Court, a baby adopted at five days old, now twenty-two months old, and the biological father who has never seen her wants her back, and the court gave the child to him. Hillary Clinton will stop this nonsense." We were heartened by her words. Perhaps help for children would eventually come from the federal level.

Many days I felt I needed time just to sit back and enjoy Jessica, away from the distractions of the phone and the piles of legal briefs on the kitchen counter. One of our favorite things was visiting the Trellis Cafe and Tea Room with Randy and Graham. The kids would order their "special tea" (apple juice), which was served in a little tea pitcher in the shape of a kitten. The kitten was wearing a waiter's jacket, holding a bouquet of flowers. They would drink out of two white porcelain teacups, with sugar cookies on little white plates. Randy and I loved the vanilla tea and sweet scones with Devon cream. What a treat! Our trips to the Trellis Cafe always seemed to bring out the best in both of the kids. They would sit and color, play simple games, and even *share*! That was a big step for these two.

Sometimes we went to Fuller Park, which had a magnificent castle structure with a wobbly bridge leading to a tire swing. Jessi was learning to ride on the big-girl swing, and to pump by bending and straightening her knees. Jessi pulled on my skirt. "Uppa, Momma, uppa!" I put her on the swing and gave her a push. Off Pooh went, way up high into the sky. Her face beamed!

A few days before Thanksgiving, I got out Jessi's new corduroy overalls from Aunt Joan. They were lavender with dainty white flowers. Pooh exclaimed, "Pretty, Momma!" She loved new clothes! We had to laugh; it seemed funny that at this age new clothes appeared to be so significant to her. I had promised Jessi that we would make bran muffins before we walked over to

Doris's house. Jessi headed for the kitchen, ready to stir and pour—two of her favorite kitchen activities.

"Okay, Pooh, one cup of flour, please." She dug the cup into the flour canister, triumphantly lifting the measuring cup and pouring the flour into the bowl. "More?" she asked. I pointed to the sugar bowl. "Sugar!" she said. "Cup?"

"Only a half cup, Pooh. Here's the measuring cup."

She measured the sugar and poured it in. "Stir, Momma?" I handed her the wooden spoon. She stirred a bit too fast and too hard, sending the four-sugar mixture flying in clouds through the air. "Uh-oh."

"It's okay, Pooh. Let's try a bit more slowly this time." She dug in and stirred ever so slowly. What a fast learner she was, and an excellent listener! I never had to repeat instructions; she was attentive and interested the first time.

Our muffins baked, we took a plateful and went to sit on the couch to watch *Barney*. The day just would not be the same if we didn't watch our favorite show. She liked every part of her day to remain on schedule, finding any variation to be disconcerting. Jessi nibbled at her bran muffin as we watched. She was entranced by the theme song, "I love you, you love me, we're a happy family . . ." Every once in a while Jessi would sing along: ". . . ovve you . . ." I loved watching her sing. She was so beautiful.

After the show, Jessi and I strolled over to Doris's house. It was a peaceful autumn morning. The dew was heavy on the bright orange leaves. Every so often Jessi would let go of my hand, stopping to pick up a pretty leaf and put it into her pocket. Then she would hold her hand up, waiting for me to clasp it again. As we walked, we talked about what Jessi might do that day at Doris's. This would be Jessi's third visit to the play group. The last time I had to pick up Jessi early. She was crying for her momma, and Doris felt that it would be best if I stopped by to pick her up. Today we hoped things would be better. Maybe we could make it through one visit without one of us being upset! As I walked home, I felt much more confident in myself and Jessica than I had before. I knew we could both survive Jessi's going to day care! Three and a half hours later, when I returned to pick Jessi up, she was happy and excited. The children had been working on various craft projects and Jessi was anxious to show me what she had made.

As we pulled out onto Pontiac Trail Road, I thought I noticed a car following us. I drove around the block just to make sure. There was no doubt in my mind that we were being followed. I was so nervous! I struggled to identify the car but I didn't recognize it. As the car drew nearer, I was able to see the man's face. He looked strangely familiar. My mind flashed back to the night before in the grocery store, when a man had been following us around in the store. I noticed him because he didn't have a cart, and no matter what aisle we were in, he was there. Seeing his face in the rearview mirror, I became frightened for Jessica's safety. I drove home, knowing that if Dan and Cara had sent him, he would know where we lived anyway. I called Doris and told her that Jessi would not be coming back because I did not want to risk the security of the other children. The driver circled the block once, and we didn't see him after that.

Jessi had eaten lunch at Doris's, so I told her it was time for a nap. Jessi showed me the way to her big-girl bed. I told her, "Just for today maybe you could sleep in Momma's bed if you want to, Jessi." Off she ran to the steps! It was a special treat to be able to sleep in Momma's bed; she didn't want to wait around for me to change my mind. Upstairs I took off Jessi's overalls and put on her soft cotton red-and-blue-striped pajamas. I told myself I was letting Jessi sleep upstairs as a treat, but in my heart I knew it was because I was afraid for her and felt she would be safer upstairs. Miles padded along behind us, positioning himself in his spot at the end of the bed where he would wait for his buddy to awaken. Snug under the covers, Jessi and I watched *Winnie the Pooh and the Honey Tree* before she drifted off to sleep. Jessi had recently started imitating Winnie the Pooh, keeping a tiny "honey jar" in her own little cupboard. Gramps had started to rip on his back seam from all of Jessi's love, and we would often laugh about how he had eaten too much honey from her cupboard. One of the most endearing traits that Jessi had picked up was walking with her hands behind her back, just like Winnie the Pooh.

I had a radio interview scheduled for four o'clock. Putting Jessi down for her nap late, I hoped she would sleep long enough to allow me to get through the interview. Jan would be home shortly after four, so he would be there for Jessi when she woke up. At about three-thirty Randy knocked on the door, and I asked her to join me for a cup of tea. Still a bit shaken, I was very happy to see her. Just as I started to tell her about the man in the car, the phone rang. It was Kim. "Robby, Dan and Cara might be in Ann Arbor."

"What?"

"I received a call from the Ann Arbor City Attorney's Office, notifying us that Dan and Cara might be in Ann Arbor."

I called Suellyn to see if she knew about the Schmidts' being in town. Suellyn said she would call me back as soon as she called the Ann Arbor police to verify what was happening. Within minutes, a call came in from an Ann Arbor *News* reporter: "Robby, Dan and Cara are down here at the courthouse. Dan is furious. He just backed me into the wall and began shouting at me."

I didn't know what was happening. What were Cara and Dan doing here? Why was Dan so confrontational with the reporter? Did they think they could just waltz into town, grab Jessi, and leave? Randy and I were here alone. What would we do if Dan and Cara came to the door? I wished that Jan were home. Randy thought I should call the police for protection. Just as I was about to place the call, the phone rang. It was the radio station calling to begin the interview. I panicked, telling them that Dan and Cara were in town. I could not believe that they would just come into town and try to pick Jessi up. The interviewer suggested I call the police.

I went upstairs to make sure Jessi was still sleeping. There she was, the most radiant child I had ever seen. In her hand she held her most precious security object, her pacifier. As she slept, she would roll the pacifier around between her fingers, totally unconscious of what she was doing. As I stepped a little closer to kiss her soft cheek, the floor creaked ever so slightly. She opened her eyes, smiled, and asked her favorite question: "Go to the park, Momma?" As Jessi spoke, I heard someone knocking on the door. Randy called upstairs to see if she should answer it. I looked out the upstairs window and saw a woman standing at the front door. Scooping up Jessi, I came downstairs to open the door myself. The woman was a reporter from the Ann Arbor *News*. I invited her to come in and sit down. She wanted to let us know that she had met Dan and Cara at the courthouse, where she had been assigned to go and talk to them. She had asked them what they were doing in town and how they felt. Dan told her that she couldn't understand his feelings, and he was sick and tired of the media always swarming around him. He just wanted his daughter. He stated, "I keep winning in court, and I still don't have my child."

Dan and Cara had come into town with a document, petitioning the Circuit Court of Ann Arbor to register the Iowa custody order. "Come now Daniel L. Schmidt, hereby registers the attached certified copy of a custody decree and judgment from the state of Iowa." The certified copy was of Judge Kilburg's order from December 30, 1991. The Supreme Court of Iowa had not yet made a new ruling as to when or how Jessi would be transferred back to Iowa. Judge Kilburg was expected to have a Show Cause hearing in one week, on December 3, 1992, to arrange the transfer agreement. Our appeal for a stay from the U.S. Supreme Court had been filed, and we were waiting for their response. Dan and Cara were trying to act on the original Iowa order.

By the time Jan arrived home from work, the reporters had come and gone. Having discovered where Dan and Cara were staying, most of the reporters left our house to see if they could talk to both of them. When I told Jan about having been followed, he wanted us to leave the house immediately and not take any chances. Dan later confirmed to a reporter that he had hired a private detective to watch us.

Suellyn and I went to the Circuit Court the next morning to file a restraining order restricting Dan from removing Jessica from our custody. The Schmidts had spent the day going back and forth between the Ann Arbor police station and the Circuit Court, asking that they be provided an official escort to assist in obtaining Jessi. The police told Dan that he should contact the City Attorney's Office before attempting to remove Jessica. Neither office agreed to assist in the withdrawal of Jessica from our home, since they questioned whether or not Dan had a valid custody order.

That day, the Ann Arbor *News* ran an article about our case. It began: "After a long battle in Iowa's courts Daniel and Cara Schmidt gathered the essentials and came to Ann Arbor on Tuesday. They arrived with legal papers, a child's car seat, saltine crackers and a package of diapers."

Were these really the essentials? Weren't love and family the true necessities? The inhumane way that the Schmidts had chosen to come and pick Jessi up made us wonder if they thought at all about Jessica and what this transfer would mean to her. Up until this point we had put most of the blame for the tactics used on their attorney and on members of the CUB organization. This was the first direct action by the Schmidts, and we couldn't get over their insensitivity to Jessica. Did they really believe that Jessica would be just fine? Did they think they could whisk her away from her family and her home with no warning and not traumatize her beyond description? They had never contacted us directly. They had never asked how Jessi was doing, had never written her a card, had never called. They simply showed up in town to take her away.

It was hard to feel at all festive at Thanksgiving, but I felt we had to try to rally for the sake of our family. My mother's enjoyment of Thanksgiving had diminished since my father's death; Joan and I usually had to persuade her to have a traditional Thanksgiving dinner. My mother thought that we should spend this Thanksgiving in a restaurant, because of the stress we were all under. Somehow, this was not our idea of Thanksgiving, so I picked up a beautiful fresh turkey and cooked it myself. It was a good decision. Somehow, spending time together around the holiday table made us all feel better.

After dinner Joan, Scott, and I took Jessi to the park to get some fresh air. It was freezing outside, but that made no difference to Jessi. As always, she wanted to swing! Joan and Scott could swing with her, but it was my job to push her. Higher and higher she would go, yelling, "Scott! Scott!" He waved to her and clapped when she managed to pump hard enough to soar on her own. We made our way back home across the ball field, which had turned into an ice-skating rink after the last storm. Scott pulled Jessi around by the arms, sliding her across the ice. She trusted him to pull her just hard enough so that she could glide, but not fall. They were wonderful together, just like brother and sister.

Just after Thanksgiving, we found out that U.S. Supreme Court Justice Harry Blackmun had turned down our request for a stay. Refusing to give up, Gary filed again, this time to Justice Sandra Day O'Connor. We continued to hope that a stay would be granted, at least until the court could look into the matter. In the meantime, Mary Anne and a friend of hers named Jody began a petition drive, urging the U.S. Supreme Court to grant our request for a stay. Mary Anne and Jody wanted the petitions to go out on December 1. They went door to door handing out petitions. Mary Anne commented to the newspaper that she was "interested in the case as a citizen who was outraged by this entire situation." She went on to say, "The best interest of this child is in jeopardy. This situation impacts more than just adoptive families. This could happen to any third-party custodian, and there are 200,000 such families in Michigan alone. The system is letting down our most innocent citizens."

Within six days Mary Anne, Jody, and the other petition workers had collected four thousand signatures. They made copies of all the petitions and sent them to Michigan's governor, John Engler, to U.S. Supreme Court Justice Sandra Day O'Connor, and to Hillary Rodham Clinton. Other concerned citizens had contacted us asking what they could do to help, including Joan Pheney Engstrom, a mother of a young child. She said that she could not bear to see this kind of injustice happening to a child. Mary Anne suggested that she might try to organize an event to raise money for the Baby DeBoer Legal Fund, which had been established at a local bank to help with legal expenses.

Diary, December:

Dear Jessi,

Oh, honey, we've reached the stage of the terrible twos. You are not a very happy camper. I cringe as I watch your frustration level skyrocket, knowing in advance that there is nothing I can do to help you through this stage of growing autonomy. Independence is your major goal; you become very anxious when you cannot achieve your tasks. Your expectation level seems pretty high! You begin to cry when you cannot put on your own diaper. It is difficult for you to understand that you are only twenty-two months old. The words "I do it! I do it!" are often heard throughout the day.

Despite the "terrible" times, Jessi was still thoroughly enjoyable. We had many moments of great humor, the kind you share with someone you've known for many years. I felt as if I'd known Jessi for a lifetime. One day we were upstairs watching a Winnie the Pooh video, *Winnie the Pooh and the Blustery Day,* one of Jessi's favorites. There is a delightful song in it about rain, which was enhanced on this particular day by a heavy rainstorm outside. In the story, a great flood takes place after the rainstorm. Jessi and I sang along: "The rain, rain, rain came down, down, down . . ." We bounced around on the bed as the song went on. "Jessi," I said, "you know what? I think I really hear some water dripping downstairs." Jessi looked at me, listening intensely. "Rain, Momma?" she said.

"I think we'd better go see what's going on." She slid off the bed and took my hand. Together we crept down the steps, as if sneaking up on someone. "Shhhhh . . ." I said. "Shhhhhhh . . ." said Jessi. We arrived at the bottom step to quite a surprise: the rain had flooded into our house, and the floor was covered with water! Jessi looked up at me and tried to read my reaction to the flood. Seeing that I was a bit shocked, and a bit confused, she hesitatingly and sweetly began to sing: "Rain, rain, rain, came down, down, down . . ." I burst into laughter, and so did Jessi. We danced around on the wet floor, singing our rain song, until Jan got home from work. He looked at the floor, looked at us, and burst out laughing. The three of us had quite a moment together, laughing, dancing, singing, and loving.

The press continued to show an interest in our case, and specifically in Jessi's welfare. The essence of the case was well captured by Mona Charen and Anna Quindlen, two Associated Press columnists.

Mona Charen:

Taking Baby from DeBoers Would Be a Travesty of Justice

> *Unless the Governor of Michigan or the Supreme Court of the United States intervenes, the baby will be taken from her parents and handed over permanently to two people she has never met. This amounts to a legal kidnapping.*

Anna Quindlen, in a New York *Times* article, wrote:

> *The DeBoers are now trying to move the proceedings to Michigan. There, they hope a judge will consider the best interests of the child . . . They hope to find a judge willing to marry humanity, discretion and statute to argue persuasively for keeping this little girl with the people she now calls Mama and Papa. The courts have relied on the letter of the law when perhaps no situation cries out more clearly for its spirit. Not to*

*determine which parents are richer, better educated or better
situated in life, but what course of action now will leave the
smallest hole in this little girl's heart in the years to come.*

Two columnists, varied in their styles and political ideals,
stepped forward and looked at Jessica's plight. In doing so, they
didn't have to choose sides. Their articles brought the real issue to
light. The courts owed Jessica some respect, a chance to have her
own rights and needs addressed independently of any adults.

After these articles were published, phone calls came in from
across the United States from families struggling through the same
kind of crisis as ours. As we listened to their passionate portrayals
of their own situations, our hearts reached out to them. We were
eternally linked through the same cruel and heartless nightmare.
One conversation which I will never forget was with Pilar Rice, a
kind, soft-spoken woman from Grand Rapids, Michigan. She
called one evening in tears, saying that she was very sorry to hear
that we might lose Jessica. She spoke of losing her own son,
Christopher, when he was thirteen months old. The adoption
proceedings in her case were held in Arizona. Pilar and her
husband, Richard, received a fax on a Wednesday saying that they
were not to leave the house in which they were staying with
Christopher. On Thursday morning a social worker arrived and
told them that they had one more hour with their son. As the
social worker drove away with Christopher, Richard and Pilar
could see him screaming frantically in the back seat. Pilar and
Richard were never allowed to see their child again. Christopher
was placed in a foster home until the court ruled that his birth
father, a priest, could have the child returned to him. The priest
then turned the child over to the birth mother, whose rights had
been terminated.

Pilar's cries were piercing. It was as if I were hearing myself
through the receiver. The court had acted irresponsibly, taking a
thirteen-month-old child out of his mother's arms, believing that
the child was resilient enough to survive such a separation. How
could they impose this kind of responsibility on a child? I tried to
comfort her, knowing that there really wasn't much I could say to
make her feel better. Pilar encouraged us to remain strong in our
quest to protect Jessica, to search for the justice which was due to
these children. I felt a strong kinship to this woman I had never

met. I knew exactly what she was saying even before the words passed her lips.

On December 3, Judge Kilburg of the District Court of Iowa held a Show Cause hearing to arrange for Jessica's transfer back to Iowa. He gave no indication that he would grant an extended transfer period, nor did he indicate that a Best Interest hearing would be held. The hearing was scheduled for 9:30 A.M. Jan and I chose not to attend the hearing. We did not feel secure leaving Jessica home in our absence in view of the Schmidts' prior actions, and we certainly did not feel comfortable bringing her with us. We feared a scenario like the Rices' tragic separation from Christopher; it seemed to us that Judge Kilburg had every intention of taking Jessica that very day. Suellyn and her students were ready to proceed in the Michigan courts. We would wait until Judge Kilburg issued his order; then we would go into the Circuit Court and file a petition requesting that Michigan take jurisdiction in the case.

Judge Kilburg's order stated:

> *The rights of Jan and Roberta DeBoer . . . are hereby terminated. The birth father, Mr. Daniel Schmidt, is given legal authority to proceed under any legal means to enforce this order directing that Jan and Roberta DeBoer relinquish immediate physical custody and possession of the child to him or his designee. The court specifically finds that Mr. and Mrs. DeBoer have no legal right or claim to the physical custody of this child. They are acting outside any legal claim to physical control and possession of this child.*

Judge Kilburg was amazing. He had once spoken of social engineering and taking a child away from her parents. In Jessi's eyes, *we* were her only parents. The judge was giving Dan full authority to do whatever he could within the confines of the law to gain immediate custody. This irresponsible action confirmed in our minds that the court system truly thought of Jessi as no more than a piece of luggage. I could only wonder how Judge Kilburg would feel if someone were to come and take his adopted son out of his hands, tell him that the birth mother had lied and there was a new birth father who wanted custody. Would he think of himself as someone who was acting outside of the law by protecting his only child?

Kim called Suellyn's office to say that Judge Kilburg had ordered a Show Cause hearing to be held on December 18. We were to appear before him to explain why we should not be held in contempt of court for not bringing Jessi back to Iowa. During this conversation Kim mentioned that although in an earlier decision Judge Kilburg had ordered an investigation of Dan Schmidt through a Child in Need of Assistance proceeding to be conducted by the County Attorney's Office and the Juvenile Court, he had now dropped that order.

We were relieved and encouraged when Judge William F. Ager, of the Washtenaw County (Michigan) Circuit Court, stated his intent to review the case on December 3, 1992. He issued an order restraining Dan from removing Jessica from our home. A Show Cause hearing was set for January 5. For the interim period Judge Ager ordered that custody of Jessica remain with us. Michigan was on its way to accepting Jessica's case! We looked forward to January 5, hoping that Michigan would order a Best Interest hearing and assign a Guardian ad Litem to oversee Jessica's case.

During this period of confusion in our lives came Peter Jennings's "American Agenda," the first national television news story about our case. The reporters and camera crew came to film Jessi in her natural surroundings. We did not allow the interview to begin until Joan had come to take Jessi over to Mom's house for her nap. The story aired within days of the interview. The camera crew had also gone to Blairstown to get Dan and Cara's side of the story.

The interview opened with Cara explaining what had happened. "I was like a completely different person, I don't even know that person. It was just a very confusing time." The camera switched to Dan for a comment. "It's our child. Why shouldn't we be given the chance to love her, raise her, teach her things?"

The reporter asked why we had not given Jessi back to Dan initially. "I'm not going to hand this child over to a man who has abandoned children," I said.

The reporter let Dan respond: "I should be judged for something I did sixteen and twelve years ago? You know I don't think so. I have an opportunity now to prove myself and now they're not going to give me that."

The reporter pointed out that what the courts refused to

address is the larger issue, the best interest of this child. With my anger at an all-time high, I proclaimed, "This child is a hundred percent ours, in this child's *mind*. That's the important issue here, *her mind*. What's going to happen to it when you take *her only parents away?*"

After this national exposure, several newspapers and talk show producers from across the country called wanting to arrange interviews. We did not have the stamina for the interviews, nor did we want to fritter away our remaining time with Jessica, who remained our most important focus. We would not exploit Jessi; that was our most important guideline. Yet we wanted to keep the public eye on the issue. Eventually we decided that if the interviewer wanted to talk about a child's best interest, we would talk; but if they wanted to pit us against the Schmidts, we would not be involved. That kind of interview would benefit no one, and would take the focus off the real issue, the opportunity for a child's best interest to be considered in the courts.

We received a call from the producer of the ABC television show *20/20*. They wanted to send their reporter Tom Jarriel to interview us. After speaking with Suellyn, Jan and I decided that we would go ahead and do this show, but this would be our last interview. The producer set a time right before Christmas to come and meet Jessica and do the taping.

The Christmas season of 1992 held some of the loveliest, most magical moments that we ever spent with Jessi. Though we were always very grateful for her presence in our lives, our sense of thanks and appreciation for her was somehow heightened during this season. We chose a cold, snowy day to go and pick our Christmas tree from a nearby tree farm. Jessi's eyes opened wide as she ran through the snow, pointing her little finger at the trees she liked the most. Finally she found her very favorite one, a fat eight-foot tree.

When we got our tree home, Jessi wanted to decorate it right away! She wanted lots of lights and snow on the tree. Whipping Ivory flakes into frothy snow was an old family tradition which I had always enjoyed. It was like lathering shaving cream onto the tree. We all started to put it on the tree together, but Jessi, always anxious to show her independence, stated, "I do it myself." We watched her with joy as she covered the tree. Jessi's favorite ornaments were the pale pink bulbs with little wires on them. She hung them all by herself!

After Jan got home from work one night, we went to the mall to do some Christmas shopping. Jessi's eyes danced when she saw the special Christmas train that was running. She dashed over to the waiting line and said, "Daddy go, too?" Jan suggested that Jessi sit on Santa's lap first, but she wanted no part of that. Although she loved Santa in her Christmas books and videos, she had no interest in meeting him personally! The train, however, was another story. Off she ran to pay her dollar. Once she and Jan got on the train, I thought they'd never get off! They waved to me each time they went by, with Jessi shouting, "Hi, Momma!" Finally Jan convinced Jessi that we would come back to the mall another day, and home we went.

At the family Christmas party, Jessi enjoyed showing all of her little cousins around Grandma Jo's house. We were all settled in there for the evening, planning on spending the night after opening our presents. Will and Jessi led the kids downstairs. Uncle Barry lived down there, and she was proud to show off the hiding places that only Jessi and Barry usually shared. Maura's children, Caili and Christopher, who had just turned one, found it tempting to follow their buddy Jessi down the stairs. Roaming in and out of each room, Jessi hosted the tour. Scott went with them, encouraging Jessi along. As the evening drew to an end, Jessi grew tired of her party dress, choosing to run around the house in her pretty slip, showing off its ruffles and sliding on the wood floors in her pink tights. Jerry's son, Gabe, had shown a great interest in Jessi, and spent the rest of the evening playing with her and the toy harmonica that she had gotten during the gift exchange.

Mom gave Jessi a pearl necklace just like the one I had. Jessi delighted in her new piece of jewelry. She put the necklace on each one of us, admiring how it looked and asking if we liked it. Aunt Joan gave Jessi a Little Tikes car. Nick, Ben, and Graham had one at their house which had become Jessi's favorite toy. Jessi adored any kind of car, especially *real* ones! She always wanted to drive our car. She had already learned how to put the key in the car door and was attempting to learn how the foot pedals worked. Aunt Joan had picked a perfect gift for Jessi. When she saw the huge box she was so excited, asking us to help her rip off the paper right away. She enjoyed the paper-ripping process so much that she seemed content when she got to the bottom of it and found a cardboard box. Jan told her that she might want to look inside the box, and we helped her open up the side of the carton. There it was, in all of its splendor: a car! Pooh knew exactly what it was. "Fix it, Daddy," she begged. "Fix it!" Daddy's little helper got a screwdriver and gave it to him as she pranced around him begging him to hurry up. When it was all put together, Jessi was so excited, so happy to be able to ride around on the carpet showing off her new present.

When it was Jan's turn to open his gifts, I grabbed the camera. Barry walked over to Jan and handed him something, then gave Jan a great big hug and told him to enjoy it. Jan looked at the envelope and slowly opened it. Inside were a set of keys and a green slip. Looking very puzzled, Jan just stared at the keys, saying, "I don't get it!" Barry said, "Keys, you know, keys!" Hearing the word "keys," Jessi ran over and tried to take them out of Jan's hand to start her car. Barry said, "Come on, it's outside!" Jan put his head down and started crying. Barry came over and gave Jan another hug and said, "Take it easy, come on outside!" We all followed Barry to the garage, where, to our amazement, there was a 1987 Chevy station wagon! Since the Dishmans' car had broken down in October, Jessi and I had been getting up in the morning and taking Jan to work. Seeing this perfect gift from Barry, Jan was so happy, so excited! It was a marvelous ending for this warm family night.

On Christmas morning Jessi gave Jan and me a great big hug, then off she went down the hall to find her new car. I heard her "drive" it down to Grandma's room. She pranced up to her sleeping Grandma and stood next to her dressed in her red cotton pajamas. "Gamma, Gamma, goo mornen." Grandma, startled by the little voice, turned to greet her Sunshine. "Oh, there she is, did you sleep well last night in Grandma's big bed?"

"Goo mornen, I've got my car, Gamma. Get uppa, Gamma, get uppa," Jessi exclaimed. Jessi lay down next to Grandma and snuggled for just a minute before jumping out of bed and running back to her car. Coming to the stairs, Jessi pointed down and called out for her Uncle Barry and Uncle Jerry. "You down dere?" Hearing no response, she headed down to see what they were up to. She wanted to share her new car with her uncles. At Uncle Jerry's door she knocked and said, "Goo mornen, Unka Der-rey.

You okay? You hap-pee?" Uncle Jerry said "Yes" and asked for a kiss. "You get uppa and see my car, Unka Der-rey." Jerry told her he would be up in a short while to play with her car, and out of the room she went, going on to see her Uncle Barry. She knocked on the bathroom door. I told her that Barry was taking a shower. "Unka Ber-rey take a shower, I take a shower, too?"

"Later, Pooh. Let's go find your car," I said. Back upstairs we went to find her car parked right where she left it. Jan was having his coffee. "See my car, Daddy!" said Jessi.

Jan said, "I sure do, Jessi, and now I'm going outside now to see *my* car!"

Later that morning, we went to church for a special mass that was being said in Jessi's honor. A longtime friend from St. Thomas's had offered up the Christmas mass for Jessi. She had gotten to know Jessi at Uncle Chuck's baseball games and was very fond of her. It felt strange being back in the church that I had grown up in. I remembered how my father used to drop off my brothers and sisters and me before school, telling us to go in and say our prayers for the day before going into our classrooms. So many mornings during my adolescence I had knelt in these same pews praying to God to give me a special boy whom I could love. Today I knelt there thanking God for my husband and the love that we shared for one another and for Jessi. And I prayed that God would not take our beautiful little daughter away.

Ten

EARLY ON NEW YEAR'S EVE morning, Jessi got out of
bed and turned the TV on. Climbing up into our bed, she
began singing "I love you, you love me, we're a happy
family" as *Barney* came on the air. "Hi, Daddy! Goo mornen,"
she said, beaming up at Jan.

"Hello, sweetheart, good morning!" said Jan, scooping her
up into his arms and giving her a kiss. Then she plopped into my
lap. I hugged her as we talked about where Jessi was born. She
said, "I born at St. Luke's, Momma?" "Yes, Jessi, you were born
at St. Luke's Hospital in Iowa." She reiterated, "I born at St.
Luke's Hospital, Iowa." As she talked, she pointed her finger and
tapped it lightly on her tummy.

She jumped down when the commercials came on and ran
around to turn on the light, anxious to rouse her parents from
bed. No longer interested in the TV, she climbed into the closet
and began going through the clothes. "This my towwew [towel],
look at all these cowths, Momma!" She buried herself under the
heap of garments and lay very still. We could hear her little
voice saying, "Bye-bye, Mom . . . Bye-bye, Djessi." Jan started
downstairs to make coffee, saying, "Well, I guess since Jessi isn't
in our room anymore, I'll go downstairs and make the coffee." A
little hand reached out of the big pile and closed the door as Jessi
said, "Bye, Dad . . . I close the door."

"Hey, who said that?" teased Jan. Jessi laughed as she came

darting out of the closet and dashed across the room to the desk. Watching her in this mood was such a delight. Her energy was exhilarating. "This On's mail, On's mail." She was trying hard to say Jan's name.

"Whose mail, Jessi? Whose?"

"This Dad's mail, Mom."

"Yes, Jessi, it is Dad's mail."

"I give it to him. Dadda, my dad!" Jessi called as she headed down the stairs. She stopped halfway down and turned around to me. "This Dad's mail, Mom?"

"Yes, honey, it is."

"I give it to him. Hi, Myse! Myse!" Jessi's buddy was waiting for her at the bottom of the stairs.

"Dad, here's your mail!"

"Oh, Jessi," said Jan, "thank you soooooo much for these letters. I needed these!"

From upstairs I heard their easy conversation, the implicit trust and understanding that had always been there for Jan and Jessi. I felt my throat tighten with sadness. No, I told myself, I won't let my sadness come to the surface right now. There's enough time for that! I want to give Jan and Jessi my best energy today.

I came down to the kitchen and said, "Hey, what's for breakfast?" Jessi raced to the refrigerator. "Muffins, Momma!" She pulled out the plate of muffins and placed one in front of me with a smile. "Good muffins, Momma."

"Should we take some to Grandma today, Pooh?" I asked her.

"Muffins for Gamma! Now, Momma?"

"Well, Jessi, we'll have to get you dressed first, unless you want to go there in your pink sleeper!" Jessi looked down at her pajamas. "Cowths, Momma." She turned on her heels and raced to find some clothes for the day, choosing her purple overalls. I dressed her, with the exception of her shoes. Pooh would want to put on her own shoes. "Neat, huh? I got a pink one, a blue one," she said as she busily attempted one shoe after another.

When we arrived at my mom's house, Jessi proudly presented the muffins and insisted, "Gamma eat one now!" My mother was happy to oblige, praising Jessi as she tasted the muffin. "Well, I'll bet some pretty special bakers are responsible for these, Jessi. Do you know who made them?"

"Momma and Djessi!" she said, glowing.

"Well, Momma and Jessi are very good at making muffins!"

Jessi raced over to me and gave me a kiss and jumped into my arms. "You gonna go now, Momma?" I had told Jessi that Grandma would be taking care of her today for a while, then Aunt Joan and Uncle Barry. She was excited to spend time with all of them.

"I'll be going now, Pooh, but I'll see you soon, when Aunt Joan brings you home. I love you!"

"Love you, Momma!"

I needed a few hours to organize all our paperwork and documents. I wanted to be fully prepared for whatever might happen next in our legal journey. We were awaiting the Circuit Court hearing with Judge Ager at which he would decide if Jessica was entitled to a Best Interest hearing. Somehow it helped to sort through all our old documents, giving me a sense that I was ready for the hearing, even though I would not be called upon to speak.

We had started quite a file of newspaper articles from all across the country. Magazines had become interested in our case as well. The New York *Times* published an article which elaborated on the CUB organization's convictions. Carol Anderson, a woman who had befriended Cara, was quoted as saying, "No woman should have to have a child for someone else. It used to be that we looked for a family who could take care of the child. Now it has shifted to finding a baby for a couple that wants one. That's a very troubling shift." What was troubling was CUB's twisting of the truth. We did not search out Cara Clausen. It was she who acted unselfishly and made a decision which she felt was best for her child. That decision was to place her child in the care of a family who would be able to love and protect her baby at a time when she could not. The article also quoted Suellyn Scarnecchia: "It is the birth mother's fraud that set this all up and has made it so heart-wrenching. My concern is that it will set a very bad precedent for rewarding her for that kind of fraud. She made a big mistake, and her child shouldn't have to pay for it."

After seeing the New York *Times* article, a producer from *Good Morning America* wanted to know if we would be interested in doing an interview in New York on January 4, the morning before the Circuit Court hearing. Jan and I agreed to go, provided it could be a very short trip. Not wanting to spend any time away from Jessi, we set things up so that we could fly to New York after putting her to bed, then fly home the next morning.

Joan and Chuck came over to take care of Jessi in our absence. I had just given Jessi a bath, and she was getting ready for bed. "Momma did my hair!" she told Joan, pointing up at the big pink bow on top of her head. Jessi had played dress-up at Gramma's house that afternoon, and she was still wearing the pearl necklace which Mom had given her for Christmas. She was so proud to show off her things to Aunt Joan. "See, see my nekass, Aunt Doawwn!"

Jessi lay on the couch kicking her feet, "Aunt Doawwn, Aunt Doawwn, dikkle me, dikkle me!" Joan zoomed in for her feet, tickling her and laughing. Jessi rolled around and around, and begging, "Do it again! Do it again! Myse, lick my toe!" Miles hardly needed any encouragement! It took quite some time after the tickling episode to calm our little Pooh down. Joan had Jessi on her shoulders as they searched in the closet for a book to read. Jessi picked a family favorite, *The Red Balloon*, from the top shelf. This copy of *The Red Balloon* had been in our family forever, it seemed. Jessi and Joan sat quietly on the couch as Jessi licked her finger, mimicking Joan as they turned the pages. We gave Jessi a hug and kissed her good night, then we slipped out the door.

The staff of *Good Morning America* could not have been nicer to us, helping us through a bad case of nerves before the show. This was the first time we had been to a studio, and we were deeply concerned about how we would articulate our concerns on-camera. Joan Lunden kindly asked us about Jessi before we went on the air. Charles Gibson conducted the interview, which included questions for their legal adviser, Arthur Miller. We stated clearly that children should have rights of their own, and that Jessi had not received due process under the law. We wanted Michigan to take jurisdiction and grant a Best Interest hearing for Jessi. Mr. Miller said that taking on a Best Interest hearing at this point would be a "gutsy" thing for a judge to do. When the interview was over and we were about to leave, the producer asked if we would agree to be interviewed from our home in two days, after Judge Ager's decision about the hearing. We agreed.

The next morning, Jan and I met Suellyn outside the courthouse. We were full of trepidation, yet very confident in Suellyn's ability to present her argument supporting a Best Interest hearing. My mother, Aunt Mary Jane, Joan, and Steve Cummings, Jan's best friend, planned to come for support. Members of Dan's and Cara's families were also present as we entered the courtroom, which was filled with family members, neighbors, friends, and supporters as well as a large media contingent. Suellyn's statement said it all: "Jessica is not a piece of property which can be owned by someone. She's not a prize to be won in a custody game." Judge Ager ruled that a Best Interest hearing would be held, starting on January 29.

Jan and I looked at each other in disbelief. We held each other as tears formed in our eyes. We were ushered out of the courtroom and into another room, where the press sat waiting for our comments. Jan spoke first, holding back the tears: "I am thankful to Judge Ager and to the state of Michigan for deciding that our daughter has a right to a Best Interest hearing." I felt the light of the cameras beating down on me as a reporter stepped forward and inquired as to what I thought about Cara. My voice cracked as I began to speak: "I do not know what made her name the wrong birth father, whether she was having a bad day, was on medication, or she just lied. I cannot and I will not judge her on any of that . . . Jessica is an innocent party in all of this. She should be given a chance to live her life free of any suffering surrounding that decision."

Dan and Cara had been waiting in another room. After we exited they came in. Dan held Cara in his arms as she cried. He said, "It is hard to say anything. We want our daughter, she belongs with us. She is family and that is where children belong, with their roots."

The hearing was over; we could go home and be with Jessica. It was a very small victory. It was imperative that Jessica's life be considered. All of the adults could articulate their personal pain and suffering, but what about Jessica? Who was speaking for her? We realized that our lives would be closely scrutinized during the Best Interest proceedings, but we were willing to make whatever sacrifices were necessary to see that Jessica's interests were served. Dan and Cara, along with members of their families, would stay in town, submitting an immediate appeal to the Michigan Court of Appeals to avoid the Best Interest hearing.

We were beginning to have quite a few supporters in Ann

Arbor and around the country. Letters poured in asking, "What about Jessi's rights? Is the biological father the only one with rights? Doesn't Jessi have a right to stay with the only parents she has ever known?" Following Mary Anne's advice, Joan Pheney Engstrom contacted me about doing a fund-raising event. She invited me to meet her in her home to discuss fund-raising ideas. Joan was a high-spirited woman who enjoyed working on events of this nature. She put an ad in the newspaper to see if people would be interested in helping. Quite a few people answered her ad, and they arranged a benefit concert to be held in late February.

I had fully intended to stay as closely involved in the legal proceedings as I had in the past, but with each passing day I lost interest and motivation. The emotional roller coaster was too much to handle, and I wanted to conserve my energy for Jessi. I was no longer able to keep track of every brief and to research legal arguments which were unclear in my mind. Realizing I had to put my trust in someone, I began to rely upon Suellyn. She communicated well with Jan and me, understanding that our primary concern was for Jessica, not ourselves. Our own network of professional advisers now expanded as we benefited from the experience of Suellyn and the other staff members of the Child Advocacy Clinic.

After our experience in the Iowa courts, we no longer had much faith in the system. Our understanding of the law had changed. Our eyes had been pried open, and what we saw was ugly and deceitful. Jessica would not stay with us. The rights of biological parents were paramount. Jan and I could not move such a mountain, but we could let the world know of its existence.

On January 14, the Schmidts' new attorney filed six motions in Judge Ager's court requesting: visitation; the cessation of all photographing of Jessica; issuance of a restraining order against the removal of Jessi from the county; bond on both Jan and me in the amount of $100,000 to secure the Schmidts' legal costs; a change of venue, asking that the hearing be moved to another county, stating that the Schmidts would not receive a fair trial in Washtenaw County; and a final order from the court allowing the attorney to file a brief in a federal court. Judge Ager dismissed a number of the motions, but granted a restraining order limiting Jessica's travel to Washtenaw County and an order prohibiting new photographs of Jessi for public use.

Bombarded with made-for-TV movie deals, we were very confused about what to do. After ten different movie production companies tried to reach us, we started to keep our answering machine on all the time. Somehow our unlisted phone number had become public knowledge. Most of the production companies tried to get us to sign by saying that the Schmidts were about to sign a deal, and that once they signed, our side of the story would never be told, because the movie industry wouldn't be able to handle two movies on the same subject. We didn't need this kind of pressure, having neither the time nor the inclination to think about a movie. No longer able to deal with all the calls, we contacted an agent who had been recommended to us. He reassured us that he would not commit to anything, and that we could move slowly. We were relieved to let someone else deal with the pressure tactics being used to pit the Schmidts and the DeBoers against one another. Both families already had to live through the real-life drama of this legal nightmare; the last thing any of us needed was to deal with a movie about it.

One Saturday afternoon Mom dropped by during Jessi's nap. Jan and I had just been discussing the movie question. We told her about our indecision.

"Why would you even consider signing a deal for a movie?" she asked. "That's the last thing you need to think about now."

Jan responded: "We felt the same way at first. But the more we've talked about it, the more we've wondered if a movie might help keep alive the issue of a child having no voice in the courts. That's the most important issue that we're trying to stress."

"But what do you know about all of this? How do you know whom to trust?"

I explained that we had an agent. "Mom, we're not going to jump into anything. We're totally inexperienced in the realm of production companies, contracts, and all the rest. One thing we do know is that we won't commit ourselves to anything at this time. As things progress, our agent will keep us informed."

"Robby," said Mom, "I just don't want you to get hurt. You'll be careful, won't you?"

I assured her that we would. "Meanwhile, Mom, do you want to see the pictures of Jessi that we just had developed?"

"You bet I would. I'd rather talk about Jessi than any of these other things anyway."

I couldn't have agreed more.

In the middle of January, the Schmidts' attorney issued sub-
poenas requesting personal information about Jan and me. We
received several calls from former employers, school administra-
tors, and banking institutions informing us of the investigation
being conducted. A call came in from Frank Santiago at the end
of the month concerning a police record of Jan's. When I returned
his call, Frank said he was calling to check something out with us.
He had gotten a call from an informer indicating that Jan had a
criminal record. I laughed. "Oh, so the Schmidts' attorney called
you?" Frank chuckled. Jan had just walked in the room. I said,
"Jan, Frank Santiago wants to know about a criminal record of
yours." Jan didn't think it was so funny.

Jan explained that when he was seventeen he had gone on a
bike ride with his friend to a takeout restaurant where they
worked. They gained access to the building and his friend went in
and stole three hundred dollars out of the register; he split the
money; and then they returned to their homes. In the morning the
police showed up at Jan's house. Jan confessed, was taken to the
police station, and was told to return to court once he turned
eighteen. He did so, with a court-appointed attorney. The judge
ordered Jan to pay back the money and charged Jan with illegal
entry, and he did return the money. He thought the record had
been expunged, but apparently it had not. There were also some
drinking charges from when Jan was an adolescent and a charge
of throwing eggs at a neighbor's yard. None of these charges were
felony convictions. I told Frank the news over the phone as Jan
reported it to me. The next day Frank wrote that I had confessed
for my husband about his police record, and the information was
openly shared with other media members.

The Schmidts' attorney was suggesting that Jan had committed fraud by falsifying the adoption records. *I* was the one who
had completed the forms. I checked "no" in response to the
question "Have you ever been convicted of a felony?" After
reviewing our adoption paperwork, I remembered that we had
submitted to the Adoption Cradle police records from the state of
Michigan and the city of Ann Arbor. They had asked for social
security numbers to cross-reference any irregularities. No criminal
record showed up. We had also given the agency the court

documentation pertaining to Jan's change of first name. It was completely legal and fully documented.

The Schmidts' attorney still wanted to make a public mockery of Jan. She went to the press claiming that Jan was a criminal. It was now twenty-some years later, and there had been no further incidents with the law since his teenage years. None of it was relevant. Dan had a record much more relevant to the case. After seeing Frank Santiago's article, Jan began to cry, feeling as if he had somehow misled people. I tried to comfort him, telling him that none of it mattered, because deep inside we both knew that it was just an attorney's vengeful tactic.

Judge Ager requested the attorneys to meet him in his chambers before starting the Best Interest hearing, including the Guardian ad Litems he had chosen for Jessi, Peter Darrow and Sally Rutzky, specialists in family law. He wanted to ask the attorneys to try to persuade the Schmidts and the DeBoers to go into mediation to work things out before going into the trial. We told Suellyn that we would be happy to meet with the Schmidts, and then they could meet Jessi. After several rounds, with the attorneys going back and forth, it was clear that Cara and Dan didn't want to meet with us. They wanted to meet only with Jessica.

I was adamantly opposed to this idea, feeling that it was imperative that Jan and I have a chance to meet with Dan and Cara prior to their meeting Jessica. No biological parents would ever consider submitting their child to such an encounter before meeting with the people first. The bottom line was that we were no different; we were Jessica's parents and we felt that it was important for Jessica's sake that we meet with Dan and Cara first. I asked Suellyn, "Would you take your son to a babysitter that you hadn't met, drop your child off, walk away, and come back in a few hours?" She answered, "That's different." When I asked her to explain why, she could not. Adoptive parents are sometimes made out to have less of an emotional attachment to their children than biological parents. That's just not so. You feel the instinct to protect your child whether there are chromosomes involved or not.

As we prepared for the upcoming hearing, one of the things we wanted to take care of first was finding a babysitter for Jessi. A friend of ours recommended her sitter, Christine, a third-year student at the University of Michigan. Christine agreed to come over one evening and babysit at my mother's while Mom was there. The evening went wonderfully. Mom was very impressed with Christine. She said it seemed as if Jessi and Christine had been friends for a long time.

The Best Interest hearing began on January 29. As we arrived at the courthouse, we purposely sidestepped the large crowd of reporters, having decided not to talk during the hearing to any of the media. Court TV filmed the whole trial.

Expert witnesses would be an important source of information during the trial. Psychologist Beth Clark had been hired by the court to compile a psychological profile on each of the parties. First she spoke of Jan: "I found him, of the four people, perhaps the most willing of all to be open to the other couple . . . His marriage appears to be stable . . . A good grasp of social judgment . . . individualistic person . . . pretty self-confident . . . Sensitive to rejection . . . He's very interested in having Jessica know all about the Schmidts . . . I found him realistic about what the possible outcomes may be in this case and planful in terms of how to deal with it in Jessica's best interest . . . No history of mental or emotional disorder . . . Generally healthy person with an adult history of stability preceded by a period of adolescent rebellion."

Ms. Clark spoke next about me: "She's one of nine children . . . She was not a particularly good student . . . she may have a mild learning disability . . . Got along well with her family and was taught by her father, whom she was quite close to, to stand up for her beliefs . . . I found her willing to be involved in treatment . . . in fact she currently is in psychotherapy with her husband . . . I felt she had a good sense of who Jessica is, a good sense of herself as a parent . . . not too inappropriately attached to the child. She is able to be self-critical . . . She felt her biggest mistake in the course of this whole situation was not having talked to Mrs. Schmidt . . . This is not someone who schemes or plots . . . Very strong views and is very assertive about them . . . stable marriage . . . very good emotional control . . . She appears to be able to put the child's interests ahead of her own, even if it would mean tremendous loss to her."

She spoke next of Cara: "Very friendly . . . dry sense of humor . . . She seems to have relationships with men who don't treat her well . . . She also has a history of becoming immobilized and depressed at times . . . She has very reasonable ideas about how she would raise a child . . . I found her to have quite a naive view of the impact on Jessica if Jessica was returned to her . . . She feels that Jessica would bond to her immediately; she feels that she would recognize her voice and be comforted; she feels if Jessica is surrounded with love and affection that will be enough to have her be all right . . . I found her to be somewhat ambivalent about whether Jessica would need treatment . . . she did say she would take Jessica to treatment . . . She was of the opinion that the DeBoers are the equivalent of foster parents to the child and do not have a legitimate attachment . . . She's still unclear about why she gave the baby up . . . a bit vague as to why she was married . . . She did not go to the CUB meeting with the idea of finding an attorney or doing anything about it; she went for support . . . She is quite passive and dependent on others . . . underachiever . . . has trouble believing in herself . . . she is a person who will act in a self-defeating way . . . Can be uncomfortable with responsibility . . . prefers others to make decisions for her . . . She has a good family history . . . A bit unrealistic in what the child will need and how she'll be able to meet those needs."

Finally she spoke about Dan: "He was separated from his mother when he was sent to live with his grandparents after the divorce . . . I think it was age eleven, he was removed from his grandparents and his mother and sister and sent to live with an uncle in a most traumatic way . . . The family had gone to the state fair and he was told that his uncle would give him a ride; when he got in the car, his uncle said, 'You're coming to live with me' . . . His history is also remarkable for . . . poor self-control and poor judgment . . . during the course of the divorce he was arrested for breaking the windshield of his first wife's car . . . had been arrested early in his adulthood for writing bad checks . . . He's lost his driver's license for habitual speeding violations, and has been fired from several jobs . . . On the positive side . . . he attended the Job Corps and he has maintained contact with his mother, his father, and his siblings throughout his life. I think those are all quite positive. Around the issue of his loss of contact with his children: I see that more as an issue of his not initiating or maintaining support and difficulties in getting along with the mothers of the children and a tendency to blame others for his problems . . . I see Mr. Schmidt as having pretty poor insight into this current situation . . . He appears to not have very much concept of what Jessica would be facing . . . If they love her she'll be okay . . . he had little sense of what the impact on the child would be if she were immediately removed from the DeBoers."

The first couple days of the hearing were very stressful. It was a relief at the end of the day to go home and be with Jessica. We planned a wonderful birthday party for Jessica at my mom's for Sunday, February 7, to celebrate her second birthday. Waking up that morning, Jan and I decided to give Jessi her big gift from us before we got to the party. It was a beautiful little pink jacket and bonnet. Jessi looked gorgeous in them! She had loved hats ever since she started wearing her bike helmet. "I tie um, Mommy, I tie um!" she exclaimed. Pooh pranced around the living room showing Miles her new coat and the special buttons. On and off the coat would go as she tried to dress herself. "Put my coat on, I do it! I coat on!"

My niece Kalise opened the door when we knocked at Grandma's house, with Jessi all dressed in her new outfit. She walked in the living room with a very shy look on her face. "Happy birthday to you . . ." everyone began to sing. Jessi stood examining everyone, then twirled around to show off her new coat. Kalise helped take off her coat, and then her bonnet. "This Djessi coat and hat!" she proclaimed to Kalise. Jessi was squatting on the floor as Joan came into the room and gave her a great big kiss. Grandma commented on how nice it would be to be able to squat down at her age like Jessi; all her worries would be gone if she could accomplish that one thing.

The sleigh was adorned with twenty helium balloons of all different shades of red, pink, and blue. Jessi pointed to the balloons and asked Angel's daughter Gina, "Dowes bawwowens mine?" Gina responded, "Yes!" Gina was one year older than Jessi and looked very much like her. When Jessi had gone to Gina's third birthday only months before, Gina had received a baby doll and stroller. Jessi mentioned she wanted one just like Gina's.

Scott sat patiently waiting for his kiss and hug from his cousin. Scott, now ten years old, would allow very few people to kiss him, but Jessi had managed to win him over! She would approach him, hold his hand, stand on her tiptoes, purse her lips, and kiss his cheek. Jessi had brought a gift for Scott; his birthday was February 12. "Come sit, Scott, dis is mine present. You open it!"

Afterward Scott helped her unwrap her baby doll. Jessi beamed. Grandma Jo had given Jessi a purse with a brush, mirror, and comb. Sweet Pea started handing out all of her presents to have everyone help her open them, and with each one she would proclaim, "Dis mine!" She sat next to Gina and asked her to open a gift from my brother Tom and his wife, Kathy. "Dina open it, Dina helpa me." It was a soft, stuffed music box of a baby sleeping. "Rock-a-bye, Baby," Jessi announced. Then came Kalise and her husband David's gift, a Fisher-Price farm, with little animals and farmers to match.

It was a wonderful birthday. Jessi was so satisfied to be two years old! She was very happy playing with all of her friends, jumping around in the sleigh, bouncing balloons against the wall, and running about the house.

As the trial started up again on Monday, February 8, Jessica's second birthday, Cara was put on the stand. She described an incident at the hospital after Jessi's birth: "They wheeled me down the hall. All I could think of was 'This isn't right,' and I didn't know that I could just jump out of my wheelchair and go down to get her [Jessica] and say, 'She's going with me.'" Suellyn cross-examined her. Cara answered most of the questions indirectly. Suellyn asked, "You don't have any problem reading; so when you signed the consent-to-adoption form, you could read the part that said you had ninety-six hours to change your mind?" Her response was "I have no idea what it said." She avoided every question that Suellyn asked her about the first days of Jessica's life and all the documents that she signed.

Cara had talked to the Ann Arbor *News* over the weekend. On the front page of the paper they had quoted her as stating that Jessica missed her, Jessica would know Cara whenever they met, and that "she will not be screaming, she will not be confused and traumatized" when and if the transfer took place. Cara also admitted that she was four and a half months pregnant and due in June, and that she'd had no prenatal care as of yet for her second child. She never saw a doctor for Jessica until three weeks before Jessica was born.

The Schmidts' attorney called me to the stand several times. Her approach was rude and antagonistic. She also called Jessica's doctor to the stand. Dr. Dumont testified that Jan and I had been textbook parents in caring for Jessica.

Dan also testified, commenting on his parenting skills with his other two children. He said that he loved his son, and he would like to meet his daughter Amanda and have some type of relationship with her. Dan also testified that there were times when he would hit his ex-wife, Joanne, stating that he had to defend himself.

Jan spent his time on the stand hearing a lengthy monologue from the Schmidts' attorney. She ridiculed Jan, rarely asking a question; rather, using the opportunity to belittle him and expound on his "wild exploits as a criminal." Judge Ager had to mention that past histories going back as far as twenty years were not relevant.

At the end of the trial that day Dan approached us with a bag of birthday presents for Jessica. As he asked if I would please give the presents to her, tears welled up in his eyes. I felt terrible seeing Dan in that kind of pain. I said, "Dan, why don't you call this evening and we could arrange for you to come over and give them to Jessi yourself?" Dan said that he didn't know our phone number, so I looked around for a pen to write it down. The Schmidts' attorney saw us talking and she dashed over. "What are you doing, Dan? She is just trying to get you to break a court order. There is no visitation!" she exclaimed. I was furious with her! I had begun to realize that this whole case was only strategy to her. She didn't care about Dan and Cara, or Jessica for that matter. Dan and Cara probably would have gotten together with us before the hearing for mediation, but their attorney must have stopped them. I remember a remark that she had made in the Ann Arbor *News*: that during the Best Interest hearing she would go and pull down the pants of all four adults, and a blood war would begin. It was as if she were in this case for an agenda all of her own. What did she hope to gain from all of this and at whose expense?

Dan's ex-wife, Joanne, called us one night during the trial, crying. I could hardly understand a word she was saying. I told her to try to take some deep breaths and tell me what was wrong. "He's gone, Robby. I don't know where Travis is. He never came home from school today. I don't know where he is." Joanne thought that Travis might have been kidnapped.

"Try to hold yourself together, Joanne. Call the police. Maybe they could help you find him." The police did show up at Joanne's house and a report was filed. I called Suellyn to ask her advice. She wondered if perhaps he was in Ann Arbor with Dan and Cara. I couldn't believe that could be the case, because Travis certainly would have told his mother that he was leaving for Michigan. When I called Joanne back, she said she had gotten a call from Travis since our last phone call. He was in Ann Arbor. Cara's father had picked Travis up at school and taken him to the airport to fly there. Dan had never asked Joanne if Travis could come to Ann Arbor. I couldn't believe that Dan would be so insensitive. Joanne was so afraid that someone had abducted her son! Travis did testify the next day that his father was a great guy and that he loved their reunion.

The most significant testimonies of the hearing were delivered by several mental health professionals. Dr. Gerald Smith of Indiana University testified about several personal assessments of Jessica's bonding with Jan and me. Dr. David Brodzinsky, a professor at Rutgers University, focused his research on the psychology of adoption, separation, and loss. Vicki Bennett, a clinical social worker and private practitioner dealing in infant mental health, also testified. But the most significant testimony came from Dr. Jack Novick. He had served as the Chief Psychologist for Youth Services, Children's Psychiatric Hospital of the University of Michigan Medical School. Currently he was a professor of psychiatry at the University of Michigan and Wayne State University.

Suellyn asked Dr. Novick if he had ever testified as an expert witness before. He responded that he had not, because he felt that both parents in other cases had a stake, and he hadn't felt comfortable supporting one or the other parent in those situations. In our case he felt that the psychological issue was clear, that we had a primary relationship with Jessica, as she did with us. Removing Jessi would cause long-term harm if she were to be taken away from us. He began to speak about Jessica: "She is shaped completely by these people. Everything is attached to these people. I would say that if Jessica was brought into this room, she would look to her mother immediately, Mrs. DeBoer, to see if it is safe or not safe. Her whole world is determined by her mother at this point . . . By the age of two, all the things which she has come into the world with, her capacities to think, to feel, to love, all get attached to these primary people. Not to anyone else."

Dr. Novick went on, speaking metaphorically: "It's like if you think of a house. The foundation, the frame of the house, is the first thing you build. And you won't know the nature of the foundation until a storm comes. And it's only whether or not it can weather the storm that will tell you how strong the foundation is." Suellyn asked him about having people like Dan and Cara stepping into our place. He responded: "It's like taking a kid who has a terrible beginning, or has a very poor psychological foundation, and sending them to the best schools and sending them, then, to the best colleges and giving them the best of everything, and a lot of money so they're wearing beautiful clothes. They'll look terrific, but the first strain and they will break. That will tell you about the foundation."

Suellyn asked if Dr. Novick felt it would be possible to have Jessica moved at this point and develop a primary attachment (like the one Jan and I had with Jessica) with any new caretakers? Dr. Novick responded: "No."

"What would happen in the short term to Jessica?" Suellyn asked.

". . . anxious nightmares . . . whatever she has achieved developmentally, she'll probably go backwards," he said. "When something big happens she [Jessica] makes a theory to explain it, because she can't exist in a world without an explanation. Her explanation here may be . . . 'I'm sure she has had fights with Mrs. DeBoer . . . she had a cookie for supper and then she wanted another cookie . . . Mrs. DeBoer gave her another cookie . . . Then Jessica wanted another one and Mrs. DeBoer said, 'No. That's enough.' Jessica could have a temper tantrum. Mrs. DeBoer said, 'I know you're angry, I'll give you a cookie tomorrow, but you can't have a cookie now.' Jessica was in a rage, and her feelings would be 'Go away. I don't want to see you anymore. I hate you.' But what she learns repeatedly at this age is that she can be furious, she can hate her mother, and Mother won't disappear. If something catastrophic happened, she'll make a theory. 'I got angry at Mom and Mom sent me away, or they took me away, Jessica's a bad girl and so they took her away from Mommy.' It's the only thing that makes sense. 'If Mommy disappears, it's my fault.' And that's what she's going to feel."

Suellyn asked Dr. Novick if anybody would be able to explain to Jessica at her age that it wasn't her fault, that it was because of the law, and because of mistakes adults made earlier on.

"No," he answered, "because she won't understand that. What does she understand about the law? She knows that she was angry at Mom, she knows she hated her, she said, 'Go away,' and what happened? Mommy went away."

Feeling very sick, I had to get up and leave the courtroom. The thought of Jessi blaming herself was too overwhelming. I wondered how Cara could sit and listen to all of this and not feel any compassion for Jessica. She wanted Jessica because she loved her, but I could not understand what kind of love drives a person to such a point. My mother took me home. I just wanted to hold Jessica and tell her how much we loved her.

On the last day of the Michigan trial, the Iowa Juvenile Court ruled that Cara's parental rights had been reinstated. The order stated, "At the present time Dan and Cara are married. To terminate Cara's parental rights would lead to the potentially ludicrous result of a birth mother adopting her own child as the child's stepmother, thus becoming not only the child's birth mother but the adoptive mother as well." It went on to say, "The court emphasizes that it is making no findings or determination . . . of Cara's contention that fraud, coercion and/or misrepresentation on [John Monroe's] part . . . to sign the consent to terminate [her] parental rights." Two and a half years later the court had ruled that it would never determine whether John Monroe had done anything wrong. Cara's rights were reinstated because she had married Dan; that was the only reason the court could come up with to give her rights back.

The judge specifically stated in the order that in reinstating Cara's rights he would not determine her custodial rights, meaning that just having her rights reinstated did not give her the ultimate control of Jessica's custody. It was amazing that Judge Kilburg would determine that Dan deserved to have custody of his child because his rights had never been terminated; but in the same state, after two years, the courts still would not determine that once Cara's rights had been reinstated she would have custodial rights. How could they have such double standards? What would happen if Cara and Dan ever got divorced? Would Jessi automatically go to Dan because the Juvenile Court never ruled on her custodial rights?

Suellyn spoke eloquently in her closing arguments in the Best Interest hearing, ending the exhausting eight-day trial:

> *The question of who was actually at fault in this case, your honor, is irrelevant to the issue of best interest. There is no evidence that this child's life has been affected by the mistakes that the adults have made in her life . . . This child has grown and developed well and in a loving situation . . .*
>
> *Your honor, many people have referred to this case as being like King Solomon's decision . . . Solomon's wise decision was based on the assumption that a biological mother will put her child's best interest first, at the time of birth. That she will give her child up if it is best for the child. In 1993 we know that the DeBoers love this child as their own. They are willing to fight for her best interest, and if they ultimately lose custody, [they plan] to put the child's best interest first in making decisions for her.*
>
> *Dr. Clark reported that Jan said that he would start a college fund for Jessica if he lost her. Robby said that she would stay away from Jessica, the child she loves, if it was in Jessica's best interest . . . The Schmidts' attorney, I must say, very callously argues: What mother would drop out? That's the very point of this case, your honor. Mrs. DeBoer has the love for this child and the courage to know that she would drop out if, indeed, it was best for the child.*
>
> *We also know, sad as it is, that Dan and Cara Schmidt repeatedly state that the child should be with them because she belongs to them. They do not say it's because it's in the child's best interest. This Court must make a decision much like Solomon's. Like Solomon, this Court can make a decision based on which parents will best meet the child's needs and put her needs first. And those parents are the DeBoers.*
>
> *Unlike Solomon, you have evidence that this child is two years old, not a new baby, and will actually, really, be damaged by the change of custody. You have more information than Solomon did. And based on the harm to the child and the DeBoers' ability to put Jessica's needs first, we ask this Court to modify the Iowa order and order custody with Jan and Roberta DeBoer. Thank you, your honor.*

Judge Ager adjourned for a day and returned on February 12 with his verdict:

The child has been in Michigan two years. Michigan courts . . . have been in the forefront in protecting the rights of children. In Michigan not only the rights of parents are . . . protected but the rights of the child . . . are paramount. Daniel Schmidt, I realize it was very important that you bring your son, Travis, to testify in your behalf . . . But it bothered me that he was brought from the state of Iowa without his mother's consent . . . In fact, she didn't know where he had gone . . . And this person as primary caretaker since his birth is going to have trouble in raising this lad in the future . . . He's [Dan] testified that he will give love and affection to the child involved in this suit. And I believe him, but love is not enough. Guidance is required.

Cara Schmidt didn't provide adequate prenatal care for the child in this case. The Court feels deep sympathy with Mrs. Schmidt . . . But the Court must consider this when the Court is deciding care that might be provided to the child in the future . . . The Guardian ad Litems [Peter Darrow and Sally Rutzky] pointed out in their report to the Court . . . I feel that it is an excellent report . . . that even though Mr. and Mrs. Schmidt believe in their minds that the child would feel a natural bond immediately with them, or that their love would be enough to establish a bond, that they [the Guardian ad Litems] felt that the expert testimony did not support this feeling or this belief.

The Court has to take into account, regarding Mr. Schmidt, that he didn't have contact with his son, Travis, between five and fourteen years, has had no contact with his daughter Amanda. He has to be commended for reestablishing his relationship with Travis and hopefully will establish a relationship with Amanda. Mr. and Mrs. DeBoer have been married for about ten years. Their marriage appears strong. The Guardian ad Litems have pointed out that they believe that Mr. and Mrs. Schmidt, as to permanent relationships, do raise some concerns.

The Court is placing a great deal of importance on the damage that would be done to the child if she were plucked from [Jan and Robby] DeBoer's custody and suddenly placed in a strange environment . . . Every expert testified that there would be serious traumatic injury to the child at this time. Certainly everybody is usually able to recover from traumatic injuries . . . But they are going to have permanent damage . . . It was reported that removing the child from Mr. and Mrs. DeBoer would break her primary relationship at a time when she had not yet become independent, but still experiences much of her life as part of her relationship with these two particular people. This would severely weaken the foundation of her psychological development.

I find that the evidence is clear and convincing that Mr. and Mrs. DeBoer have sustained their burden of proof for the best interest of this child.

I know how deeply hurt Mr. and Mrs. Schmidt are at this time. But I would ask you to maybe consider a suggestion that the Court has to think of the possibility of saying "enough." The Schmidts' attorney asked at least one of the witnesses about what could you tell this child when she grows up and says "Oh, you gave up. You didn't want me, you gave up in your fight"? I have no hesitancy in telling you what to say. Tell this young woman that you fought your hardest for this child. That you went all the way to the Supreme Court in Iowa. You fought in the courts in Ann Arbor, Michigan, and finally some experts told you, and some old gray-haired judge who you didn't agree with said that for the best interest of the child the child should remain where she is.

I remember what Mr. DeBoer said when he was testifying . . . I think my eyes glazed over as his did. He said that "someday, when this is done and over with, I pray that all four of us and this young girl will have a relationship." And I think this is possible, but I don't think it's possible if you're going to continue fighting.

But I would suggest if you consider this advice, that so far as you, Mr. and Mrs. Schmidt, are concerned, you'd be heroes. People all over the United States would say, "These people have acted in the best interest of the child."

Jan and I fell into each other's arms. All of the emotions of the last weeks came pouring out. We prayed that Dan and Cara would hear the judge's plea for Jessica and maybe we would all start to get along, for Jessica's sake. Dan and Cara, sitting across the room, appeared to be snickering. We wondered how they could have sat through a week of testimony, heard the judgment of a knowledgeable judge, and think this was all so funny.

At the news conference that day, Dan declared: "I will never abandon this. I can't believe a judge would ask us not to pursue our legal rights."

We spoke very little at the press conference. Jan thanked the courts of Michigan for finally ruling in Jessica's best interest. Feeling pain about moving forward and knowing I could not change the course of what had already happened, I said, "They are not losers and we are not the winners. We are all losers in this battle."

Eleven

G AMMA, want muffin?" Jessi asked, holding a plate of freshly baked corn muffins right up under my mom's nose. "Well, Jessi, they smell so good, I guess I'll just have to have one!" Jessi scurried to the dish drainer and took out a clean plate. "Juice, Gamma?"

"Why, yes, Jessi, I'd love some apple juice." Again Jessi raced to the dish drainer. "Momma pour the juice?"

As I poured three tall glasses of juice, I reflected aloud on Judge Ager's ruling. "He understands. He really understands that children are people. They have feelings. They have rights."

"Robby, do you think his ruling will hold up on appeal?" asked Mom.

"The problem is even deeper than that, Mom. It's a bit confusing, but I'll try to tell it to you the way Suellyn told it to Jan and me. The Best Interest hearing could be held because Judge Ager agreed to take jurisdiction. The question that the Schmidts are appealing now is his right to jurisdiction. Michigan's right to jurisdiction. They actually filed that appeal while the Best Interest hearing was going on. They also questioned whether Jan and I have standing to bring a custody case to court. Imagine that, after two years of being Jessi's mommy and daddy, we still may not have the right to bring a custody action for her."

Mom asked, "When will the decision come through on jurisdiction and standing?"

"The Michigan Supreme Court said that the Appeals Court will hear the appeal. Suellyn has to file her briefs in the next few days. I don't know when we'll hear, but I can tell you this: I'm scared."

"Robby, you just have to hang in there, as you have all along. I've never seen anyone stronger than you. I'm proud of you, Robby, I'm proud of the way you love Jessi." Her eyes filled with tears. I got up and walked over to her and held her hand. "There's one more thing I have to ask you, Robby. What was it that Jan told me yesterday about an arrest warrant in Iowa?"

"I can't even think about that, Mom. It sounds so awful, doesn't it? Judge Kilburg entered a contempt charge on Jan and me for not returning Jessi on December 3, 1992. An arrest warrant was issued in the state of Iowa, and the judge set a bond of ten thousand dollars apiece on Jan and me."

"That doesn't affect you in Michigan, does it?" she asked.

"No, but we cannot go into Iowa as long as the warrant stands. Please don't worry, though, Mom. I can't stand to see you this way."

Things were a mess. Instead of celebrating the justice of Judge Ager's decision, we were deeply concerned about what would happen next.

Dressed in her hot-pink snowsuit, Jessi headed outside to the hill. "Go sledding on Gamma's hill!" she exclaimed as we ran through the newly fallen snow. It was a delightful sunny day, and Jessi was ready for some outdoor fun. She wanted to try sledding in preparation for the little sledding party that the boys were having in a few days. Jan carried my childhood toboggan out to the slopes, calling to Jessi, "Anyone who wants a ride, you'd better come now! Sled's leaving in ten seconds! One, two, three, four . . ." Jessi ran gleefully to Jan and hopped onto the toboggan. Barry followed with the video camera with Miles by his side, nipping at his pant leg, wanting to be a part of the fun.

The fresh air was so exhilarating! Jessi and I sat together with Jan in front of us in the toboggan. "You all ready?" Barry shouted as he bent over to give us a great big push. Down the hill we zoomed, with Miles sprinting vigorously from side to side around us, trying to hop onto the sled, barking all the way to the bottom of the hill. I remembered the thrill of taking this ride down the hill as a child. My brothers used to try to stand up on the toboggan and surf down the hill, thrilling me and my sisters. For us it was daring enough sitting down. The part we hated the most was having to drag the toboggan back up the hill. We used to draw intricate plans for contraptions that could pull it back up to the top, hoping that someday we could really build one. Little did I know that someday I'd find the "contraption" in my dog! Jan hooked the rope to Miles's collar, and the St. Bernard in Miles shined through as he pranced happily up the hill dragging the toboggan behind him. Barry and I commented that we should have gotten a dog long ago.

Jessi decided she would rather watch than go down the hill the next time. Jan had jumped onto the toboggan and headed down at warp speed, only to crash into the pines at the bottom of the hill. Pooh hurried down the hill to help her dad, shouting, "*Mom* commawn, Mom commawn, *peeze!*" Jessi and I ran down together to rescue Jan, who was shaken but not injured. Jessi said "Ugs an kisses, Dad!" and gave him the best medicine of all. He miraculously "recovered" under Jessi's fine care. "Got Dad better, Momma!" she exclaimed.

Jessi had a little hiding place under the catwalk of the house, a forty-foot corridor of little pebbles that she could play with while watching the activities on the hill. As I sat and watched Jessi pick up the little pebbles and throw them into the air, Barry zoomed in on his little snow bunny, as she said, "I take my goves off, kay, Mom?"

"No, Jessi, it's cold out here; your little fingers will freeze. Maybe we should go in the house and see if Gramma has made us some hot chocolate."

When we went in, we found Grandma pouring some apple juice for Jessi. She said, "Tank you, Gamma." Grandma Jo went over to the stove. In turning to respond to Jessi, she burned her finger on the boiling coffeepot. "Ooh, that's smart," she said. Jessi waved her hand at Grandma Jo and responded, "Time out, Gamma, you not spose to play with the stove."

Jessi's trip to the boys' sledding party proved to be very exciting. She knew now what it was like to sled, and she opted just to ride in Graham's little children's sled with Graham instead of sitting close to me in the big one. I was proud of her sense of independence and adventure. She and Graham enjoyed sledding so much, neither one of them wanted to go home.

As the story of our family's struggle to stay together became increasingly well known, many people across the country began to reach out to us. We received heartwarming letters from birth parents, adoptive parents, grandmothers, schoolchildren, professionals, teenagers—all expressing their hopes and prayers that Jessica could stay with us. People in the Ann Arbor area continued to show their support as well. The group of supporters who were planning the fund-raising concert met weekly, gathering momentum as they worked. Jan and I were very touched by their commitment. Some of them wrote us notes of encouragement every few days; others baked bread or cookies and left them at our door. We did not know any of them well, yet they were completely dedicated to our case and to Jessi.

One of the committee members, Annie Rose, wrote and recorded a song for us called "Child of My Soul." As I listened to the tape, the tears fell like a waterfall. "Child of my soul, child of my heart, child of my lifetime, we will never be apart." I had never met this woman, yet she sang as if she knew me, as if she could feel my pain and my love for my little daughter. I felt the same way about some of the letters we received. What was it that gave people the insight to understand what we were going through? It was as if our situation touched a raw nerve in people and they had to reach out to us. Sometimes I wished I could meet all the kind people who had written and called. I felt as if they were a part of our lives. I knew I would never be able to thank them all in person, but I did try to answer as many letters as I could. Many days, as Jessi napped, I wrote short notes of thanks, hoping to make a dent in the piles of letters we had received.

Jan, Jessi, and I got to meet Annie Rose and many of the other committee members at a children's concert that Annie was giving at one of Jessi's favorite toy stores. As we walked into the store, Annie was setting up her instruments. She recognized me and came right over to me to give me a hug. I felt as if I had known her for a long time. All the committee members had something special to say about why they had gotten involved in helping us. It was a very therapeutic experience for us; we saw the depth of the committee members' commitment and compassion.

At the end of February, the committee put on the fund-raising concert that they had worked on with such energy. Grandma Jo babysat Jessi so that Jan and I could stay as late as we wanted at the concert. The stage was decorated with a rainbow of balloons and flowers. More than fifty area businesses had donated goods and services for the evening, including a marvelous buffet at intermission. Judy Dow Alexander, a philanthropist and performer who is known and loved in Michigan, was the master of ceremonies. Judy had met Jessica over at Grandma Jo's house one day, and they became fast friends. In her role as emcee, Judy was able to light up the stage and bring humor to the crowd, which was something we all needed.

We met a wonderful couple that night—the Martins, from Utica, Michigan. Mrs. Martin worked in a Ford factory there and many of the employees had generously donated to the Baby DeBoer Legal Fund. In an emotional moment, Mrs. Martin presented the money to us onstage. Jan and I were so touched by the generosity of these people who did not know us.

The Monday after the concert, the committee members got together for their weekly meeting. They had successfully raised ten thousand dollars for the fund; now they wanted to do more. They began to brainstorm about what steps they might take. What else could they do for Jessi? Could they urge changes in legislation that might help us? Could they run petition campaigns? Together as a group they decided to take the name Justice for Jessi. Simultaneously a group of concerned citizens in Iowa decided to formalize their structure as well. Following the lead of the Ann Arbor group, they called their committee Justice for Jessi. Donations of bumper stickers and phone lines came in from generous businesspeople who sympathized with our family's struggle to stay together.

20/20 aired the first of their stories about our case on March 5. I felt they did a good job of sticking to the issues, presenting both sides of the story, and not exploiting the parties involved. Tom Jarriel interviewed all of us. He asked me whether I thought Cara would be a good mother. I said that although I thought that Cara probably had the ability to be a good mother, that was not the issue. "We've got to look out for Jessica, and watch out for Jessica's well-being, especially with the massive amount of knowledge that we now have about the permanent damage she will go through if put in a stranger's home, and that is exactly what Dan and Cara are to Jessica. There might be blood ties, but that does not change anything psychologically in Jessica's mind. We are her parents. We are her only parents."

Tom Jarriel said to Cara, "She [Jessica] spent two years in another home. When she looks upon the face of another woman, she says 'Mother.' " Cara closed her eyes, as if she were trying to block out what he was saying. Tom continued: "When she looks upon another man, she says 'Father.' Can that be reversed? Can you recapture what they spent two years building in terms of a relationship with this child?"

Cara responded: "She'll never be able to regain it with us, but when she comes home she'll be surrounded by love, and that's the best building block there is. She'll feel safe. She'll be able to explore. She can ask us questions and we'll say, 'You did that because your grandpa did that.' All her missing parts are here." Dan's response was "I'm her father; her roots are here."

My last comment was "Jessica is as much of my blood, sweat, and tears, I have given all of myself like any birth mother. I have given my heart and soul to this little girl; she is a part of me."

Tom asked Cara why she gave Jessica up. "There was no thought, and my mind clicked off, and it was just this adoption thought popped into my head, and I have no idea why. I was a completely different person. I wasn't during my pregnancy that person before and it wasn't me after."

Tom had asked, "Why did you name a different man as the father?"

Cara responded: "Since he was the man I was dating. It was just that, just happened, and when the lawyer made me name a father, that's what I said."

We were deluged with mail and calls after the show aired. Members of the Justice for Jessi committee started helping us handle the calls; many of them gave out their home phone numbers to many people around the country. Soon they were all receiving hundreds of calls each week from people who wanted to help us. They advised the callers to write to their legislators and governors, and even to the White House. Their opinions needed to be heard. The committee members also sent out petitions to callers, many of whom photocopied them and went door to door in their own communities gathering signatures.

Stephanie advised us to start thinking about writing a "goodbye" letter to Jessica. In the event that we were to win, Jessi would know in the future what it was like during the time we thought we might have lost her.

Diary, March 9:

Dearest Jessica,

The time has come, Jessi, for you to pack up your life and for us to let you go free. It's something we must do; however, we can only do this in our minds. We pray that the day never comes when the boxes will be sitting by the door. I've been up nights trying to find a way to tell you that I'm scared to death of what will happen to my little Pooh Bear. We want all this pain to stop. I sit in your "big girl" room only hoping to hold back the inevitable and never having to turn this page to what lies ahead. I see your childhood unfolding. I see you playing dress-up wearing an old dress that you've stumbled upon in the attic, holding an old straw hat and putting Mommy's shoes on, running around the house with Miles behind you. Oh, my little Pooh, what has happened to our days together? To our lives?

Diary, March 12:

Dearest Jessi,

It is hard to face the true reality that it is over. Letting go is too much to confront all at one time. I just can't do this letter, Jessi. I've thought of every last detail, and I can't get past the final piece. I envision Dan and Cara coming and taking your crib . . . That damn crib. I remember the moment we bought it, thinking it was too much money, thinking you would never sleep in it. It sat empty for several months. The trials and tribulations of going from your little crib to the new crib! What a memory. I think Dad and I cried more than you ever did trying to teach you to sleep on your own, in that crib. I've realized one thing, that you will always be in my heart, and no pieces of wood put together to resemble a bed are really you; it is only an object that resembled a part of your life. A very small part. You're one of the kindest people I know. Your love pats and comforting words have always brought me such joy. I'll miss you always, Jessi, FOREVER . . .

Diary, March 17:

The road we've traveled upon has been rocky, but your spirit has always pulled us through. I think of every day as

*being the last one that I'll ever spend with you. I want to make
every moment special, and to comfort you through the hard
times of your new independence and frustration. I love your
warmth and strength. I pray to God that you won't suffer, that
you will not have to pay the price for all of our mistakes. I
would sacrifice any possession or part of me to stop this from
happening to you. You're a part of my soul and my every
breath, Jessica Anne, and you will always be. I thank you for
restoring my faith in so many things and for clearing my mind
of other, less important things in life.*

God bless my little Jess. Love, Momma—

Diary, March 26:

Dearest Sweetheart,

*Why? Why were you meant to be the sacrificial lamb? Why
has this thing called the law not protected you? I want so much
to be strong, to stand against the blasting winds of Justice, but
the system is too strong. I'm torn between the cause and my
love for you. I can never say I'm sorry enough. I feel as if you
have the strength to tear down the walls of Justice, to reveal the
blindness that exists to those who govern and control the lives
of so many innocent children. I'm so sorry. I can still remember
the day when I came home thinking that I had lost you, you
heard me crying and came down and asked if "Momma's okay,
Momma's heart broken?" I told you Momma's heart would
mend. Afterward you still worried if I truly had repaired my
broken heart.*

Love, Momma—

I kept writing the letters, but none of them satisfied the
assignment. The more I wrote, the more the pain poured out
through my pen. I wanted to tell Jessica how much joy she had
brought into our lives, but instead I could only see the pain that
we had brought into her life.

Jessica continued to grow and thrive as if none of these
problems existed. She had begun to train herself at using the potty.
I was so proud of her, doing it all by herself. She had learned by
watching Graham use the potty, in his very special potty chair.
Jessi had to have the same brand of potty as Graham, of course,
and whenever she went in her potty she would make sure Graham
knew about it.

One morning I got up and was making tea when I heard "Mom! Mom! You down dere?"

"Yes, Jessi," I answered. "I'm in the kitchen." I heard a noise; it sounded as if Jessi was dragging something. I filled up the teapot and was wondering if I should go check on Jessi to make sure that she was okay. I turned around and almost tripped over my little angel. Jessi grabbed my hand and led me into the living room. There it was, her little potty. She had dragged it out of the bathroom and placed it smack-dab in the middle of the living room. "See, Momma, see?" She bent over and lifted up the top, which had closed as she pushed it into the room. "Poopen, Momma, poopen!" Jessi's little face beamed; she spoke with such joy. I couldn't believe how well she had done. Jan and I had not even begun to train her, but Jessica was not going to wait around for her parents to initiate this process. She had a goal, to beat Graham; this was competition, and she really wanted to succeed.

We wanted to reward Jessi for her fine accomplishment by buying her a present of her own choosing. One day when we were out running errands, Jessi and I stopped at Pier One. Jessi sat and relaxed in the little wicker couch that was next to a chair like one we had bought for her earlier that year. I told Jessi that she had done such a wonderful job with her potty that Daddy and I wanted to buy her a special present. Jessi was so excited; she started dragging the couch up to the register. I asked if I could help. "No, mine!" she declared. Kalise had set aside money every month to buy things that Jessi needed, and it certainly came in handy when we bought Jessi her little couch.

Diary, March 28:

Dear Jessi,

I've been trying for a long time to compose a letter to say goodbye to you. I have failed. I've always thought up to this point that you would forget me if you were to be taken away. I know now you will never forget me; you'll never allow your mother's heart to be broken for any length of time. You check often and ask Momma if everything is okay. "Momma's heart kay?" Yes, sweet Jessi, Momma's heart's all better . . .

Love, Momma—

Jessi and I always liked to go down to Randy's house so she could play with Nick and I could sit and talk with Randy. Jessi also had an ulterior motive: graham crackers. She knew where Randy kept the crackers, and she would stroll into the kitchen with her hands grasped behind her back and stand under the cupboard saying, "Kacker, kacker—peeze, Ree, Ree, peeze?" Randy would give her all the graham crackers she wanted. "What do you say, Jessi?" Randy would ask, with love in her eyes and voice. Jessi would stop and give Randy an inquisitive look. "Djessi says 'tankouw.'"

Jessi had such good manners, and was proud when she said 'thank you.' The boys were usually busy playing games in the living room. If they didn't want her to join in, she would end up back in the kitchen and go over to her favorite drawer to get out the Tupperware. She would set places for herself and the Cabbage Patch doll that Randy had gotten for her, and they would have tea together as Randy and I talked.

One day Jan and I had a meeting at Joan Pheney Engstrom's home with Norm Nickin and John Israel, two licensed private investigators who wanted to offer their services to us. When I first met them, I was a bit hesitant. I couldn't figure out why they would want to help us, although we certainly needed help. We were probably being watched all the time, since some people suspected that we would leave the country. We thought that our phone was being tapped; we heard clicking noises on it, and had trouble getting a dial tone after hanging up from one call and trying to place another.

I thought that I should check out John and Norm, to see if they were legitimate. I called the commander at the Sheriff's Department of Washtenaw County, who was very helpful. He said that John Israel had been an outstanding police officer for twenty-four years. That's all I needed to hear. Jan and I decided that it would be a good idea to have someone watch out for us, especially for Jessi's sake.

John and Norm's first step was to check our phone lines, on which they discovered some type of frequency interference. They explained how someone could tap into a frequency and listen to our phone conversations, and advised us to get rid of all cordless phones and to be careful about what we said on the phone. We wouldn't have believed this could happen, but Mary Beth Seader, of the National Council for Adoption, had advised us that it might. She told us about the Musser Foundation, an organization that believes in opening adoption records in this country. Two people from the organization were up on charges for allegedly stealing files and engaging in wiretapping.

One rainy day Jessi really wanted to go outside and play in the park. I tried to explain to her that it was just too wet and muddy, but she was inconsolable. After much deliberation, I came up with an alternative. I ran down to Randy's and picked up the plastic slide that she had gotten for the boys when they were younger. I brought it into the house and Jessi and I played "park" in the house. Pooh was so elated to see the slide in her living room. Up she climbed on the slide. "Hi, Mom! I'm so high, Mom! You takin' care of me!" Jessi loved to ramble on. "Whatta our daddy dowen?" I told her that Dad was taking a shower. "I wanna take a showder?" The way she emphasized her words, most of what she said at this point came out as a question. "He's no . . . He's not done with showder? Myse done. He's all done?"

"Where is Miles, Jessi?" I asked.

"Uppa nordth with Unka Barry?"

"And where is Uncle Jerry, Jessi?"

"Uppa the poppertee with Unka Barry. One more time the slide, Momma!" She wanted the slide to stay in the house permanently. Jan came out and asked Jessi if she knew where we were going that day.

"Farmer market, Dad, witha *boys!*" she replied, and then she broke into a song, "Baby Ba Ouga . . ."

Jan and I were having a great deal of trouble dealing with the movie contract. It was all so foreign to us, and we just couldn't make the effort to figure it all out. We talked it over with Suellyn and decided that we just weren't ready to sign any deals. Seeing our need for help, Suellyn called the media consultant at the University of Michigan Law School and asked her to meet with us. She felt that we probably couldn't handle all the stress of the movie and our legal struggles at the same time. We agreed. When he found out how we felt, the agent was upset. I couldn't deal with his anger, so I asked Suellyn if she could talk to him. She asked him if he had ever told us what our responsibilities would be. He responded: "They never asked." After their conversation, Suellyn recommended that we get an attorney specializing in entertainment. We had not signed any agreement with the agent, and we felt that we should not have to commit to a movie unless we were ready. We spoke with representatives from three production companies to try to figure out how they would handle our story. I didn't want them tearing apart the lives of the four adults involved. We felt that the story should focus on Jessi and the fact that her rights had not been addressed by the courts, except for the Best Interest hearing in Ann Arbor. We decided on Bernie Sofronsky, a very kind man who had a great portfolio of other productions, to handle the movie. One of the other producers actually admitted to being an "ambulance chaser," but Mr. Sofronsky was not that kind of man.

The most in-depth story written about Jan and me, Dan and Cara, and the genesis of Jessi's legal nightmare was by Lucinda Franks from *The New Yorker*. Suellyn had accepted the interview with Lucinda on our behalf, and I was glad she did. Lucinda spent several days with us, getting to know us and asking important and incisive questions. She also spent time with Cara and Dan. Lucinda was the first reporter to spend more than a few hours interviewing all of us. She was kind enough to call us one day after she had been with Dan and Cara, and told us that despite the fact that they had always been painted as a little shady by the press, they were actually decent people. I'll never forget that conversation.

I spoke with Lucinda for hours, crying most of the time. I told her I felt terrible about what had happened to Dan and Cara, and blamed myself for everything. When Lucinda told me the things she had discovered about CUB, I recalled that I had always seen that organization as the villain in all of this. Lucinda exposed CUB in her article, detailing its history, and explaining the devastating effect it has had on adoption. In the article, Mary Beth Seader stated: "Many of the pregnant women that I counsel are terrified of choosing adoption, because they've seen or read some CUB propaganda. The members of the anti-adoption groups come from great pain, and their pain is real, but it has made them into predators. They have never worked through the normal process of grieving, which moves from anger to acceptance of loss. Their message is that they have suffered the one unrecoverable loss of a lifetime and that the only treatment is to undo all adoptions. The troubling thing is how they pose as support groups, when they are really just the opposite. Their purpose is to fasten on to women who are in the same vulnerable and formative stages they were once in. They suck them into their passionate obsession, so that they, too, will get stuck in pathological grief that lasts a lifetime."

The article went on to say that during the Best Interest hearing in Ann Arbor, Dan and Cara were ready to give up their fight, but a CUB member, "Laurie Parker, who had befriended Cara," came to the trial and stayed in their room. Laurie had also given up a child for adoption years before, and now she stood by Cara's side telling her how Jessica would be feeling: " 'Deep inside, there's a hole. Something is gone from her, but the bond will always be there.' " Laurie convinced Cara. " 'You have seen what giving up has done to me. You see me on holidays and my son's birthday. You know what I've put up with for twenty years and you are not going to go through that.' " I knew about Laurie before reading about her in *The New Yorker;* she had written to Jan and me offering her advice. The contents of her letter indicated that as I combed Jessica's hair, I was really combing Cara's hair! Laurie went on to say that as I looked into Jessica's eyes, they were not truly her eyes—they were Dan's. The note ended by telling us that Jessica would never be ours. I could only think that Laurie needed help, and I felt sorry for Cara for having been influenced by this kind of thinking. What Laurie and many other CUB members failed to see was that Jessica was a *person*, and when I combed her hair, it was Jessica's hair I was combing! No one had the right to lay claim to anyone the way CUB members did. Jessi's eyes belonged to *Jessi,* and it infuriated me that anyone would venture to lay claim to any part of her body.

We had no idea when the Appellate Court ruling would come down. People were always asking us when we thought we might hear, thinking that the court had given us an indication. They had not. Most of the time I could put it out of my mind; I had to, for Jessi's sake. I wanted to be there for her one hundred percent, and the only way to do that was to focus on her and forget the rest. But deep inside there was a gnawing fear that surfaced occasionally. Sometimes when I looked at Jessi sleeping I was overcome by a dichotomy of extremely strong emotions: love and fear.

On the morning of Monday, March 29, Suellyn appeared at our house unexpectedly with Jan. She had picked him up from work and brought him home so that he could be with me to share the bad news. I knew as soon as I saw Suellyn's car pull up that the Appellate Court had ruled against us. Jessi and I had been coloring together. When I saw Suellyn's car, I said, "Jessi, I'm going to look at something outside for just a minute. Will you draw something for me while I'm gone?"

"A red thing, Momma?"

"Sure, Jessi. Red would be great . . ." I could barely finish my thought. I felt my knees buckle as I stood up. It was almost impossible for me to walk.

"Robby . . ." Suellyn said. She didn't have to finish. Jan held me, as we both were extremely upset. Mom and Joan arrived a moment later, and Joan went right in to Jessi to take care of her. She put Jessi's jacket on her and took her out into the backyard to swing. I could hear them talking excitedly about seeing how high Jessi could swing as Suellyn explained the legal implications of the ruling. The juxtaposition of Suellyn's soft voice delivering horrible news with Jessi's happy laughing tones was too much to bear.

Members of the press were all around our house. We had already announced the location for a press conference we planned to hold as soon as we got the ruling; we thought that might encourage the media to set up the cameras and microphones there instead of on our sidewalk. I felt overwhelmed by their presence. We were grateful to the press for their coverage of a story that we felt had to be told; at the same time, it was very hard to know that there was no privacy in moments like this.

Later that day, we pulled ourselves together for the press conference. I spoke of how losing Jessi was like a death, and Jan said, "This is one of the most difficult days of my life." Again the Schmidts' attorney told the press that we were planning on going into hiding; once again I confirmed that we had no intentions of doing so. The producer of *Good Morning America* called and asked us to appear the next morning. We agreed to, as long as we could stay at home for the interview. We didn't have the strength to travel.

Charles Gibson interviewed us again. His manner was calm and compassionate. He spoke very carefully, as if the wrong phrase or tone of voice might make us break. He asked if I had anything I might want to tell everyone. I did.

"We started about a year and a half ago to try to prepare Jessica for this, trying to build up some type of character within her to withstand all of this. Jessica loved the stairs and we would allow her to play on them. She soon wanted to conquer them by going up, and now, learning to go down. Somehow in my mind I thought this was a great accomplishment, and hoped this would help her in life. She had not learned how to walk yet." I could feel myself trembling inside as I continued to talk.

"I thought it would build strength within her to get through this in her days ahead. I realized one thing this morning. The reason she could conquer those stairs, and go up and down before she had learned to walk, was because she had her mom there. Jessica had her father there. We won't be there. The courts of Michigan and Iowa have made sure of that. We plan on making an appeal to the Michigan Supreme Court. If we lose, I ask the people of Iowa to take our place on the stairs. To help Jessica conquer all of what lies ahead for her. For everyone who's for children, I ask that they understand this whole process. The law has done a terrible thing. They've condemned this child, and with this child go many more down this road. Just don't sit back in your chairs and take it. Stand up, write the Michigan Supreme Court. Protest if you have to on April 17 at twelve o'clock in front of the City Hall in Ann Arbor. Protest at the Michigan Supreme Court up in Lansing. Protest in your state. Don't let this happen to another child . . ."

Jan said that the Iowa and Michigan courts had washed their hands of Jessica, and he responded to what Cara had requested: "I would like to make an appeal to end it, and to the DeBoers to please let her come home."

Jan said, "Jessica *is* in her home, and if they were to come and visit her they might realize this is her home. She's *always* been home."

People from all over the country were outraged. After our appearance on the show, ABC got flooded with phone calls, jamming the phone lines. People also called the Michigan Supreme Court; never in the history of the court had they received so many calls. The Justice for Jessi line that had been set up with an answering service had to be canceled because the system was so overloaded. The committee members had to implement an elaborate system of dealing with phone calls, which poured into their homes around the clock, from all over the country and around the world. They all used answering machines, and had volunteers from all over the area returning calls. At home we received crates of mail every week, some merely addressed to "Baby Jessica's parents in Michigan."

The Justice for Jessi committee organized a candlelight vigil at the state capitol in Lansing, as well as beginning plans for a rally in Ann Arbor on April 17. The candlelight vigil was held on a cool evening in early April, several weeks before the rally. About a hundred and fifty people gathered on the steps of the capitol building. It was a very moving experience. As the sun went down, one person lit a candle to begin. We passed the flame from one candle to the next, saying "Justice for Jessi" as each candle joined in the glow. We stood in silence for quite a while, just feeling the strength of each other's support. Then we sang a few songs together, including "We Shall Overcome" and a new song that Annie Rose had written, entitled "Hear My Voice." It was written from the child's point of view:

> *Does anyone see what I see with my eyes?*
> *Did you know I have eyes too?*
> *I already see my life clearly, but no one's asking me.*
> *HEAR MY VOICE. CHILDREN HAVE VOICES TOO.*
> *HEAR MY VOICE. CHILDREN HAVE VOICES TOO.*

The last verses were especially poignant:

> *Does anyone know what I know deep inside?*
> *Did you know my choice is clear?*
> *You know very well if you'd only ask.*
> *I'd say, "Of course I'm staying here."*

> *Can anyone say what I say with my voice?*
> *Did you know I have a voice too?*
> *Before it's too late please listen to me.*
> *Please listen, won't you?*
> *LISTEN AND HEAR MY VOICE.*
> *CHILDREN HAVE VOICES TOO . . .*

After Annie taught us the refrain, we were able to join in with her. We stood in the candlelight well into the evening singing the refrain over and over again. After we let our voices fade away, we extinguished the candles one by one, repeating our words, "Justice for Jessi." Jan and I were so moved by the experience that we sat in the car in silence for the hour's drive home, just holding hands and hearing the echoes of loving voices.

Suellyn appealed to the Michigan Supreme Court. As was the case in the past, we had no idea how long it would take for them to make a decision. We had to go on with our lives, and keep a sense of faith. Perhaps the Michigan Supreme Court would rule positively.

Pooh Bear was all prepared, bathtub paints in hand, as she headed for the bathroom, looking as if she had no time to waste. "Momma, you commin'?" she said, and jumped into the warm bath. Tubby time was one of our favorite times together. We had figured out a technique of painting in the tub; we could paint all over the place and not have to worry about the mess. I hopped into the tub and we began our little mural on the plastic wall liner. Jessi asked me to draw our house, the tree out front, and the sun. Jan walked in. "Draw a flower, Dad! I need a buew one, Dad. Sit down!"

"Where's Jessi's house?" Jan asked.

"Right there, and dis is my sun. I need a green and eddow [yellow] color," she explained as she painted little flowers in her garden. "You like a finger painten? See a picture of Djessi!"

"It's beautiful, Jessi. Did you paint that?" Jan asked.

"Mom paint that one."

"Jessi, you're like a beautiful flower always in bloom, you know that?" said Jan. As Jessi sat on my lap patiently painting, she dipped her paintbrush into the purple and started to paint the moon. "See, Mom, dis is the moon. See?"

"Oh, yes, Jessi, that is a beautiful moon," I said. After the moon came the inevitable, painting on my face.

"I put polka dots all over!" Jessi said.

"I like the fuchsia color," I told her. "You could paint your little belly button fuchsia."

"I like pusschia, too, Mom."

Satisfied with our painting experience and feeling very clean, we decided to get out of the bath, wrap up in our robes, and have some tea before bed.

We were blessed to have a lot of visitors for Easter this year. Jan's brother Richard and his wife, Rhonda, flew in from Iowa. My brother Tom, his wife, Cathy, and all of their family came from the West Coast. Jan's parents also came. Jessi was very excited about having so many people in her Grandma Jo's house, and she made sure everyone was welcome. My niece Korie catered to Jessi's every need. If Jessi wanted to play the piano, the two would disappear into the music room and begin playing their masterpieces; if Jessi wanted a snack, Korie would sit down and eat with her.

One afternoon I told Jessi that it was time to go buy a piñata for our Easter celebration. "Korie come, too?" she asked. We had decided that this year we would fill a large piñata with candy instead of hiding eggs; it would be a new experience for Jessi. Korie and Jessi looked at all the piñatas, carefully considering each one. They chose a brightly colored horse which Jessi could hardly carry.

On Easter morning, Tom's son Robert and my brother Barry secured the piñata out on the deck as all the cousins gathered around and got in line. Robert held Jessi's hand and led her to the front of the line, handing her the stick and showing her how to swing it at the piñata, reminding her that it was full of candy, so she should swing as hard as she could to break the horse open. There was no way Jessi was going to hit the horse. The look on her face was a combination of surprise and horror. She wanted no part of it. She came and sat on the sidelines in my lap while the other children broke open the horse and ran for the candy. Scott led Jessi over to get some of the treats, but Jessi was more interested in repairing the horse than eating.

Opa and Oma were so delighted to see Jessi again. They took her out to breakfast one morning, went on bike rides with us, and played with Jessi for hours on end. As an Easter surprise, Jan hopped out of the back room one day wearing my old bunny suit from Halloween. Jessi was just tickled. She jumped into his lap for a big kiss.

In the midst of all our legal troubles we had reason to be grateful for so many people who had helped us through this traumatic time. One of them was Peter Darrow, one of Jessi's Michigan Guardian ad Litems. In April he asked the court if he could be Jessi's Next Friend; this would give him an expanded legal role, allowing him to represent Jessi's voice in a court action of her own. Prior to this, all court actions had been brought by adults. We did not know if the court would allow such a case, but it was worth a try. Peter hired attorneys Scott Bassett and Richard Victor, from suburban Detroit, to represent Jessica. They brought the action to Judge Ager, who accepted it in the Circuit Court on Jessica's behalf.

At least ten attorneys from all over the country contacted Suellyn through the Child Advocacy Clinic to say that they wanted to file amicus briefs with the Michigan Supreme Court on Jessi's behalf or our behalf. Don Duquette, director of the clinic, helped coordinate everyone's efforts.

On April 8 we received a fax from an entertainment agency telling us that the Schmidts were on their way to having a movie produced about their story. The press release announced: "The agency is now handling the exclusive rights to Cara and Dan Schmidt's story, and will be negotiating television and film offers for the Iowa couple.

"The Schmidts' heartbreaking story has only been partially exposed, although widely publicized . . . Although the DeBoers, the couple who attempted to adopt the Schmidts' baby, have sold the rights to their side of the story, the Schmidts have not, and unlike the DeBoers, the Schmidts have full cooperation from the Michigan and Iowa attorneys as well as various family members who have been involved in this case for two years.

"The Schmidts have an extraordinary story to tell, and it is one that has not been heard before . . . The Schmidts now seek vindication for the mudslinging and hateful assaults on their character. They are now free to explain why the Iowa Supreme Court has demanded that the DeBoers release the baby back to Dan and Cara. The Schmidts want what they believe to be the realities of this cause célèbre to be portrayed appropriately and accurately."

Everyone assumed that we had already signed a contract for a movie, when in fact we were having a lot of conflicts with even doing the movie. We just couldn't take the pressure. Our new entertainment attorney was trying to figure out what had happened thus far when I contacted him and asked him to put everything on hold; we were not going to sign anything. Within a few days a letter came to the house. Our entertainment attorney had written us to say that he could not predict what would happen if he were to go back to the production company and tell them that we didn't want to sign yet.

The letter signified that he could not guarantee that the production company would not just go ahead with the movie without our rights. Our attorney went on to say that the company could claim that we had an oral contract. He explained that Kim Basinger had recently been sued for eight million dollars due to an oral contract that she had not upheld. What he was trying to tell us was that there was no way to predict what the production company would do, but he felt obligated to tell us that the possibility existed.

Jan and I were scared. We were in over our heads. We decided that we would sign the agreement with the production company, not wanting to take our chances with any more litigation. We were relieved that at least we had gotten a good producer, so we could rely on his integrity and good taste. We were reassured when the production company purchased the rights to the *New Yorker* article, which was an excellent piece in its own right. We did not sign the contract for the movie until the end of June, although it had always been reported that it was signed months before.

The morning of April 17 we awoke to one of the coldest April days on record in Ann Arbor (with the windchill factored in). It was the day of the rally at the Ann Arbor City Hall, sponsored by Justice for Jessi. They had done an excellent job of planning the rally. Despite the cold weather, over six hundred people showed up to support the cause. As they cried out "Justice for Jessi! Justice for Jessi!" tears flowed from nearly everyone there—tears of anger, pain, and frustration. It was at this rally that the idea rose of taping together all the petitions that had been signed for this cause and rolling them up into a scroll. Petitions had been coming in from all over the country. Ultimately over a quarter of a million signatures would come in supporting Jessi's right to stay with us, and a child's right to be heard in the courts.

The rally speakers were excellent. Michigan's lieutenant governor, Connie Binsfeld, a longtime proponent of children's rights and adoption reform, gave an enlightening speech about the many children who have to wait far too long to be adopted, while, simultaneously, many couples have to wait far too long to adopt. Judge Charles D. Gill, who had flown in from Connecticut, spoke passionately of the need for children to be represented in the United States Constitution. Attorney George Russ, from Florida, had firsthand experience with a children's rights case; his son "Gregory K" had "divorced" his mother and been adopted into the Russ family shortly after Jessica's case came to the Iowa Supreme Court. George's speech touched the hearts of many. Mary Beth Seader also spoke of the adoption process from the perspectives of both birth mothers and adoptive mothers, and the effects on the children. Nannette Bowler, director of the Children's Law Center in Grand Rapids, Michigan, spoke eloquently of her experiences in representing children. I could not speak. I was too overwhelmed by the crowd and thoughts of losing Jessica. Jan did speak, and told of his love for Jessica: "Our love for you comes over us like a strong wind and holds us to this battle . . . Jessi, never forget how much we love you or that when our last breath escapes us in this life . . . it will be your name that I will call."

Supporters of the Schmidts also had a gathering at a nearby park on the same day. They called it a baby shower for Jessica and the baby that Cara was about to give birth to. The sign hanging over a table at the shower read: "Jessica's Homecoming Shower. Let the healing begin."

Later that week, spring was finally in the air. Jan, Jessi, and I went to a nursery to buy a tree to plant in Jessica's honor. Stephanie had suggested it as a way of dealing with the grieving and helping Jessi understand that she would always be a part of our lives. Jessi ran in and out of the bushes that sat on the ground. We had no idea what kind of tree we would buy; we thought we'd let Jessi help choose it. When she ran over to show me that she had found a swing set, I told her I would be over in a minute, and that we were trying to find a perfect tree so that we could all plant it when we got home. Jessi stood patiently next to a little soft pink flowering crab apple tree. One look at it and Jan and I knew that was the one. It was Jessi's height, and she loved its "little ball" buds. It would be perfect. Jessi had pulled a little bud off the tree and was asking me why the tree had balls on it. I explained that if we loved the tree enough, it would produce beautiful flowers from the little balls. Jessi vowed that she would give the tree all of her love once it was home.

We brought it home and Jan started digging the hole for the tree in the front flower bed. Jessi was excited to be outside helping her dad. Michael was outside playing next door, and Jessi kept running over to the fence and telling him all about her little tree and how proud she was of it. As she watched Jan dig, Jessi said to him, "Why that hole so big, Dad? It's a little tree!"

Jan said, "The roots need lots of room to breathe, and to be protected. It's just like with a person, Jessi. The stronger the roots, the more they can flower." Jan looked at me with tears in his eyes. We both hoped that Jessi's roots were strong enough to help her flower, no matter where she was.

When the hole was ready, we told Jessi that we would have to be very careful and spread out the roots so that they would have enough room. Jan held the tree in place and Jessi and I poured dirt all around it and stomped the dirt down around the edges. Jessi loved playing in all the dirt. We fertilized it, explaining to Jessi that the tree needed lots of food and love to grow. It was in a perfect place; Jessi could look out of her favorite window and talk to her little tree whenever she wanted to. I told her that if we loved it enough, perhaps the buds would flower this year and there would be beautiful blossoms all over it.

The next morning Jessi and I decided to spend the day outside working in the yard, planting flowers all around the tree. Jessi had her own little shovel and bucket. Spring had come early this year, so we felt safe planting the flowers. I told her that we could have our little Jessi's Grove in the front garden, just as we had one up north. We stayed outside all day, not paying any attention to the phone, for once. Around six in the evening I noticed that the answering machine had several calls.

Suellyn had left several messages. She had flown to Washington, D.C., to go to a convention and to meet with a law firm about our case. I called her back and was relieved to be able to reach her. She told me that the Michigan Supreme Court had taken the case, and had taken Jessica's case with Peter Darrow as Next Friend. I was thrilled that they took our case, of course. However, I was very disappointed that they had taken Jessica's case without letting Judge Ager make a custody decision in that case first. No one was sure why the Supreme Court took Jessica's case, but I felt the Justices wanted to bring the court actions to an end.

Oral arguments were heard before the Michigan Supreme Court on June 3. Jan and I attended the hearing with my mother and Joan. Dan's and Cara's mothers came to the hearing in their place; Cara was soon to be delivering her second child and could not travel. The media was also present on this day, as were several members of the Justice for Jessi committee. Suellyn had asked us to be careful not to respond to any of the Justices' comments. It was rare that Supreme Court Justices ever had to deal with an audience. They prefer that the clients not attend, so they can concentrate on the legal issues and not be swayed by any emotional reactions.

Suellyn said, "Jan and Roberta DeBoer became Jessica's legal parents on February 25, 1991, when the Iowa Juvenile Court terminated Cara Clausen's parental rights to Jessica and named them the legal custodians of the seventeen-day-old baby. Jessica is now two years and three months old. She has lived continuously with the DeBoers in Michigan, always pursuant to custody orders provided by the courts of Iowa and then the court of Michigan . . . The loss of her present family would be devastating to Jessica. This is a very important point to make, not only because we have already had a Best Interest hearing in this case and the court has found by clear and convincing evidence that it would be harmful, not just better for Jessica to stay with the DeBoers, but harmful to move her. We must take into account just how bad it is for a child to have a custody decision made where her best interests are not considered at all."

Justice Riley said, "I'm curious as to why there has been no contact with the child and the Schmidts up until now."

Suellyn answered, "Quite frankly, that when a visitation request was made in Iowa, late in the appeals process, that was the first time Mr. Schmidt requested visitation; it was denied by the Iowa Supreme Court . . . There are major security issues, obviously, for both parents that need to be worked out. When I went to the trial court and said 'Visitation should be granted if it is in the best interest of the child, but please consider security, and whether or not the visits are handled correctly.' I did not adamantly argue: We will never have visitation and we shouldn't have visitation. The judge said, 'We're not going to have visitation for now.'"

Scott Bassett spoke next, arguing Jessica's case: "I'd like to start out by pointing out what this case is not. This is not a foster parent case. This is not an adoption case. This is not a termination of parental rights case. This is plain and simply a child custody case, to be decided upon the best interests of a two-year-old girl."

In her brief in Jessi's case, Suellyn wrote passionately about the rights of a child. She cited legal history that said: "A child is a person, and not a subperson over whom the parent has an absolute possessory interest. A child has rights, too, some of which are of constitutional magnitude."

In her own words, Suellyn went on: "If the law recognizes rights in children at all, the most basic must be the right to a hearing on her best interest when her custody is at issue . . . Our current family law is the descendant of common law which gave the father absolute control over children . . . The father's 'entitlement' to his children and the succession of those rights to his wife upon his death reflected a property interest in his children. A man's control over all of the 'property' of the family was also reflected in common-law marital property rights . . ."

She quoted former Michigan Supreme Court Justice Mary Coleman: "Many eloquent words have been written and spoken concerning 'the best interest of the child,' only to evolve into an analysis of rights of parents and others as to a piece of property. To minimize these regrettable results, the Child Custody Act was passed and hailed as implanting in our statutes the humane and progressive mandate that children are people who have the same unalienable rights as all other citizens. As such, children are deserving of the right to those liberties in which physical, mental, and emotional growth is essential. They are endowed with a right to the 'pursuit of happiness.' "

Jan and I felt good about the oral arguments. They seemed to go much better here than they had in the Court of Appeals. We would hear the ruling in four to six weeks if we were lucky.

The next morning I was lying in bed with Jessi and she rolled over, put her little hand on my cheek, and said, "Hi, Momma! I love you, Momma!" I lay there and thanked her for her kindness. All the stressful days in courts and the fear of losing Jessica disappeared for a moment as I realized that I had Jessi in my heart forever. She would always remain in my life, no matter where she was.

I told her that she would always be in my heart. Stephanie had urged us to show Jessica that our love was in our hearts, and she could always keep our love in her heart. I showed her where my heart was by pretending to reach inside and hold it in my hands. I asked her where her heart was, and she showed me. I said, "Now we're going to put all of Mommy's love inside of

Jessica." When Jan came home that afternoon, Jessi told him that she needed to put all her love in his heart, and put his in hers.

Later in the afternoon, Jan took Jessi to the hardware store to buy some supplies for Jessi's little house, which he was working on. Just after they left, the phone rang. As I picked it up and started talking, the doorbell rang. I answered it without looking through the window first. There stood Earlene Clausen and Mary Dickerson, Dan's and Cara's mothers. I froze, my insides trembling, not knowing what to do next.

Twelve

EARLENE SPOKE FIRST: "We would like to see Jessica." I didn't know what to say. Mary Dickerson reiterated what Earlene had said. My palms felt sweaty as I spoke. "I'm sorry, Jessica isn't here right now." Both seemed a little puzzled at my response. "I'm sorry. I'm not just saying this; she really is not here. Would you like to come in for a second? I'm on the phone and I'll be with you in a minute." Earlene and Mary stepped into the house. Jessica's toys were scattered about and the swimming bag sat next to the door ready for our evening swim. I was glad the house looked like this today; I wanted them to see how we lived. I wanted them to be able to see Jessica's life firsthand. I went back into the kitchen and told the person I was speaking to that I would call her back. My heart was pounding as I returned to the living room.

Earlene asked when they might stop by to see Jessi. I said I wasn't sure, but if she would leave a number where they could be reached, I would be more than happy to call them after talking it over with Jan. Earlene mentioned that she didn't know the phone number of the people with whom they were staying. I told her she could call us back later that night. I knew Cara had access to our phone number, because it was on the adoption papers, but I gave them our number anyway, and thanked them for stopping by. When they walked out to the sidewalk, I realized they had not parked near the house. They were parked around the corner on a side street. It was so strange. Why would they do that? I felt a wave of discomfort come over me.

I felt confused and scared. I called Suellyn, but she was out of town, so I called Norm and John to ask them what we should do. Norm told me he never would have allowed them into the house; he felt Jessica's personal security was at risk. John mentioned that there were many incidents of grandparents kidnapping their grandchildren. They had read an article in the Ann Arbor *News* which acknowledged that Earlene had wanted to take her granddaughter home. Norm encouraged us to stay somewhere else that evening.

When I reached Suellyn later in the day, she echoed what Norm and John had said. She said that Judge Ager had specifically ruled that there would be no visitation, since he was concerned about security. Suellyn wondered why the Schmidts' attorney had not contacted her about arranging a visit for the grandparents. She felt that if they wanted visitation, they should ask for it through Dan and Cara's attorney.

We went to my mom's house, having decided that was the safest thing to do. After we sat and talked with her for a while about what was going on, I wanted to go back home to pick up a few things; I thought I'd go alone while Jessi and Jan stayed at Mom's and played. It was getting dark and starting to rain as I drove home. When I got there, the phone was ringing. It was Jan. "Robby, listen to me. Someone followed us over here. They parked out on the street, and they've been watching this house. I want you to leave our house right away and come back here. Please don't worry about packing anything. We'll make do with what we have here. I'm going to call Norm." I couldn't even answer him. I just hung up the phone and went right to my car. As I pulled out of the driveway, a car which had been parked down the street started to advance. I drove around the block to see if it would follow me. It did. I felt trapped; I could feel my heart beating quickly. I lingered at the stop sign on the corner, hoping it would pass. It drove around me and stopped on the next street. I pulled up behind the car, hoping that it would move on, but it didn't. The driver got out of the car, lifted up the hood, and just stood there. What was I doing? Someone could attempt to harm me. How would I defend myself? I heard Jan's words in my mind: "I want you to leave our house right away and come back here." There was no reason for me to play detective; I should just get to Mom's as soon as possible. I drove off quickly. The car didn't follow me, or at least I didn't see it behind me. When I got to Mom's, Jan said that he had scared the other car off by going outside and walking up to it. It had driven away as he approached. We were convinced that our actions were being monitored.

Jan and I felt threatened by Earlene and Mary's presence. Why had they come to the house and parked around the block? Who was following us? Jan was angry and shaken. He felt a great deal of resentment having to leave our home every time something like this happened. He swore that it would be the last time he would leave his home.

I nestled up next to my little Pooh as we played with a farm animal puzzle in my mom's living room. "Djessi watch tape, Mom." I pulled out *Winnie the Pooh and the Honey Tree*. Jessi looked at the cover and said, "Not this one, Momma, not this one." She ran to the tape bag and pulled out *Winnie the Pooh and the Blustery Day*. Prancing back into the room, she went up to the VCR and announced, "I do it, I do it all by myself." Jessica loved sitting in my lap while watching this movie. She grabbed the pillows and threw them on the floor and said, "Banky, Momma, we need the banky." She threw the blanket over me as she plopped down on the floor. Toward the end of the movie Jessi began to anticipate Christopher Robin's party. She could reenact step by step what was going to happen. It was funny how the movie mirrored our lives in some respects: we seemed to encounter those blustery days, and Jessi, like Pooh, was often the hero of the day, capable of erasing the sadness from our lives by simply being herself.

That night at about three in the morning I woke up and went to the living room. I had found through all these months of turmoil that sometimes I found the greatest clarity in the stillness of the night, after having slept for a couple of hours. As I sat in my mom's favorite chair, I found myself thinking how Jessica would feel if she knew that her grandmothers had come to the house to see her and we didn't allow that reunion to happen. I couldn't do that to her. Jan and I had a responsibility to Jessica. During the Best Interest hearing we saw the pain in Mary's and Earlene's eyes; we saw their tears. We had agreed never to block her biological family from entering her life. Requests for visitation had been denied by the courts. However, we did have very strong feelings about how the process should evolve if visitation was to occur. We felt that it was important for the adults to come together prior to direct contact with Jessi. So much tension had built up over the past two and a half years, and we couldn't pretend that nothing had ever happened. We needed to confront each other and address the issues with the assistance of a mediator. This would protect Jessi from having to be exposed to those raw feelings. We had hoped we would be meeting with Dan and Cara directly, but for now we should welcome the opportunity for Jessica's grandmothers to enter her life. I would not let a possible security problem stand in our way. I could always call the police if I had to, and John or Norm could stop by to monitor the situation.

In the morning I felt prepared to propose my idea to Suellyn. I first called a therapist by the name of Irv Leon, who had attended some sessions of the Best Interest hearing. Irv was more than willing to be present during the visitation. I then called the Ann Arbor Police Department to identify what type of assistance they might be able to provide. I also called Norm and John, but was unable to reach them. When I called Suellyn and told her that we intended to have Jessica meet her grandmothers, she said she was uncomfortable with our proceeding without participation by both attorneys. She was still puzzled why the Schmidts' attorney had not requested this visitation. I hung up the phone feeling discouraged. I struggled between the reality of Suellyn's and Norm's arguments and my own gut instincts to proceed. Suellyn mentioned that this would be the perfect time to grab Jessi because once the Schmidts or the grandparents were out of the state of Michigan, there would be no recourse.

Earlene called. I advised her to contact their lawyer because arrangements would have to be worked out between the lawyers before the visitation. Once things were worked out, we would be more than happy to let them see Jessica. Earlene called several times the next day to tell me that she was unable to reach Suellyn, and that they had planned to leave Monday morning. I explained how important it was to work it out through the attorneys because of prior misunderstandings. I reminded her of the photos of Jessica which I had given her during the Best Interest hearing. The Schmidts' attorney had misconstrued the gesture, saying that we were only trying to hurt their feelings by not bringing a picture for each family member. I told her that I knew this whole thing was hard for her but it was equally hard for us. I reminisced about the letters she had written in February 1991, and how grateful we had been. "I know your tears have not stopped," I told her. "Our tears haven't stopped either. I want this to work out for Jessi. I am not concerned with what is best for us or you. I want to make sure that this is not a traumatic event for Jessi."

The delay in meeting with them made me very uncomfortable. I felt it would be our fault if Jessi did not see them. I put another call in to Suellyn late that night and told her I was going ahead with the visit; I would make the appropriate security arrangements and Irv would be there to facilitate.

The next morning I called Earlene to arrange a meeting. I expressed our desire to meet with her and Mary alone initially; if things went well, then they could see Jessi after her nap. Irv would be present during all of the interactions. Earlene seemed thrown by the idea, but agreed, saying that she just wanted to see her granddaughter and would do anything to make it work. I said, "I think we just need to sit down and spend some time with each other. If you start to feel uncomfortable, let us know; if we feel uncomfortable, we'll let you know. Let's just work all of this out for Jessica. I don't think she needs any of us to have any hostility toward each other. I want us all to be calm around Jessi."

Diary, June 6:

Dearest Jessi,

Today you will meet your biological grandmothers. Last night I couldn't leave your bedside. I kissed you good night many times. Nothing in the world makes me feel better than telling you how much we love you, more than anything else in our lives. My fears of this day seem almost unrealistic, for I know that the love I have given you cannot be broken by the mere vision of two women who are your biological grandmothers. I hope and pray that I can do everything to make this a good day for you. I know you will enjoy the time you spend with them. Your precious smile will bring the sunshine into everyone's day. I know Earlene and Mary will be forever grateful for having this time with you. You have accomplished pushing the pedals on your trike and that has brought you a great feeling of accomplishment. Your grandmothers will be so

*pleased to see how coordinated you are, and how you have
grown into a big girl.*

> *God bless my little Pooh,*
> *I will always love you. Momma—*

Earlene and Mary arrived at noon, as planned. We invited
them in, showed them around the house, and then spent a great
deal of time looking at photo albums and Jessi's baby book. Irv
Leon patiently explained that it would be best if everyone knew a
lot about Jessi's life, her habits, her likes and dislikes, in case a
transfer would occur. He told Mary and Earlene that if Jessi were
to return to Iowa, Dan and Cara would be taking on the roles and
responsibilities of an adoptive family because Jessica would be
unable to perceive them as her biological family. In order to
minimize the effects such a transition would have on Jessi, Dan
and Cara and other family members would have to reinforce
the idea that Jan and I loved Jessi very much, but because of
circumstances that were out of our control we had to let Jessi go
to Iowa. Earlene and Mary said they understood, and would do
their best to make sure this happened.

This first leg of the visit had gone well. I felt that we
were communicating important ideas as well as getting more
comfortable with each other's style. We arranged for them to
return when Jessi's nap was over. A little while later Joan and
Chuck came by to see how things were going. I told them that
things were fine, but Joan could see I wasn't saying all that I felt.
She led me out to the kitchen and said, "Okay, how do you *really*
feel? What's going on?"

"Oh, Joan, I just want it to go well with Jessi, and I'm
scared."

"Look, Robby, as long as you are comfortable with them,
Jessi will be, too. She'll follow your lead," said Joan.

"I just want Jessi to know that we all want the best for her.
I'm afraid she might sense my ambivalence about them and
the situation."

Joan was very reassuring. "Robby, you know Jessi. She'll
probably be asking them to push her on the swing after five
minutes!" I felt better after talking with Joan; I felt more centered
and ready for the next step.

As Joan and Chuck were getting ready to go, Mary and

Earlene arrived. A police car was parked in front of our neighbor's home. Seeing the police car, Earlene refused to get out of the car. Joan went out to tell her that everything was fine; the police were there as a reassurance for all of us. Joan was able to coax them out of the car.

As soon as they came in, I brought Jessi downstairs. Mary was very excited to see her, and started to talk to her immediately. Earlene was much more reserved. Just as Joan had predicted, Jessi carefully watched my reactions, and followed suit. She was quite comfortable. All of us went out to the yard so Jessi could play on the swings. She ran to the swing, climbed up, and asked to be pushed. Jan grabbed the video camera. Everyone watched and cheered Jessi on. "Swing high!"

When Jessi had finished swinging, she said "Carry me, Dad, peez!" to Jan. He responded, "Carry you? Okay, Jessi." Then Mary told Jessi in a loving voice that she would like to carry her. She asked Jessi if she would let her. Jan reassured Jessi, "It will be okay, honey." Irv said, "Is it okay, Jessi, if Mary carries you?" Jessi seemed comfortable with the idea, so Mary picked Jessi up. Once Jessi was in her arms she started to push at Mary's chest, shouting, "No! My Mommy! No!" Mary tried to get Jessi to laugh by saying "Here we go, let's get Daddy!" and swooping her through the air. She was able to get Jessi to giggle as she handed Jessi over to Jan.

We all went inside, and after Jessi ate some dinner, we asked if they would like to stay for tubby time. They happily accepted. Mary helped Jessi into the tub and Earlene sat and watched Jessi play. The sparkle in their eyes made me feel as if we had done a very good thing that day. They seemed to enjoy every last minute of being with Jessi. They both thanked us as they headed out the door. I could tell they appreciated our having welcomed them into our home. Jan held Jessi as I gave them both a hug. Earlene walked up to Jessi and shook her little bare toes, saying to Jan, "You take care of my grandchild." The words hit me the wrong way. I questioned her: "Well, don't you think we have done a pretty good job so far?" Earlene just looked back at me in silence. I felt wounded. I took Jessi in my arms as Jan walked them to the car. He told them that we would do anything to make this relationship work, no matter what the courts decided. If Jessi were to stay with us, they could visit whenever they wanted to. When

Jan came back in, we held each other with Jessi between us for quite a while. We felt a combination of relief, fear, and exhaustion.

I don't often receive letters from my brothers and sisters, so I was happily surprised one day to get a letter from my sister Liz. She wrote:

> *Dear Robby, Jan, and Jessi,*
>
> *I've enrolled you with the Jesuit Seminary Association as I think you need a little influence from above. Enjoy Father's Day, Jan! I know Jessi brings you great joy. Remember, regardless of what the outcome is I can guarantee you that it will be the most meaningful time of Jessica's life. You should both feel proud of what you have done to raise such a beautiful child. Jessica looks like she's pretty much captured everybody's heart. I will say an extra novena for all of you. I thought I would send you the words to a song I wrote, it seems to portray your lives. Remember you are the ones who taught Jessica to fly.*
>
> *Teach Me to Fly*
>
> *Dark is the night without your sun, things don't go my way I need your light to lead me on, spend the time, please stay.*
> *I've seen summer winds that blow across the golden sky. Spread those beautiful wings of yours and teach me how to fly.*
> *Soon I'll be leaving for parts unknown, what direction I don't know.*
> *Share your wisdom while there is time, show me which way to go.*
> *I will remember the days we spent, just counting endless sands. I'll fly among the weightless clouds, and watch the spot where you stand.*
> *Each door we open leads to new paths, which we must walk alone, but you have given me newfound strength, and now I'm off to roam.*
> *You taught me to fly . . .*

The letter sent chills up my spine. It was as if she knew what the future would hold, and she was trying to share a way to reach out to the child in ourselves and in Jessi. Liz's letter reinforced my feeling that we should now prepare Jessica emotionally as much as we could for whatever was to come. We had already begun teaching Jessica about love, happiness, sadness, anger, and hurt.

We wanted her to be able to verbalize her feelings. She had started using the words, and seemed to understand them very well. Like most parents, I loved hearing my child use new words and demonstrate comprehension of new concepts.

Jan's sister Nelli came to visit in mid-June with her son, Corie, who loved playing with Jessi. Even though they were only in town for a day, they made the most of it. Both Corie and Jessi had grown a lot since their last meeting. They often spoke on the phone, so they were by no means strangers. Jessi went up in her bedroom with Corie, pulling out every toy she had. They ran around the house all afternoon, tiring themselves out. By the end of the evening Corie was ready to settle down and read Jessica a book of her choice. She selected *Goodnight Moon*. They lay down on Jessica's bed looking up at the stars on the ceiling and Corie read the book while Jessica pointed out where the mouse was hiding. Corie kissed his cousin goodbye, as if he knew that it might be the last time he would see her. Nelli and Mel had always been honest with him about what could happen to Jessica. It was as if he was giving her his love, forever.

Nelli dropped by the next morning to spend time with Jessi by herself. They sat on the floor and played with the building blocks that Jessi had received from her grandmother Earlene. Jessi was busy building a sidewalk, talking on and on with Nelli. "You like a sidewalks, you like 'em? I like a sidewalks, you like 'em?" She tilted her head ever so slightly waiting for Aunt Nelli to respond. Nelli spoke with a very enthusiastic voice. "Oh, I love sidewalks! And towers, too!" As Nelli started building a tower of blocks, she paused for a moment and yawned. Jessi looked over, again tilting her head to the side, and asked Nelli, "You sad?" Surprised that Jessi asked the question, Nelli explained that she was just tired. "Oh, you tired!" Jessi responded. "Yes," said Nelli. Jessi still wanted to pursue how Nelli was truly feeling. "You happy?"

"Oh yes, I'm very happy," said Nelli. "I'm very happy that I can spend this time with you."

"I'm happy, too," Jessi responded, and they gave each other a kiss. I was so proud of Jessi. Jan and I had started to accomplish what we set out to do, to have Jessi speak openly about feelings.

In one of our meetings in her office, Suellyn recommended finding a therapist to do a baseline analysis of Jessica to help us assess how she was doing developmentally and what her needs might be in the future. A therapist named Kerry Novick had offered her services to us in a letter to Suellyn. Kerry specialized in child, adolescent, and adult psychoanalysis. She had studied at the Anna Freud Center in London, England, under the supervision of Anna Freud, and had twenty-five subsequent years of experience with normal and pathological child development. Jan and I talked it over and felt that she would be the best for the job.

Kerry's office was in her home. Our first visit with her was extremely pleasant. Kerry had a soft and relaxing quality to her voice. Jessi liked her right away. She played with the toys that Kerry kept in her office as we carried on a playful conversation. One of the main attractions was a large plastic house that was set up on a little table with chairs. Jessica was instantly attracted to it because it was just like the one that Graham had. My inquisitive little Pooh found a basket of toys in the corner near the end of the visit. When Kerry asked if she would like to play with one of the toys, Jessi responded politely "Yes!" and reached for the little baby doll. After Kerry pointed out that the baby doll had a little blue blanket, Jessi covered the little doll, wanting to keep her warm. Kerry told her that she could come back and visit the baby doll if she wanted to. Jessi gave the doll a hug and started picking up the toys before leaving.

One Saturday morning Kerry stopped by to see Jessica. When Jessi saw who our visitor was, her face lit up. Kerry brought along the little doll that Jessi had played with at her home. Jessi remembered it and wanted to take the doll and Kerry up to her room to show them her bed and toys. Kerry was very pleased to accompany her upstairs. The two of them sat near the stairs talking about the baby doll, and Jessi's own doll, which was a bit bigger than Kerry's. I told Jessi that I had to go to the basement and I would be right back. "Be right back, kay?" Jessi said as I walked down the stairs.

Jessi noticed that Kerry had a notebook organizer with her, and asked if she could see it. When I came back up the stairs, Jessi was talking about the purple and orange tabs, showing Kerry how she could turn the pages, opening and closing the zipper. I asked Jessi if she wanted to go for a ride outside on her bike. "Go outside, Mom!" Jessi said. First she had to put the doll down for her nap. She wrapped her up in the little blanket that Kerry had brought with her, and covered her little toes so that they wouldn't get cold as she gently placed her in bed.

It was a beautiful summer day. The birds were chirping away as Jessi dashed for the backyard to show Kerry how high she could swing. I had become very fond of Kerry, even though I had met her only a few times. She explained to me why children love to swing, and how it involves all of their senses. It was so enlightening to listen as she explained the child's world from the child's point of view. It gave me an even greater appreciation of the things Jessi had learned and all that she could do. Jessi eventually grew tired of the swing and we went to the front yard to get Jessi's bike out so she could ride.

Jessi exclaimed that she could maneuver the bike around the car and didn't need any help. When she had any trouble, she said, "Mom, Mom, can you helpa me, peez?" and off she went down the sidewalk. Jessi had learned to steer somewhat and was able to pedal down an incline. She told Kerry that her daddy was "up at the poppertee" and that "Myse and Unka Barry" had gone along with Daddy.

Kerry explained to me as we walked behind Jessi that I was all of Jessica's world. The two of us were one. I had read that all mothers and their children maintained that level of oneness for up to three years, before the children learn that they can function as separate entities. Yet I was surprised, mostly because of my self-doubts, that a professional saw Jessica and me as being one person. The problem with most literature on adoption is that it implies that the child is a separate entity, even at a very young age. Kerry was the first person who helped me come to terms with that oneness that I had always felt, the closeness and bonding that I had felt but for some reason didn't fully accept. Kerry had validated the one most important thing in Jessica's and my relationship. I had heard it so many times before, but this time it had penetrated into my consciousness.

Before saying goodbye to Jessi, Kerry said she was finished with the baseline and would prepare a copy for me and one for Suellyn and get them to us soon.

There was some progress in the Michigan legislature that gave Jan and me hope for a while. They were working on a bill which would grant third parties (nonbiological parents) standing to file a custody case. The Schmidts' attorney had argued before the Court of Appeals and the Michigan Supreme Court that Jan and I were no longer Jessica's custodial parents, since the courts of Iowa had thrown out the adoption on December 3, 1992. This was the same day that Michigan agreed to evaluate whether they could take jurisdiction and address Jessica's best interests, since Jessica was a Michigan resident.

If Jan and I were not Jessica's legal custodial parents, the law considered us to be third parties. Michigan had a recent case history stating that third parties do not have standing to bring child custody action to the court. In April, Senator Jack Welborn introduced a bill to the Senate which raised the issue of third-party custody. We had gone to the Senate hearing the day the bill was to be voted on to listen to the testimony. I wanted to have a better understanding of what we were up against if the Michigan courts decided that we were third parties. Members of the Justice for Jessi committee attended the hearing as well. They had been working diligently with the legislators, encouraging them to grant third-party standing. Many of them talked with their legislators three or four times each week, in addition to running letter-writing campaigns to legislators within their own districts.

Senator Dingell's statement that day was as follows: "This bill deals with a situation which recurs. It's just that the press noticed it for the first time in the DeBoer case . . . The legislature does not have the power to do much here, but we are going to do all that we can. We don't have the ability to solve the problem. We do have the ability to give the DeBoers standing to have the question of the best interest of the child heard in court. Ladies and gentlemen, under current circumstances, the best interest of the child will not be heard in Iowa. It will not be heard in Michigan. That particular question will not be heard anywhere. Is there anyone here who is not offended by that situation? . . . The (Senate) committee worked hard . . . to work a statutory fix for this kind of situation that does not conflict with constitutional protections of the biological father, that does not conflict with the constitutional requirement of full faith and credits to judgment in other states. We protect parental rights and at the same time protect the rights of children."

Senator Jack Welborn, who initiated the bill, also spoke: "What this law will do is give standing, merely allowing the court to consider the UCCJA [Uniform Child Custody Jurisdiction Act] by giving prospective adoptive parents standing to bring a child custody action so that the court then can rule in the best interest of the child."

Senator Vernon J. Ehler's statement followed: "This is not a Jessica DeBoer bill. It is not a bill to decide custody between the state of Iowa and the state of Michigan, or who has jurisdiction. That is going to be settled ultimately, I suspect, by the U.S. Supreme Court. What that case has pointed out to us is a flaw in our current law. Our current law gives no standing in court to the prospective adoptive parent. That is all that this bill is designed to correct, and to insure that the adoptive parents have standing in court just as the biological parents do, so that the court indeed has the freedom, the power, and the ability to adjudicate this matter with the best interest of the child in mind. That is not happening under current law. I support this bill because I believe that it will act in the best interest of any child, not just Jessica DeBoer, but in the interest of any child where a custody case is being heard. I hope that everyone also recognizes that this is not, in any way, going to resolve that dispute between Michigan and Iowa."

For the first time in the entire two years of our struggle, I was proud to be a part of the process of the law. For once a group of people talking together made sense of this entire issue. No matter what political party they belonged to, the senators stood up and spoke about the best interest of all children. That was the true issue. I applauded all of them along with the members of the Justice for Jessi committee who were there. The bill passed almost unanimously, with only two senators protesting.

It was very painful for us when, after the bill passed the Senate, the House of Representatives sat on it, often stating that they were not going to pass a "Jessica DeBoer bill." Even though the Supreme Court Justices had urged the legislature to pass a bill addressing the problem of third parties over two years before Jessica's case had arrived in the Michigan courts, the representatives somehow saw this as special legislation for our family.

Judge Ager in the Circuit Court had already ruled that Jessica should not be removed from her home and her family. But if we didn't have standing, it wouldn't matter what Judge Ager ruled. We would lose and Jessica would be removed like a piece of furniture, to be put in another room, just to make things look better. The only question would be who would think the furniture looked better in that other room. Certainly not Jessica . . .

The Justice for Jessi committee worked on many different levels, both in Iowa and in Michigan. From the nationally broadcast television shows that were done on our case, the country became familiar with the efforts of the group. Committee phone numbers having already been established in both states, a number was also added out in California, with the help of my sister Pam and a group of women who had gotten together to start their group. Bridget helped with a few rallies, along with an old neighbor of my parents', Loretti McCook. It was as if the nation was reaching out to help Jessica in any way that it could.

The support the group provided was uplifting, and gave us strength to keep pushing ahead. And yet it was difficult to convey to them that our possibilities of winning were so very slim. The public just had not experienced the injustice that Jan and I had, and we knew from all the attorneys we spoke to that we would most likely lose. I remembered the reaction of Justice for Jessi members when the decision came down from the Appeals Court of Michigan. They were devastated. Joan Pheney Engstrom had stopped by, with tears in her eyes, telling me that the group would not give up.

In addition to all the other things they were doing for us, the group members tried hard to find us a getaway vacation spot in Washtenaw County. We still were under Judge Ager's order restraining us from leaving the county with Jessica. It was as if we had become prisoners inside an invisible electric fence. There was no way to escape. My mother had become really good at knowing where the boundaries of the county were. Often she would take Jessi and me out for jaunts to have a change of scenery. Maura and her children, Caili and Christopher, had become a major part of Jessica's life. They lived in the county and we began to visit them more often at their home on the lake. Caili and Christopher looked up to Jessi and tried to do everything that she did. Jessi was a great teacher and, being one year older than they were, she could often accomplish much more advanced tasks than they could, like getting in the baby pool all by herself. Christopher and Caili were determined to hop in that pool the same way, no matter how many times they wiped out.

I was very excited to receive the baseline assessment of Jessi when Kerry dropped it by one day. I made myself a cup of tea during Jessi's nap and sat down to read about my daughter's development.

"The overall first impression of Jessica is of a sturdy, alert, well-grown toddler, confident in her movements and her regard, but reserving judgment and expression in an unfamiliar situation." Kerry went on to explain that her evaluation had taken place over three different visits, and that she would describe Jessi's gross and fine motor development, cognitive development, speech, self-care, affective development, and relationships.

> *Jessica is well-coordinated, sure in her gait and fluent in her movements. Jessica has not yet completely established lateral dominance: she does things with both hands, somewhat favoring her left. Jessica's speech development is good, with a large and varied vocabulary. She knows many words and many kinds of words. She can understand others easily and make herself understood, both in terms of her syntax and her articulation. Jessica shows good and varied range of feelings, from reserved alertness and curiosity when faced with a new person and a new setting to enthusiastic exuberance.*
>
> *This brings us to the last and most important dimension of Jessica's current functioning, that is, the level of her emotional development and relations with others and herself. Jessica's general high level of development and functioning exists in the context of a rich and strong relationship with her mother. As I did not see her with her father, I am not making explicit reference to his role with her here, but we should note that she would not function as she does if her relationship with him were radically different in quality.*
>
> *Toddlers need a firm base from which to venture out into the world . . . The way she finds out is through her mother's help, support, explanation and reassurance: with these available, she can safely explore and experiment. Jessica's sequence of behaviors and reactions to meeting me and becoming comfortable with me . . . perfectly exemplified the way a toddler secure in her reliance on her mother's continued availability feels able to include a new person in her world. Jessica is able to enjoy herself and integrate her growing capacities harmoniously at this point in the context of her dependable ongoing*

relationship with her parents. The excellent quality of Jessica's way of relating and the "well-put-together" feel of her personality demonstrate the solidity of the foundation of her personality in her early experience.

I began to feel nervous about what the future would hold after getting the report from Kerry. Acting on the assumption that we would lose, we wanted to start to work out the visitation issue before the ruling came down. Jan and I scheduled a meeting with Stephanie, Kerry, and Suellyn to discuss what would be in Jessica's best interest. The point of the meeting was to help Suellyn understand Jessica's developmental position and for us to understand Suellyn's legal position. The meeting proved to be extremely beneficial.

We needed Suellyn to understand that Jessica saw us as her parents. I asked Suellyn if she truly felt that I was Jessica's mother. I had a feeling she wouldn't be able to answer. I wanted her to put herself in our shoes, and tell me what she would do on behalf of her son if he was going to be torn out of her arms. Suellyn could not respond as she attempted to hold back the tears. The law saw Jan and me differently. We were not Jessica's parents in the eyes of the law. We were seen as third parties.

Seeing how difficult this was for Suellyn, Kerry explained that perhaps what Suellyn needed was an understanding of how Jessica perceived us, so that she could reasonably argue solely on Jessica's behalf, thereby representing the connection of the true parentage that Jessica felt to Jan and me.

Modeling everything upon the grandmothers' visit, which we felt had been pretty much a success, we came up with a formula to introduce Jessica to the Schmidts. They would visit in our home, helping Jessica feel at home and comfortable. We all felt that someone like Irv Leon, who had done an exceptional job with the grandmothers' visit, would work well once again. Irv told us it would be hard for him to follow up in the future with the visitation if Jessica was really to be removed from our home. It went against most of his beliefs, and therefore he didn't feel he would be the right person. Stephanie, Kerry, and Suellyn all said they would look for someone they could recommend to take Irv's place in the visitation.

Kerry advised Jan and me to be truthful with Jessica if the

ruling were to go against us in the Supreme Court. She explained to all of us that a child cannot deal with the unknown, so we should not tell Jessica that she might be going away until we knew for sure that she would be leaving us. Kerry wanted us not to hold back the tears, to explain that we were sad and that none of the sadness was from anything that Jessica had done wrong. She told us how important it was to Jessica that her relationship remain on the same truthful level that it had always been; she needed to feel as if she could always depend on us to speak the truth, no matter what happened.

On the morning of July 2, Maura called to ask if Jessi and I could spend the day with her and her kids at the park, and out at the lake near their house. Jessi and I both liked that idea, but we were hungry and hadn't had lunch yet, so we drove through McDonald's on the way to the park. Jessi educated Caili and Christopher in the art of eating french fries. It seemed like yesterday that Jessi first had french fries with cousins Colleen and Riley. Now she was an "old pro," showing her little buddies how to eat theirs. Caili and Christopher were so good at following Jessi's instructions. "Like dis," she would say, and hold a french fry in front of her mouth. She inserted it between her molars and did an exaggerated chewing motion to demonstrate. Caili and Christopher watched carefully and mimicked everything that Jessi did.

After we were done, the kids ran down to the jungle gym and swings, and entertained themselves for quite a while. Christopher started getting tired, so we left the park and headed out to the lake. As we passed through downtown, I said, "Maura, maybe we should stop by the Law School." I had a premonition that something was going to happen that day. I told Maura that I would just run in and be out in a few minutes.

When I walked into the clinic, Cindy and Lou Anne, the legal secretaries, looked shocked to see me. The looks on their faces sent chills down my spine. "Hi," I said slowly. "Have you heard any news from the Supreme Court?" It seemed as if they were afraid to say anything. "What?" I demanded. "What's wrong?"

"Robby, sit down. We just got word that the ruling will be coming down any minute and they will fax it to us right away." The phone rang as a fax started to come in. It was the Ann Arbor *News*, wanting to know our reaction to the ruling. It was amazing that the court could not have the common decency to let the clients know first, before telling the press. We had even petitioned the court in the proper manner, asking to be informed in advance. One of the other lawyers in the clinic told Cindy that she didn't want me to see the order before the lawyers, and they sent me into Don Duquette's office.

Furious that I couldn't see the order right away, I became extremely anxious just sitting in Don's office. Something was wrong; I knew that. I got up and went back into Cindy and Lou Anne's office. "What is going on?" I was almost shouting. Cindy jumped up and said that there was no news yet; she suggested that she could go outside and tell Maura to bring the kids and come inside for a few minutes.

Maura brought Jessi in and gave her to me to hold. Cindy had already asked Maura if she could take Jessi home for a while after she came in to see me, since a decision was coming in from the Michigan Supreme Court. Maura gave me a big hug and told me that everything would be fine, to keep my chin up. Jessi kissed me on the lips and put her little hand on my cheek. "It be okay, Momma, it be okay." She always could read deep inside my thoughts. I gave her another bear hug and told her that I'd see her in a little while.

After they left, Cindy said, "Robby, we're trying to find Suellyn," as tears welled up in her eyes. Through all the months of my visits to Suellyn's office, we had become pretty close, and I knew that if she was crying, something was very wrong. The other lawyer came back into the room.

"Robby, you have got to go into the other room now," she said with frustration. "The press is coming down here, and we don't want them to see you." She followed me down to Don's office.

"Robby, listen . . ." The lawyer's voice trailed off. I had begun crying. My head was on the table and I couldn't look up.

"We can always appeal." I'll never forget those words as long as I live. I couldn't breathe; my head had begun pounding. Cindy contacted my doctor to try to get me some medication. It was as if nothing else mattered; I could let go, I could scream as loud as I wanted to. They had taken Jessica away and I wasn't going to remain calm anymore. A scream came from the base of my lungs, a noise unlike anything I had ever heard. I didn't even have to know what the order said. I could not stand to hear the word "appeal" one more time. I was in a state of panic, wailing at the top of my lungs. The sounds echoed throughout the clinic and out into the courtyard of the Law School.

Robby and Jessi—six months old.

At Randy's house—Jessi is fourteen and three-quarters months here.

Aunt Joan with her little angel.

Jessi loved
Disney World.
May 1992.

Cousin Scott with
his pal Jessi.

Even angels can
screech as loud as
the boys.

Uncle Jerry and Jessi horsing around.

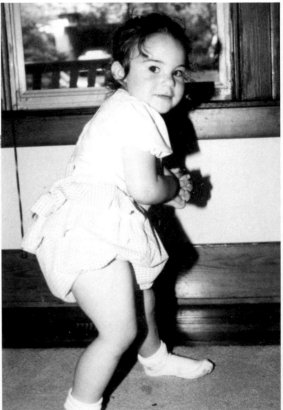

"You put your left foot out and you do the hokey-pokey and you turn yourself about."

Jessi's first tricycle! May 1993.

Jessi and I at the park. May 1993.

Jessi and I often took naps together. June 1993.

Jessi and her best buddy Gina (Angel's daughter) at Jessi's farewell party for family and friends. August 1, 1993.

Miles sits with Pinky looking over some of the mail we received, mostly wonderful letters of support and encouragement.

April 1993 rally for Jessi.

Thirteen

I WISH I COULD DESCRIBE the anguish I felt that day, but no words can ever capture the fear and the sadness I felt for Jessica. My need to protect her overwhelmed me, emotionally and physically. We had to attend a press conference, but I felt I couldn't even move. I needed Jan. I needed to look into his eyes and connect with the one other person who would lay down his life for Jessica.

"Robby . . . Robby, try to stand up. We're going to your mom's house. Jan will meet us there," said Suellyn. She had arrived at the Law School a few minutes earlier, prepared to help us through the day. "Come on, Robby," she said gently, "we have to go now. The press will be swarming all over here any minute. We'll go to your mom's and prepare for the press conference there."

When we arrived at my mom's, Jan was already there. I felt my body starting to tremble inside at the thought of seeing him and acknowledging what had happened. As we walked toward each other, I could see something in his eyes that I had not seen before, even after the other court rulings. His eyes looked like those of a man who had just been shot and was about to collapse and die. They were wounded, pained, ravaged. It was as if each ruling had debilitated our tolerance for dealing with the next one. We held each other and trembled together. Jan spoke a single word: "Jessi."

As we walked into the press conference, I saw that the first two rows of seats were occupied by Justice for Jessi members. They were all crying softly. They had been racing around ever since the ruling, gathering information sheets to make press packets for the media. I tried not to look directly at them, sensing that they were trying to compose themselves. Suellyn spoke first, commenting on the ruling: "The decision affirms the [Michigan] Supreme Court's belief that children are the property of their parents. The transfer date has been set for August 2, 1993. It's our hope the [U.S. Supreme Court] will see the rights of the child to assert what is in her best interest, even when it goes against the desires of her biological parents."

Jan made a brief statement. "We are considered second-class citizens. The bottom line is that no matter what outrageous things [the biological parents] have done, the unwritten law of biology supersedes reality in every part of the law. We are parents whether the system sees us that way or not. We are good parents."

It was hard for me to speak. I felt my throat tighten as I began: "I will always, as Jessica's mother, hear her cries. I will always be with her to help her through those times of isolation and loneliness . . . Parenting is an action. It is not a title to be given to someone. It is not a title given because you have a blood [relationship]; it is a process, developed over time through caring and nurturing."

I implored the Schmidts to seek psychological help for Jessica. The next day in the Ann Arbor *News*, in response, the Schmidts' attorney mocked the offer, saying that it came with strings attached. She quoted us as saying we wanted updates on Jessi's condition to come directly back to us, and went on to say, "We're not going to have [Jessica] held hostage," then added: "If [the DeBoers] want to escrow $35,000, I'd accept it." This was not our intent. How would Jessica benefit from this? The information would need to be provided to Dan and Cara so they would be able to help Jessi through the difficult periods. They would have to be the ones responsible for working through the pain which the separation would inevitably bring.

Later that evening, I finally had an opportunity to sit down and read the Michigan Supreme Court order. It cited case history dating back to 1961, *Herbstman* v. *Shiftan*:

It is a well-established principle of law that the parents, whether rich or poor, have the natural right to the custody of their children. The rights of parents are entitled to great consideration, and the court should not deprive them of custody of their children without extremely good cause. A child also has rights, which include . . . the right to proper custody by his parents, guardian, or other custodian . . . and the right to live . . . free from neglect, and cruelty.

I read these words with disbelief. Had the Justices considered the expert witnesses' testimony when making their decision? Or had they pursued independent psychological evaluation? How could they be so confident that this judgment itself was not a case of cruelty? The following affidavit had been submitted to the Michigan Supreme Court, by Dr. Jeree H. Pawl, of the University of California:

The loss of a potential parental figure or figures when a child is in the first few years of life is among the most devastating life experiences that a human being can have . . . A small child torn from the tapestry of relationships into which she is so completely woven, loses not only that familiar world, but herself . . . When the parents are permanently absent and a child of 2, like Jessica, is removed from all familiar adults there is no one who knows her or who knows her unique language—a language not of speech but a language of love learned in intimate and repeated interaction with those who have nurtured her.

How can one expect a small child to cope with this? Is it possible that the judicial system that should be devoted to the well-being and protection of children should itself inflict so dreadful a punishment?

Dr. Pawl continued:

Adults seem to imagine that their suffering is somehow more important than that of children and that the smaller the child, the less the suffering counts. Children, it is said, will "get over it" just because they are children. From Jessica's point of view, she was already with her parents. She knew and felt nothing but the absolute rightness of her life as it was then.

I found it disconcerting that the courts could not acknowledge the difference in our society over the span of thirty years. The whole definition of family has changed. There are many new living arrangements determining what now constitutes a family. This decision failed to recognize parents other than those who are biologically related. The court had neglected this child's best interest by ignoring her as a human being, not acknowledging her *own* definition of who her "mommy" and "daddy" were.

We decided to let Jessi sleep at Maura's house that night. She was having a good time with Caili and Christopher, and Maura was delighted to have Jessi there. I missed her terribly as I tried to sleep, tossing and turning. Finally, when I drifted off to sleep, I saw my father's face as it looked the night before he died. Joan was living in Arizona then, and she had come home to spend time with Papa since his health was declining. The night before she was to return to Arizona, we all went out to an old German restaurant, a favorite of my parents. Papa was in good spirits, and feeling well that night. Before he went to bed, we hugged each other and laughed. Papa loved to laugh; it came from deep inside him. Joan and I told him how much we loved and respected him. As if he knew what was about to happen, he told us to take care of Mom.

The next morning he passed away. Even though it pained me deeply, I found great consolation in the fact that I had been able to say goodbye to my father. He had a very full life, full of laughter, love, family, friends, and many personal achievements. He was ready to say his goodbyes. It would be dramatically different for Jessica. She was just beginning to say her hellos. I wondered if I could ever say goodbye to my Jessica. Could I ever hug her for the very last time?

The sun shone into the bedroom and woke me up early the next day. Jan and I were very anxious to pick up Jessi. When we arrived at Maura's, she told me that Jessica called out in the night, wanting her mommy and daddy. This was the first night that Jessica had slept in someone else's home other than Mom's without Jan or me there. Jessica was distant that morning as I held her and asked her how she was. I felt hurt, but I could understand how she was feeling. She hadn't wanted to spend the night with Maura and Bob; she wanted to be with her parents at home. She had every reason in the world to be mad at me, and I let her keep her distance.

We spent the day at the lake with Maura and her family. Since Jessi loved the water, I thought this would be the best activity to help her feel better. We called Jerry and asked him to join us, knowing that he was very distressed over the Supreme Court ruling, and some time with Jessi in the water and on the boat would be just the remedy. There was a sandbar on the other side of the lake which was a great place to drop anchor and swim. At first Jessi wanted no part of getting into the lake, but when I took off her cumbersome life jacket, she was ready to go. As Jan and Jerry jumped into the water, Maura and I sat in the boat getting the twins prepared. Jerry came up to the boat and told Jessi he would catch her if she wanted to jump in. It took some coaxing, but eventually she felt comfortable enough to jump. She responded by giggling. "Do it again! Do it again, Unka Jerry!" We played for hours on end, none of us wanting to let go of the warmth we felt in the sunshine and in our companionship.

On Monday morning, the Schmidts and their attorney appeared on *Good Morning America*, via satellite from Iowa. The reporter asked Dan how they were preparing to bring Jessi into their home. Dan responded: "Maybe [we would] have the De-Boers come to Iowa and bring Jessica with them so she can see where she'll be moving, and have some of the family around and such before we actually bring her here so it won't be a total surprise to her." Cara added that she was ready to go today to Michigan: "We need to make the transition as quickly and as smoothly as possible; we need cooperation from everyone." When asked if they felt at all victorious, Dan answered, "It's not really a victory for Cara and Dan. It's a victory for all children and families in the world."

"Yes, it is a worldwide victory for children and families," Cara agreed.

When asked about the offer which we had made to provide professional counseling, Dan said, "We will have to discuss that, you know, between ourselves . . . I think that once she's home, as we are her parents, it will be up to us to make the decisions and whatever our therapist here says would be good for her." The reporter asked if they would give it some thought. Cara replied, "Oh, definitely, we love her with all our heart. We are not going to ignore any of her needs, emotional, physical, or spiritual."

Dan added, "Like we said all along, we will do whatever it takes to . . . help her adjust, whatever is the best for her."

The reporter asked how they would feel when Jessica says, "You are not my mom, you are not my dad."

"With a lot of patience, love, and care," Cara replied.

Dan added, "We will have to deal with it at that time the best way we know how and the best that we can."

"We are not scared of it," Cara added.

With Dan's comment in mind we began planning for the transfer, hoping that we could bring Jessica to Iowa to introduce her to her new home. We called the Riccolos and asked if we could stay at their house during the transition period. Suellyn asked the Schmidts through their attorney to have the contempt of court charges against Jan and me dropped so that we could go back into the state of Iowa. The Schmidts' attorney refused to have the charges dropped, thereby forcing the transfer to take place in Michigan.

Diary, July 5:

Dearest Jessica,

I will miss the running and jumping to catch the stars,

I will miss the glancing at the moon, thinking that we can put it in our pockets,

I will miss thinking that someday we can learn to fly.

Often you try to comfort me, washing away the tears and giving me strength,

But the next time I see you reach for my cheek with those two golden hands and say,

"It be okay, Momma," I know I will not be able to reply so reassuringly. My loving kisses will no longer be able to console you and mend all.

It will never mend Jessi,

For the law has broken you into a thousand pieces.

May my spirit hold you strong against the winds, and God be with you as I will be during your darkest moments in life.

Love, Momma—

Suellyn stopped by that afternoon to tell us that Kent Syverud, professor at the University of Michigan Law School, wanted to help us take our case to the U.S. Supreme Court. He had been encouraged by Suellyn's conversations with attorneys at a prestigious law firm in Washington, D.C., Wilmer, Cutler and Pickering. Suellyn had made contact with one of the founding partners, John Pickering, who had taken the case because he saw the injustice in the courts' treatment of Jessica.

It was extremely encouraging for us to read Michigan Supreme Court Justice Carl Levin's dissenting opinion when Suellyn brought it to us one morning. Suellyn indicated that the opinion supported our position, and his argument would help us to proceed to the U.S. Supreme Court. He stated, in part:

> *I would agree with the majority's analysis if the DeBoers had gone to Iowa, purchased a carload of hay from Cara Clausen, and then found themselves in litigation in Iowa with Daniel Schmidt, who also claimed an interest in the hay. It could then properly be said that the DeBoers "must be taken to have known" that, rightly or wrongly, the Iowa courts might rule against them, and they should, as gracefully as possible, accept an adverse decision of the Iowa courts. Michigan would then have had no interest in the outcome, and would routinely enforce a decree of the Iowa courts against the DeBoers.*
>
> *But this is not a lawsuit concerning the ownership, the legal title, to a bale of hay. This is the not usual A v. B lawsuit: Schmidts v. DeBoers, or if you prefer, DeBoers v. Schmidts.*
>
> *There is a C, the child, "a feeling, vulnerable, [and about to be] sorely put upon little human being": Baby Girl Clausen, also known as Jessica DeBoer, who will now be told, "employing all necessary resources," . . . that she is not Jessi, that the DeBoers are not Mommy and Daddy, that her name is Anna Lee Schmidt, and the Schmidts, whom she has never met, are Mommy and Daddy. This child might, indeed, as the Circuit Judge essentially concluded, have difficulty trying that on for size at two and one-half years. She might, indeed, suffer an identity crisis.*

Seeing these words in print from a respected Supreme Court Justice brought back the feelings we'd had when Judge Ager gave his opinion in the culmination of the Best Interest hearing nearly five months ago. We felt affirmed and encouraged by a voice of authority's seeing things from Jessica's perspective, finding solace in the fact that at least a few judges were able to see it that way. Perhaps the U.S. Supreme Court Justices could do the same, taking their attention out of the adult-centered arena and considering the child's rights instead.

It had been a couple of weeks since Jessi and I had shared one of our painting extravaganzas, and we both felt the need for one after her nap one day. We put on our painting clothes and collected our paints. Sitting on the floor, we decided to make Grandma Jo a card.

"Do you like to wake up and paint?" I asked Jessi.

"What's dis? Where's your paint shirts?"

"Pooh, I've got my painting shirt on just like you do. You look so pretty today. Do you know that."

Jessi cocked her head. "I know. Letter to Gamma Jo. Look, Mom, purple. Ya sure, purple, right, Mom?"

"Yes, Jessi. That is a pretty color, purple. That's Randy's and Aunt Joan's favorite color, isn't it?"

"Uh-huh," she responded.

"Okay, Pooh, here is the paper. Look, I'll write Grandma Jo's name on it, and then you can paint on a couple of other pages along with this one. We'll make a book for her and tie it together with yarn. Okay?"

"Dis your pen, Mom? Look, Mom, water! See? Ya like water? I like water." Jessi carried on her running conversation as she concentrated on her painting. She just loved to converse.

As often happened in our painting sessions, we got sidetracked from our original project. Jessi began to paint her toes, pretending that she was putting on nail polish. "You like 'em, Mom? You like purple, Mom?" Jessi giggled as her paintbrush moved from her feet to my nose, then to my cheek. I tried a dot or two on Jessi's nose, but today she wasn't interested in anything being painted on her face, just mine.

"Daddy, Daddy, you wanna paint, you gonna paint, Daddy?" Jan walked in from the kitchen.

"Sure, I'll paint with you."

"You get dat piwwow and put it here. You sitten on it." Jessi explained to Jan that she was making a book for Grandma Jo and she wanted to bring it over to her that day. "You wanna use Mommy's paintbruss?" Once again, the canvas turned from paper to Daddy's face. After all the painting was done, Jessi announced that she needed to take a tubby to wash off the paint. Jan and I were the ones who needed the tubby!

The issue of visitation had to be worked out. A closed hearing was held in Judge Ager's chambers on Friday, July 9. Suellyn planned to petition the court for authorization to have a therapist present during the visitations, to act as a mediator. We had been given the names of two local therapists. That day I quickly conducted interviews with them over the phone because of the time constraints, after which I notified Suellyn at the courthouse that I had selected Lucy Biven. Lucy and I spoke at length about what her role would be. We were looking for someone to replace Dr. Leon, who had declined to be involved in the transfer. It was our expectation that she would act as an intermediary during the visitation sessions as Dr. Leon had done with Earlene and Mary, standing back and letting the adults get acquainted while offering support. I also explained that Jessi was already being seen by a therapist, Kerry Novick, and that we planned on continuing that relationship. Lucy said she could work within that framework.

On Saturday, July 10, Jan, Joan, and Scott boarded a plane to Washington, D.C., to participate in a rally there for Jessi which had been arranged by the Justice for Jessi committee. I had hoped to attend, but did not want to leave Jessi, so I stayed home with her. Mary Beth Seader and Bill Pierce from the National Council for Adoption had helped organize the rally, and would be among the speakers, along with Joan Pheney Engstrom and Annie Rose of Justice for Jessi, and attorneys George Russ, Lewis Pitts, and Shari Shink, and Judge Charles D. Gill, all from the National Committee for the Rights of the Child. Two large tour buses full of supporters made their way to D.C. Supporters came from as far as Iowa to be on the buses. Lorette McCook, a former neighbor, and her husband, John, an actor, pulled together a group from California to attend, including Bridget. It was sweltering as they stood before the steps of the U.S. Supreme Court.

When Jan rose to speak, the crowd chanted, "Jessi's daddy! Jessi's daddy!" He spoke with vigor and strength, stressing the injustice with which Jessica was being treated by the courts:

"Today I realize once again that your love has won my soul. It is my responsibility as your father to make you happy for today and stand by your side. It is the U.S. Supreme Court's responsibility to make sure that Jessica's happiness will be well served tomorrow. It is this country's responsibility to hear her voice and stand by her side for all the new days to come. The U.S.

Supreme Court must take this case up, and give us a stay to hear the legal arguments and let justice be served for Jessica's sake. The Michigan and Iowa Supreme Courts have forgotten the fundamental constitutional rights of this child. Let us pray that they do not walk away from Jessica. Please! Give her the justice she deserves."

The crowd applauded Jan as he spoke. Scott had talked about getting up to speak, to tell everyone how much he loved Jessica. On the plane Jan and Joan had told him he could just get up and say something impromptu, but he didn't care for that idea. He wanted to prepare a speech and deliver it himself, to show his friends back home that he was in Washington, D.C., doing his part to help Jessica. When it came time to approach the podium, he still did not feel comfortable. He stood in front of Joan, next to Jan and Bridget. Joan stepped forward. "I am Jessica's aunt, I am also her godmother, this is her daddy, and these are her cousins. This is her world, it is all she knows! We implore the Justices of the U.S. Supreme Court to hear her voice. Jessica is home!" At the end of the rally, the Justice for Jessi members unrolled the scroll of signatures, over 250,000, that had been collected from every state in the Union and around the world during the past year in support of Jessi's right to remain with us.

I was very moved when I saw the coverage of the rally on television that night. The grandeur and majesty of the Supreme Court building provided an appropriate backdrop for the issue of the day: the rights of children in America. I was particularly heartened to read the words engraved across the façade: "Equal Justice Under the Law."

While Jan was in Washington for the rally, I met Lucy Biven for the first time. We discussed the case. Lucy said she supported Jessica remaining in our home, and asked if she could meet her, so I brought her to our house. Christine and Jessica were playing on the couch with a puzzle, giggling, when we arrived. Lucy entered the room in front of me, holding a little purple stuffed dog in her hand. Enthusiastically she said, "Hi! How are you today?"

Jessi scooted closer to Christine. She said, "Hi, Mom, we playin'!"

I came in and gave Pooh a kiss. "Did you have fun with Christine while I was gone?" I asked.

"Uh-huh," she replied.

Lucy sat down, attempting to join in the merrymaking with Jessi and Christine. Jessica had never met her before and was a bit shy, looking for guidance from me, and then Christine. I introduced Lucy to her.

Lucy tossed the purple dog toward Jessica. It landed next to her. Thinking it was a game, she tossed it right back. Just then, the phone rang and I went into the kitchen to answer it. Lucy and Christine talked. When I returned a minute or two later, Jessi and Christine were getting ready to go to the park. After they went out the door, Lucy stood up and said, "Oh yes, she's depressed."

"Excuse me?" I said.

"Yes, she is depressed," she repeated.

Needless to say, her statement bothered me. I called Kerry right away to ask if she had picked up any signs of depression. Kerry indicated that she had not. I asked Lucy what had happened to make her think that. She told me most children would have wanted to keep the stuffed animal, but Jessi had not. I almost started to laugh. It didn't surprise me at all. Jessi had a few stuffed animals that she loved, but in general she wasn't really interested in them. I informed Lucy that the baseline analysis, conducted over several days, showed no sign of depression. Lucy did not alter her assessment, telling me that Jessica had picked up on our sadness and was now responding to it.

The first visitation was scheduled for Sunday, July 11. We had always hoped to meet Dan and Cara alone first, then introduce them to Jessica, as we had done with the grandmothers. This plan was unacceptable to the Schmidts. In Judge Ager's chambers there was a private hearing to discuss visitation. He ruled that Cara and I would meet, and then Jan and Dan, before meeting with Jessica.

As I tried to sleep on Saturday night, I couldn't stop worrying. How would Jessi react to Cara and Dan? I kept trying to picture things going smoothly, all of us talking and playing with Jessi. As I lay alone in our bed, I could hear Jan pacing downstairs. I knew he was having the same troubling thoughts as mine, so I finally gave up trying to sleep and went downstairs. Jan and I held each other in the kitchen as my tea water heated. "I've been thinking about those first few days," Jan said, "when Jessi was so little. God, Robby, I feel like it was just yesterday. I can still feel her little hand wrapped around my finger. Remember how she always used to hold on to my index finger and squeeze?"

"I do remember," I said softly.

"Robby, she held my finger so tight. And when we first taught her about holding our hands when she crossed the street, remember the feeling of taking that little hand in yours and dashing across the street together?"

"Yes, Jan." I was rubbing his back as we hugged.

"Robby, I just want her to be able to hold our hands forever. Now we've got to teach her that Cara has hands to hold and Dan has hands to hold, and she can trust them to guide her across the street."

"You're right, honey. If we try to show her that we trust them to care for her, she'll trust them, too."

"Can we do it, Robby?" Jan's voice broke and he couldn't go on. I poured my tea and felt the steam moistening my cheeks as I took a sip.

"Jan, we'll do the best we can. That's what we've always tried to do with Jessi." We sat for a long time without saying another word, the silence broken only by the sound of Miles's occasional deep, sleepy sighs.

On Sunday morning Jan and I were very nervous. This would be the first time that either of us would actually have a conversation with Dan or Cara. The meetings were scheduled to take place at Lucy's office. I would meet Cara first, while Jessi and Jan headed to the park with Miles, taking snacks along. When I pulled into the office driveway, Cara and Dan had just arrived. They both got out of the car. I approached them and gave them both a hug. I told Dan that we needed to start over.

We talked about Chloe, her new baby, and their drive to Michigan. Lucy came out to greet us, and Cara and I walked inside together. It was the strangest feeling, being there with Cara. I began talking first. I told Cara that I had always thought of her as a caring, well-educated person who loved Jessica very much. Cara nodded her head in agreement. Lucy explained that she felt we were never true enemies, and that maybe we would be able to mend our relationship. She felt that the attorneys had been counterproductive and asked why the two of us had not met before this point. "I don't think we could have met until we got to this point," Cara replied.

Cara and I talked about her letters. Cara thought that I should have been able to read between the lines. I told her that we considered her letters to be very genuine. We recognized her struggle and the love she had for Jessica, but how could we read between the lines if we didn't even know her? I told her that we would have appreciated her calling us when she had decided that she wanted Jessica back. I played the tape recording for them of a conversation I had with Gary on January 2, 1992, during which I asked him to pursue getting Cara's rights back. Cara didn't want to listen to it or talk about it. Lucy told her we needed to work through this. I sat there crying, trying to get her to understand what it was like being trapped, not knowing what her relationship was with Scott or Dan. I wondered how she thought I could just hand Jessica over to a complete stranger. Lucy asked Cara, "Do you understand why Robby and Jan did what they had to, to protect Jessica?" Cara, showing no emotion, just nodded her head.

I talked about the role which CUB had played in all of this. We believed Cara had been manipulated by them. Cara responded by saying that she had gone to the meeting for support, and they explained that her rights had been violated. I asked her if she could look me in the face and tell me that I had kidnapped Jessica. Cara had made statements in the past to this effect. She looked up from the table. Lucy asked Cara if that was how she felt. Cara responded that the system in a way had helped in the process of the legal kidnapping of her daughter. I asked if she could just give Chloe away to a stranger at this point. Chloe was about the same age Jessi was when we were brought into litigation. Cara put her hands up to her face and began crying.

Lucy asked Cara if she now understood why I couldn't give Jessica to a perfect stranger. "Well, I don't understand why she couldn't give Jessi to her biological father." I had expressed our position as openly and honestly as I was capable of, but it wasn't having any effect. I requested the name of the therapist that she would be using to help Jessi through the transfer process. She gave me a name and told me that she had not seen the woman as yet, but if they needed her they would call. I asked how they planned to help Jessi heal the wounds that would be created by the loss of her family. Cara responded that she would be coming home to her family, and that they would love her. I told her love was not enough, Jessi would need help. Cara did not respond.

As I walked to my car, I felt a wave of intense sadness. I was so concerned about Jessi's well-being, and I understood her so well, yet in a matter of weeks I would be out of her life. I didn't have the feeling that Cara was open to my thoughts about Jessi and her welfare.

When I got home, I took Jessica upstairs and got her ready for her nap. She climbed in our bed, telling me about her wonderful trip to the park and all the things she had done with the boys there. I read her *Green Eggs and Ham* and tucked her into bed. As I lay next to her, I thanked God for letting me be Jessi's mother.

Meanwhile, Jan went to meet Dan. I was worried about their meeting, wanting so badly for them to get along, but fearing they might not. After he came home, Jan was quite taciturn, not wanting to upset me about what had obviously been a difficult time for him.

"Jan," I said, "please tell me about it. I need to know what happened."

He took a deep breath, then spoke softly. "Oh, Robby, I don't even know how to describe what happened. Dan was mad about the media coverage of the case, and he blew a fuse. He started yelling at Lucy and just couldn't quit."

"At Lucy? Why at her?"

"I guess he's upset at Lucy for bringing the media up. I don't know."

"What did Lucy do?" I asked.

"Well, that's the odd thing. She didn't really do anything. She just asked him to calm down, but didn't try to work through the situation. What scares me is Dan's anger."

"Maybe he yelled at Lucy because it's safe to yell at her. She's not going to yell back," I suggested.

"Robby, what scares me is that I feel like I can't protect Jessica."

Lucy called later and asked if Dan and Cara could see Jessica. There was no court order stating that the visitation would start yet, but I saw no reason why we should wait. Lucy said that they would arrive within the hour. I contacted Norm and John and asked them to come over. Arriving before the others, Lucy asked if she could speak to me alone. "Now, Robby, try not to aggravate Dan," she said, explaining that Dan had been irritated at the office. She thought he would be calmed down by the time he got here, but that we wouldn't want to upset him. I responded: "Lucy, I said I have no intentions of making Dan angry, but if he does become that way in our home he will have to leave." Lucy said she thought we intimidated Dan and Cara because she felt we were more articulate than they were. I found this statement to be pretty unfair to Dan and Cara, especially since it was based on only a few hours of contact. Lucy's hasty assessments made me very uncomfortable.

Jessi was sitting outside on the stairs when Dan and Cara arrived. She didn't pay much attention to them, being thoroughly engrossed in a conversation with me about her toes. Cara spoke softly. "Hi, Jessi." Dan introduced himself. Jessi did not say anything; she just watched them, a normal response for her when meeting strangers. Cara held out a present which she had brought. "Look, Daddy, present!" Jessi chirped. I introduced Cara and Dan one more time, telling Jessi that they had come to visit her. I asked her if she would like to show them her house. She got up and opened the screen door.

"Dis is my house, my house," she said as she pointed to the floor.

I said, "Jessi, can Dan and Cara come into your house?"

"Ya, sure," she said. Jan and I showed Cara and Dan around the house, ending up in the living room, where they sat down on the couch. I sat down in the chair next to them. Jessi leaned up against my legs as Cara offered her the present again. I reassured her that it was okay to open it. Jessi moved over to the other side of my legs and began to open the present. The look in Dan's eyes was quite moving as he sat there watching his little girl open the present. You could see that he loved her deeply. Cara placed the puzzle between them on the couch. Jessica looked back to me for reassurance. I said to her, "I wonder if you can put the puzzle together?" When Cara took a piece of the puzzle out, it made a noise. Jessi remained cautious, staying back. I got out of the chair and moved the coffee table so I could sit on the floor next to her and show her the puzzle.

It took a while, as would be expected, but Jessica warmed up to the toy and to Cara and Dan. Cara spoke softly to Jessi, showing her how the puzzle worked. Jan and I could see how happy they were to be able to meet Jessica at last. After about a half hour, Jessi was standing next to Cara's leg and had rested her arm on her leg for support. It made me feel good that she trusted Cara enough to do that.

Jessi asked if she could go outside to swing, so we all followed her into the backyard. After just a short time outside, Lucy indicated that it was time for Dan and Cara to go. You could see the disappointment in their faces. Jessi walked with Cara and me to the car. Jessi asked where the handle was for the door. Cara showed her, and then Jessi dashed off, saying, "I can run fast!" While Cara got into the car, Jan stood next to Dan on the driver's side. Jan thanked them for coming, and Dan looked at Jessica and said, "You've done a wonderful job with her. She's healthy and happy." When I heard Dan say that, my fears about him dropped away. It was a very kind gesture. Dan thanked us for letting him come and see his daughter. Jan and I thought the visit went very well. We were all able to put our differences aside for the moment to enjoy Jessica. We all loved her so much. Having the visitation was simple compared to dealing with the fighting that was staged by the Schmidts' attorney.

Diary, July 12:

Dearest Jessica,

Yesterday is a day that you should always remember. You met your biological parents. You played with them and enjoyed their company. God bless you and may you have a wonderful relationship with them always. We love you and know that we've done our best to keep you happy. Remember that we will always care for you and hope that you find new love with Dan and Cara.

With the help of the law firm of Wilmer, Cutler and Pickering, and Professor Kent Syverud from the University of Michigan, Suellyn filed her brief with the U.S. Supreme Court requesting a stay that would allow Jessi to remain with us until they made a decision about her future. Seventeen of the nation's most prominent scholars of constitutional law, adoption, child welfare, and court procedure signed another brief which had been drafted by Professor Barbara Bennett Woodhouse, a family law expert at the University of Pennsylvania, with the assistance of professors from the law schools of Harvard, Duke, New York University, Stanford, Columbia, and the University of California.

Diary, July 17:

Dear Jessi,

We have spent the last few days at the pool. Christine and I are teaching you how to swim. You are definitely a water baby. It is wonderful to see you paddle your way through the water. Dad stops by at lunchtime to give his Sweet Pea a kiss, and Grandma Jo comes over to have a potato chip with you every once in a while. You are learning to swim and I am so proud of you! I don't think we could have done it without Christine's help. I can't swim too well, so I have to believe that the lessons from Christine are the ones to learn from.

Love, Momma—

As the days went by, I kept trying to picture Jessi in a different home, surrounded by new people. It was overwhelming for me to imagine her face, her confusion, her inevitable cries at bedtime. No matter how good a job Dan and Cara might do, no matter how much they loved her, Jessi would still be experiencing a more profound loss than almost any of us would ever have to endure. I made myself try to run through what a typical day might be like during her first weeks in Iowa, so that I could prepare her as well as possible. I thought it might be a good idea for her to have one of the lovely porcelain dolls from the shop in the outdoor mall she loved so much. She could take care of the doll, nurture her, and find comfort in the memories associated with her.

Jan and I took Jessi to the mall on a bright morning, having told her that we wanted to buy her a doll. "A doll for me, Mom?" she said, her eyes dancing. She was very excited in the car, talking on and on about what she might name her "baby." When we got to the store, Jessi led Jan to the crib where the dolls were sleeping. She wanted to pick one up. "Be careful, honey," said Jan. She selected the one dressed in a pink nightie, picking her up with great care. We named her Brea.

"Oh, so heavy! So heavy!" she said as she tried to boost the baby's bottom up higher, imitating me carrying her. When she grew tired of carrying her, she would drag her by the arm on the floor.

When we got out to the car, Jessi insisted that Brea have her own seat belt right next to her in the back seat. When we arrived home, Jessi said, "I do it, I do it, Mommy!" She wanted to take

Brea out by herself, with no help from Jan or me. She lifted Brea out of the seat and declared that now it was time to go to the park, and she would put Brea down inside for a little nap. "Tuck her in, Mom!" Jessi said as we took the doll upstairs. I loved watching her loving, gentle manner as she placed the blankets around Brea, saying, "I be back, soon, Brea. Goin' to da park!"

Dan and Cara returned to our home for a few more visits before Judge Ager established a regular schedule. During one of the visits, Jessi had climbed to the top of the play structure and was jumping into my arms. I would put her back up on the structure to do it again. I noticed Dan just beaming as he watched Jessi jump into my arms. I asked Jessi if Dan could catch her, but she wouldn't allow it. I felt crushed for Dan. Jessi did let Cara catch her, though, and she laughed with amusement.

During the following visit I wanted to help Jessica feel secure being around Dan. It was raining out, so we decided to stay in and paint. We sat on the floor, Jan and I encouraging Jessi to paint a picture with Dan. They hit it off right away, talking on and on about the colors and what they wanted to paint. Cara and Lucy sat in the background talking. Dan painted a star, then asked Jessi what he should do next. They painted Dan's name under the star. We hung it on the refrigerator that day to dry. Jan and I both wanted Dan and Jessi to get along; we felt that he was more vivacious than Cara. Jessi was used to expressing herself, and Dan could reinforce that quality of her personality.

Lucy was fairly removed from the interactions. She did counsel Jan and me to remove ourselves from the activities, keeping our distance from Jessi so that she could interact with Dan and Cara more. We had discussed this issue with Jessica's therapist and she felt that we needed to continue our role as Jessica's parents and introduce the Schmidts as we would with any other strangers. Over time, through our interactions independently and as a group, Jessi would begin to establish a relationship with them. By our staying in close proximity, Jessica would feel free to interact with them, knowing that we were there if she needed us.

Diary, July 20:

Dearest Jessi,
    Thirteen days left for you to enjoy your swing. Thirteen days left for you to let your spirit run free in your little park.

Thirteen days left of you learning to swim. And only thirteen days left with Momma and Daddy. How did life deal you such a hand? How can two strangers think that love will mend all? Yesterday, someone asked me, "Robby, will you ever adopt again?" It takes too much out of me to answer that question. You see, Jessi, you didn't come into our lives by mistake. You are a part of me, the same threads weave all three of us together. When I first laid eyes on you, it was as if I knew you, as if I had carried you in my womb. No other child will ever replace you. You are your own unique being.

Love, Momma—

On July 21, Christine, Maura, and I took Jessi and the twins to the Ann Arbor Art Fair. We thought that we could carry one twin in the front pack and one in the backpack. Jessi would be in the stroller. For the hour or so that we walked around we couldn't stop laughing about how heavy the twins had gotten. After buying snacks for the kids and watching people walk by for a while, we decided to go home and put the kids down for a nap. Jessi didn't get to sleep until late in the afternoon.

Jessi was just waking up when Cara and Lucy arrived for a six o'clock visit. After waking up from her naps, Jessi liked to be held for a while until she got her bearings straight. We went down to greet our visitors. Lucy had brought another therapist by to meet Jessica because she was planning on going away for the weekend and she thought her friend might be able to assist during the visitations scheduled for those days. Jessi just wanted to sit and be hugged by me as she got used to being awake and having visitors.

Once she was awake she was more than happy to talk with Cara. They played with the blocks on the floor; later we went to the park to swing for a while. Jan stayed at the house to prepare the grill for dinner. Once we were back home we asked Cara to join us for something to eat. She said she didn't care for anything to eat, but she would just come in the backyard to talk to Jessi. Lucy and her friend stayed at the side of the house talking. Jessi announced that she had to go to the bathroom, so I took her inside. Jan and Cara stayed outside talking. When I came back outside, Lucy and the other therapist were still sitting at the side of the house. As I walked toward the backyard with Jessi, I could hear Jan raising his voice. I asked him to stop. I apologized to Cara for Jan's behavior. Jan stormed away.

Within seconds Lucy and the other therapist said the visit would have to end. Cara went in the house, grabbed her purse, and came outside. Jan went up to Cara and apologized for his behavior, explaining to her that it made him angry when she had questioned his use of the word "if" when referring to Jessi going to Iowa. Apparently he had been trying to reassure her about our intentions; he had said, "If Jessica goes back to Iowa, we would do everything possible to make it go smoothly." Cara wanted to know what he meant by "if." This question set Jan off. He asked Cara why she had lied about who the birth father was. Cara was very guarded, just as she had been with me, allowing little of herself to be revealed. This angered Jan. He felt as if we were being quite open, sharing as much as we could about ourselves, but she was extremely guarded and closed.

Cara hopped in the car with Lucy and her friend. Seeing that Lucy had brought Cara to the visit angered Jan further. Lucy was supposed to be the neutral person in these exchanges. Why would she bring Cara in her car? Jan approached Lucy's window, saying he felt betrayed; he thought her purpose there was to ensure that everyone's emotions were kept in check, yet she had done nothing to help in the earlier altercation. He said he would crucify her if she mentioned any of his private conversations to anyone. Lucy was furious that Jan had threatened her. She closed the door and they drove away.

Lucy called later wanting an apology. I told her I didn't think Jan was threatening her so much as he was expressing his frustration toward Cara for getting in Lucy's car. I went on to say that I thought it would have been more appropriate for her to have gone in the backyard while Jan and Cara were alone rather than remaining at the side of the house. I thought she should have recognized the potential for a confrontation, since Jan and Cara had never talked one-on-one before. Lucy responded: "Well, Robby, obviously in retrospect you are right and I wish I had gone back; however, one doesn't know. But none of that changes the fact that Jan lost his temper . . . Frankly, an apology is in order . . . We have to have different kinds of visits, dear." I was furious with the way she was talking to me.

"Jan will apologize, and he did apologize to Cara," I said.

Lucy's response was: "The last thing said is the one that counts, dear. Don't you understand that?"

I told her I thought everything said counts, and that she put too much emphasis on the last words. I reiterated that her position, as defined by the court, was to help facilitate everyone's needs, and that she should always be close enough to stop any actions like the one that happened that day.

Lucy stated, "I am just doing my best in a very difficult situation. However, you were not doing your best today with Cara." She was referring to my holding Jessi when she was just waking up as she and Cara arrived. She said, "It was terribly uncomfortable."

I said, "Do you want me to playact? I'm sorry, I cannot. I have been told by Jessi's therapist that it is not good to act." Lucy went on to say that it would have been better if I had. I told Lucy that I was not going to change Jessi's lifestyle for these visits. I was amazed that she expected so much of people, and I found her to be very unrealistic, especially for a professional who dealt with people's feelings.

Jan and I began to feel uncomfortable in having chosen Lucy as a mediator. She did very little to facilitate conversations about Jessica, her patterns, her likes, her dislikes, and she did little to help things run smoothly. I wished that I had never given her name to Suellyn. Jessi needed help, and Lucy was not going to be the one to help her.

As we expected after the difficult visit, the Schmidts' attorney petitioned Judge Ager to have the visitations stopped, demanding that Jessi be handed over to the Schmidts immediately. I contacted one of the Guardian ad Litems asking for guidance, and discovered that the other therapist who had come over recently with Lucy reported that Lucy was being overly partial to the Schmidts. Judge Ager decided that day to request that Don Duquette be present at the rest of the visitations.

Suellyn wanted us to come up with a plan for transferring Jessica in case we lost in the U.S. Supreme Court. This was one of the hardest assignments we had ever faced. How do you devise a plan to say goodbye to your daughter? There was no magic strategy that would make it bearable. We focused on Jessi and what might be the least traumatic plan for her. Since we could not bring Jessica to Iowa, the transfer would have to take place in

Michigan. We thought the best way might be to bring Jessi down to the clinic at the Law School, say goodbye, and leave her there with someone who would hand her over to the Schmidts. Jessi had grown to like the clinic, where everyone had been friendly to her. Cindy and Lou Anne let her play with the computers and the fax machine every time we came by. That night I had nightmares of Jessica screaming in the long dark law library. I couldn't envision being so deceitful to Jessica, taking her to a place she loved and then leaving her there. When we told Suellyn the next day that we could not drop Jessi off at the Law School, she understood. The transfer would take place at our house at two o'clock on Monday, August 2. Jan and I told our family and close friends what the arrangements would be. We knew when and where this devastating event would take place. We knew who would be involved. The only question I still couldn't answer was: *Why?*

Peter Darrow, Jessi's Guardian ad Litem, had been appointed by Judge Ager as the Next Friend, and with attorneys Scott Bassett and Richard Victor he had filed an action in the U.S. Supreme Court on Jessica's behalf. Attorney William F. Abram from the law firm of Orrick, Herrington and Sutcliffe in San Francisco also presented a brief to the Supreme Court in Jessica's name, asking that her constitutional rights be addressed.

On Monday, July 26, we received notice from Justice Stevens of the Supreme Court, turning us down for a stay. Justice Stevens stated, in part:

> *Applicant's claim that Jessica's best interests will be served by allowing them to retain custody of her rest, in part, on the relationship that they have been able to develop with the child after it became clear that they were not entitled to adopt her. Neither Iowa law, Michigan law, nor federal law authorizes unrelated persons to retain custody of a child whose natural parents have not been found to be unfit simply because they may be better able to provide for her future and her education. As the Iowa Supreme Court stated: Courts are not free to take children from parents simply by deciding another home appears more advantageous.*

He had completely ignored the fact that Jessica would be harmed by losing us. The news was devastating, but expected. We had all braced ourselves for this decision.

As we snuggled in bed that night, we read *Goodnight Moon*. I told Jessi of our love for her, and Jan knelt by the side of the bed telling her that we would always love her. I spoke softly, reminding her that our love would always be in her heart, and I showed how I took the love out of my heart and put it into hers. I asked for her love, and she did the same thing; she put her love in both our hearts. Then I told her she would be going away, to stay with Dan and Cara, that the court had made up its mind that she would live there. I spoke of the love that Dan and Cara had for her, and said they would always love her and take care of her. She had a new baby sister, named Chloe, whom she could take care of, and she had a sister named Amanda and a brother named Travis. They would love her very much. She nodded her head. "Ya, sure," she said.

I told her she was going to live in Iowa. She began screaming, "No, I don't want to go to Iowa!" I held her close to my chest, as she clung to me, not wanting me to let go of her. I'll never forget the look of terror in her eyes as she screamed. I held her, rocking back and forth, trying to reassure her, telling her that Mommy and Daddy didn't want her to go, that we loved her, and this was not her fault. "Cara and Dan will love you, Jessica. They will love you."

"I'll be back, I'll be back," she kept saying. I remembered that Kerry had said to be honest with her. I held Jessi so close. Jan got on the bed and hugged us both. Jessica clung to me that night as I massaged her forehead and told her that we would always love her, and she would always be in our hearts, and ours in hers. I couldn't believe that the world could be so cruel, expecting this little child, who had always felt so secure, to understand that she could no longer have her mommy and daddy by her side. How could anyone expect her to understand this insane decision?

Suellyn and Don held a press conference, in which Suellyn said, "There are no magic words to tell her [Jessi] she's going away . . . the DeBoers decided they need to concentrate all their attention on preparing Jessica for the transfer, which will take place on Monday. They will definitely not leave the country. They are in mourning already. They will follow through, as painful as that will be."

Cara didn't show up for the next visit. We sat and waited with Don, not knowing why Cara and Lucy had not come. Don called Judge Ager the next day to help us straighten out whatever might be wrong. It turned out that Lucy had advised Cara not to come to the visit because Jessica knew that she would be going to live in Iowa, and she might be upset with Cara. Suellyn asked Judge Ager to relieve Lucy of her responsibilities, since she was only complicating the process. Judge Ager said it was too late. He no longer had jurisdiction, but he would do what he could to clarify Lucy's role.

That Friday, the full U.S. Supreme Court responded to our second request for a stay. They turned us down, but Justices Blackmun and O'Connor dissented. Justice Blackmun wrote:

> *This is a case that touches the raw nerves of life's relationships. We have before us, in Jessica, a child of tender years who for her entire life has been nurtured by the DeBoers, a loving couple led to believe, through the adoption process and the then-single biological mother's consent, that Jessica was theirs. Now, the biological father appears, marries the mother, and claims paternal status toward Jessica.*
>
> *The Supreme Court of Iowa has ruled that Jessica must be returned to her biological parents regardless of whether such action would be in her best interests. Jessica, through her Next Friend [Peter Darrow, Guardian ad Litem], filed an action in Michigan state court, claiming that she has a constitutional right to a determination of her best interest in awarding custody. The DeBoers also filed suit, arguing that federal law authorizes the Michigan state court to modify the custody decree issued in Iowa since the Iowa courts did not at all consider Jessica's best interest . . . While I am not sure where the ultimate legalities or equities lie, I am sure that I am not willing to wash my hands of this case at this stage, with the personal vulnerability of the child so much at risk.*

Justice Blackmun was not able to stop the process, but at least he looked at Jessica as a human being. Despite our devastation, we were grateful for that.

Fourteen

THE COUNTDOWN BEGAN. Jessi had lost in the Game of Law; we had lost Jessi; and Dan and Cara would also suffer the consequences of this outrageous injustice. It was July 30, and we were beginning our last weekend together. After that we would never see Jessica again. Our beautiful daughter whom we had nurtured for two and a half years would disappear.

Jan and I were determined not to spend our last weekend with Jessi lying around the house and crying. We had been a fun-loving family for two and a half years, and we wanted to stay that way as long as we could. It's hard to imagine that one of our highlights in a weekend of good times would be a trip to the dentist, but in our case, it was. Jessi's dentist, Dr. Ray Maturo, was a wonderful, caring man, and he treated each child as his favorite patient. When Dr. Maturo greeted us in his office, I saw a look of understanding and compassion in his eyes; I had to look away, or I knew I would cry. Dr. Maturo cleaned Jessi's teeth and told her she had done a great job cleaning them the last six months. She was able to pick out a toy and a new toothbrush. As Dr. Maturo walked us out into the waiting room afterward to say goodbye to Jessi, I had to give him a hug. He told me that we had done our best and we should be proud of our efforts.

After Jessi woke up from her nap, it took her a while to move about on the bed. Then that perky face came out of the clouds of pillows to say, "Hi, Mom!" I had been sitting in her room pulling clothes out of her drawers, but I stopped to greet my little Pooh. Jessi could see how distressed I was. She sat on her bed saying, "It be okay, Momma." She jumped out of bed and rummaged through the clothes in her drawers, pulling out a turtleneck. "I go dis way," she said as she twisted the shirt in and out, trying to figure out how I kept turning the clothes right side out. "See, this is how you do it," I said, showing her what I was up to. "Oh, go da ouder way," she said as she continued trying, determined to get it right.

Brea lay on the bed watching Jessi pull all of her clothes out of the drawers. "Pooh, have you found Brea's clothes yet? We can't forget to pack those clothes," I reminded her. As Jessi walked over to Brea to undress her, Jan came in and sat on Jessi's big bed next to her. "Dis is da way," she explained to Jan, lifting Brea's hat off. She put it on her own head and said, "I go on bike 'ide, dis my bike 'ide hat!" She cocked her head to the side, saying, "Dis adorable!" Jan and I looked at each other as she spoke, sharing an unspoken moment of joy. I wanted to hang on to the simplicity of this moment, spending time with my husband and daughter talking about Brea. It was all so normal that I found myself forgetting what was going to happen.

Jessi wanted to get moving, since the packing was getting boring and there were many things to do that day. She grabbed the hat off her head and turned around to find Brea fully undressed. "Now, Daddy, *I* put it on my baby." Jan tried to help. "No, no!" Jessi exclaimed. "Like *dat*, Daddy. Does it fit Brea?" Jan helped Jessi put the hat on Brea, "Dat's silly, oh, dat's silly. Put her down, Daddy. I'm going to take her on my bike 'ide, keep da sun out of her eyes. Der we go! Dis her helmet. Keep da sun out."

That evening we rode our bikes down to the park by the Huron River with Randy and the boys. Jessi enjoyed coming to this park to play in the sand, to splash in the water, and to watch the people walking their dogs. Jessi and Graham went down by the water with Jan and dug in the sand. Watching Jan and Jessi from the hill was so beautiful; I couldn't bear the loss Jan would feel when his daughter left. The thought made me tremble inside as Randy and I sat there watching the silhouette of the kids and Jan against the evening sun. That night Jan, Jessi, and I tucked ourselves into bed, and, holding one another, read *The Red Balloon* and watched *Winnie the Pooh and the Blustery Day.*

July 31

Could it really be this close to the end? I lay in bed in the morning, tortured by thoughts of inadequacy. Had I prepared Jessi for the transfer? Did she know how much she was loved? Had I made it clear that Cara and Dan would take good care of her because they loved her? Had I been a good mother? Would Jessi be strong enough to make it through the next months in one piece? In my early-morning daze, I heard a resounding "NO!" in answer to all the questions. Oh, please, God, I thought, I need more time with her. I want to make sure she'll be okay. I'm not ready yet, and neither is Jessi . . . My thoughts trailed off as Jessi woke up and looked at my tense face. "Momma! Good mornen!" I saw such strength in her eyes, such clarity. She was as prepared for this as she could be. Looking at her stripped away the confusion from my mind and I was able to say, "Good morning, Pooh. Nothing's wrong now that I've heard your sweet voice!" She smiled and said, "Snuggle, Momma!" We lay there with our arms around each other and drifted back to sleep.

It would be a busy day. The morning visit was to start at nine-thirty. We had only two more visitations. To date, Cara and Dan had not asked any questions about Jessica and her needs. I told Suellyn and Lucy that this was a problem for me, because I couldn't sit back and watch Jessi go through all of this without the Schmidts learning everything about her that they possibly could. I felt that Lucy's job was to help facilitate a successful transition, which meant, in part, addressing Jessi's personal language. The Schmidts would have to understand the context of Jessi's ideas, and her ways of expressing her feelings, her needs, her history.

I was thinking of Dr. Jeree H. Pawl's affidavit, written on Jessi's behalf, which affirmed the unique language between a parent and a child, "a language not of speech but a language of love learned in intimate and repeated interaction with those who have nurtured her." I suggested meeting with the Schmidts right after the visit and perhaps cutting the visit a little short so we would have time to address these issues, but Lucy didn't think that we could change the length of the visits.

I decided not to be a part of the next visit, but rather to spend that time writing a synopsis of Jessi's daily life. Lucy was not at all happy with the idea, but I felt if Dan and Cara were ever going to be close to Jessi they would have to get to know her language.

When I told Jessi I would be going over to Grandma Jo's house while Daddy, Cara, and Dan were with her, she said she didn't want me to go. I told her I would be back soon, and that if she needed me Daddy could call me.

Jan did call me during the visit to tell me that Jessi had announced: "Court's taking me away from my home." She went on to say that she was going to live with baby Chloe. Jan called me in great distress because soon after Jessi made the remark to Dan and Cara, Lucy entered the room and told Jessi that she was just going on a little vacation with Dan and Cara. Lucy's lie left Jessi questioning her reality. We had told her the truth, and now Lucy was telling her a lie.

When the visit ended, Cara left behind a lengthy list of things to do. On one of the pages was a reminder: Pack Anna's things. *Anna's* things? Throughout the page she referred to Jessica as Anna. During the Best Interest hearing Dan and Cara said they would not change Jessi's name. The grandmothers had said the same thing when they came for their visit. The experts had testified that changing Jessi's name would take away the one item of security she could carry with her to Iowa. Jan and I found it ironic that Cara would try to change Jessica's name after the experience she had once been through. Cara had worked as a nanny to two adopted children in another state for over a year and a half. The mother of these two children was named Cara, and she asked Cara Clausen if she would mind going by her middle name so that there would be no confusion. Cara refused, and for a year and a half she was referred to as Cara II.

When I got back from Mom's house and saw the papers in the kitchen, I became very upset. I needed to get away for a moment, to collect myself before seeing Jan and Jessi. I went down to Randy's and found that she was next door at her neighbor's house. A television station's truck sat outside the neighbor's house; I declined to talk to them and just walked inside. We talked for a while, trying to figure out how the Schmidts could possibly feel that it was okay to change her name. Later that afternoon the press was told that Dan and Cara planned to change Jessi's name. They aired the interview on television that night.

Joan called a little while later to say that she and Scott were going to the park that afternoon to watch Chuck play softball with Casey's team. Jessi overheard our conversation and got very excited. "Can I go to da ball game, Daddy?" Jessi asked as I finished talking with Joan.

"Oh yes, Pooh, we can go to the ball game."

"Momma, you ready?"

"Yes, Jessi. I'm ready if you are!"

"Is Brea going with us?" Jan asked.

"Oh sure," answered Jessi as she ran out to the kitchen to find her.

Jessi loved watching the game. She would call out Uncle Chuck's name as he ran the bases. When the game was over, Scott coaxed her onto the field to run the bases with the other kids. Uncle Jerry stopped by the park to see if he could take Jessi with him for a little while.

"Where we gonna go, Unka Jerry?" asked Jessi. He told her that he had a special mission to take her on.

"Mom, can I go on a spesha michin with Unka Jerry?" she asked, her eyes dancing with anticipation.

"You sure can, Pooh. Just remember everything you can about it so you can tell Dad and me about it later!" I kissed her and hugged her, trying not to cry.

The "spesha michin" was to Jessi's favorite pet shop. Jerry asked Jessi to pick out two parakeets that they could take home. One was bright blue, the other yellow. They named them right away: Jessi and Jerry. Jessi helped pick out a new home for the birds as Jerry explained to her that she was like the birds; she would be going to a new home, where she would be loved and cared for. All of us would always love her and no one would forget the love she had shared with us.

"Two birds, Mom! Jessi and Jerry!" Jessi announced as they carried the birds into Mom's house. We assisted in preparing the birds' new home. Jessi helped Jerry put the food in the cage.

"I help, I put it in now. We need some water," Jessi told her uncle. Jerry gave her the water and vitamins.

"See, Jessi, we want the birds to be really healthy and sing,

like you sing. It helps them get through the hard times, you see."
Jerry explained every step.

Jessi went to Jan and climbed into his lap. Joan explained
that the birds would be scared for a while. Jerry interjected,
"Yeah, then things become easier on them."

Joan went on: "And they need to feel better during that time,
and feel secure because they're nervous. It's because they have a
new home."

Jerry said, "Like anyone who goes to a new home, they're
scared for a little while. Jessi, you may be scared for a little while
when you're at your new home, too. But Dan and Cara will be
there to take good care of you."

I noticed Jessi starting to look uncomfortable, so I came and
sat down next to her and Jan. Jerry went on to say, "After a little
while, you'll discover that you're okay and that you have new
toys, new things to do, and a new sister, Chloe."

I told Jessi that she would also have her old toys and would
have her big-girl bed in her new home. I could tell that was all she
could handle for now. Kerry advised us not to overwhelm her
with information, but to intermittently tell her things about her
new life. I ended the conversation by saying she would always be
loved where she was going; I felt it was very important for her to
hear that.

Jessi had started to regress as the transfer got closer. She no
longer wanted to wear Pull-Ups; diapers were a must. She had
fallen back into using baby talk, and on occasion she would draw
inside herself, leaving an empty look on her face. Deep within her
eyes you could see her sadness. I felt tremendous responsibility for
her unhappiness, and I knew of no cure for it.

When we got back to our house, it was surrounded by the
press. They appeared to be in the same places they'd been in
earlier that day. We realized that they would probably stay there
until the transfer time on Monday. I checked the answering
machine. Dan had left a message on our private number. He had
called in response to an evening news report which indicated that
the Schmidts planned to change Jessica's name.

This is Dan Schmidt calling you two, and if you reveal any
more information and lies about what we left there, you will
deal with me tomorrow. I guarantee you, you will deal with me
tomorrow. If you reveal anything more off of it, you will be

held liable, and I am not kidding. *I am tired of it, and it's* going to stop *tonight. You lied again to Channel 7 and I'm tired of it.* You will deal with me *tomorrow before you leave.* Robby, I'll set you straight, *you got my word.* MARK IT . . . *Bye.*

I froze as I listened to it, unable to react. Jan thought we should call the police. How had Dan gotten our private number? Only family members, Lucy, Suellyn, and a few friends had it. The police listened to the message, made a report, and said they would keep it on record.

Going to bed that night, I found my breathing constricted and labored. I was in a state of intense anxiety. My body was out of control. I thought it might be a good idea to have a cup of chamomile tea, which always made me feel more relaxed. As I put the water on, I looked around the kitchen at all the things in it that were part of Jessi. The pictures on the refrigerator, all of her drawings we had proudly displayed, her special teacups, her favorite little frying pan. "Oh God," I said aloud, "my God, everything in this house is Jessi! What are we going to do?" I fell into the chair sobbing. Until this moment, I had not let myself cry over my own loss in a long time. I had cried in empathy for Jan's loss many times. I had cried endlessly for Jessi's loss. That was the most devastating thing for me. I felt that all of us adults could handle the loss eventually, but how would Jessi fare in the long run? That was my deepest concern.

But at this moment I was crying for me, for my loss of motherhood, my loss of my beloved daughter. This is what my body had needed when I couldn't breathe earlier. I was constricted inside and needed to sob over my own deep loss. "Forgive me," I thought, "for my selfish tears . . ."

It took me a long time to stop crying; even when I wanted to stop, my body would not let me. Finally I was able to pour a cup of tea and sit in the stillness of the living room. Jan was sitting by Jessi's bed, and he had not heard me crying. I was glad for that; it would have torn him apart. He was trying to be strong, but I now wished for him what I had just felt, a recognition of his own unspeakable loss.

August 1

I was awakened by the birds chirping outside our window. I thought of the parakeets and Jerry's sweet gesture. I was so lucky to have a strong and caring family. I never could have made it through these months without them. As I lay in bed looking at Jan's face, I saw lines in his face that had not been there a few months ago. He looked drawn and pale, my dear Jan, my partner in a journey that neither of us ever could have imagined before we began it. I wanted to heal his wounds, but my own were just as deep. Was I capable of helping him heal? Would he ever walk in his carefree way again, with the easy swing of his arms and his steady gait? I woke him up with a kiss, telling him I loved him. A tear ran down his cheek as he looked into my eyes in silence.

This morning's visitation was to be held at nine-thirty. There seemed to be more police out front than in days past. When Lucy arrived, I walked out to her truck and asked her how Dan got our private number. Lucy avoided answering. I told her I would not be threatened or have Jessi be threatened.

For the first time, John and Norm would be inside the house for this visit. As Dan and Cara arrived and walked toward us, I was holding Jessi, who was not in the greatest of moods that morning. I stared into Dan's eyes and he stared back, neither of us speaking. I kissed Jessi goodbye, telling her that I loved her and that I would be at Grandma Jo's house while Daddy took care of her.

I kissed Jan goodbye and asked him to call me if anything went wrong. As I drove down the street a car began to follow me, so I went around the block and the car stayed right behind me. I drove back to the house and told one of the Ann Arbor police officers that I was being followed. He provided a police escort to my mother's house.

Suellyn met me at Mom's house to help prepare the list for Cara and Dan. She had to keep asking me to sit down so we could finish the notes, but getting up and walking around was my way of coping with the situation. It felt so strange to have to sit down and write notes on how to care for Jessica, yet I wanted to say everything I could think of so that Dan and Cara would have as much information as possible. We finished just as the visitation was ending. I drove home in a daze and found Jan and Jessi sitting on the stairs waiting for me to come home. Jan was kissing Jessi's feet. She loved having her feet kissed. Jan said that the visit went well and Dan and Cara left peacefully.

The Justice for Jessi members had planned a last gathering

for us at Joan Pheney Engstrom's house. I asked a friend to invite Barbara Schlicht, Dan's ex-girlfriend, and their daughter, Amanda, to Ann Arbor for the day to see Jessica. We also asked Travis if he would like to come; he almost did, then he declined at the last moment. Jan and I wanted Jessi to be able to meet her siblings, if only briefly. Jan and I had always planned to introduce Amanda and Travis to Jessi and to encourage them to have a relationship.

Bridget, Joan, and Scott came along that day. Everyone played in the backyard. Amanda introduced herself and told Jessi that she would like to read her a book. Jan and I seemed to be floating around, not really doing or saying much. We wanted to go home and be alone with Jessi. We both felt completely isolated from what was going on around us.

As we sat in the yard, four or five of the committee members were inside on the phone to Iowa, still trying to work out a last-minute appeal. They were determined not to give up. I could see them through the window, sitting with lists in front of them, placing call after call. They were in tears. When we left to take Jessi home for her nap, Amanda gave her a hug and kiss and told her that she would always love her.

I held Jessi in my arms as she settled in for her nap, hugging her, telling her once again that I would always be in her heart. I showed her how I took a big chunk of love out of my heart to put inside of hers. We did the same for Brea, and we told Brea to watch over Jessi. I felt as though I could never let Jessi go; the tears ran down my cheeks as I slept, trying to hold on to this moment and make it last forever. Jessi moved over in the middle of the nap and wrapped her arms around my neck and wouldn't let go.

That afternoon Randy woke us up from our nap to invite us to the park to play ball with the boys. Jessi nodded under the blankets, and responded "Go see the boys!" with her eyes sparkling. "Dad come, too?"

"Sure, he'll come, Pooh. Let's get going," I said. Jessi tried to enjoy the time playing the game, but she was withdrawn, going inside herself to escape the pain. She wanted me to carry her as we ran around the bases. She snapped out of it for a moment and giggled all the way to home plate.

Joan and Bridget had gone back to Mom's to set up for Jessi's farewell Popsicle party with her friends. My cousin Pat Connors and his wife, Hyatt, had come from Washington, D.C., for the week, and stopped by to say farewell to Jessi. My cousin Ann and her husband, Tom, also dropped by with Will and their new baby, Casey. Angel brought Gina, and of course Randy came. She wanted to bring her boys, but they were so upset that they just could not come. Jessi was very happy when Caili and Christopher arrived with Maura and Bob.

Joan had brought Jessi's favorite balloons, and Uncle Barry had the Popsicles lined up for the kids, who were outside running up and down the hill. Maura and I sat on the hill watching the kids, holding back the tears, knowing that Jessi would never again see the children she loved so much. My mom kept to herself that night, thinking that if she remained calm and distanced herself emotionally from what was happening, all of us might remain calm, too. Pat told of the effect that Jessica's case would have on the laws in this country and what a difference it would make for all children.

None of that seemed to matter at this moment. Jan and I were losing our daughter, and that was all we could focus on. We had done our best to maintain our life as a family as long as we could, finding pleasure in being together, no matter what was going on. Jan and I knew there was no way we could protect Jessi completely from the bad times. We would see Jessi withdraw inside herself when she was very upset, and we knew that she would have more of that in the future.

Gabe and his girlfriend, Shannon, came to say their goodbyes. Each family member had their own individual way of approaching the transfer. Gabe pulled out Mom's atlas. He found the map of Michigan and pointed out to Jessi where her home in Ann Arbor was. He then flipped to the map of Iowa and found Blairstown. Shannon and Gabe pointed out on the U.S. map how close Iowa and Michigan were to each other, trying to reassure Jessi that we would not be so far away. Jessi followed the conversation, but she became distant and closed the atlas, trying to move on to more enjoyable moments.

As it got dark, I thought of our friends in the Justice for Jessi group. They were holding a candlelight vigil at our home, attended by friends, supporters, neighbors, and members of the press. They wanted to have some time together in the yard they'd seen Jessi in so many times as they dropped by with petitions to show us, gifts of food or flowers. They had worked harder than anyone could have imagined, and Jan and I were eternally grateful.

Jessi hugged her buddies on the hill that night and said farewell to all of them. She kissed Gina and told her that she "oved her." The day had drawn to an end. We went home for Jessi's last night in her own house. Randy couldn't bear to leave Jessi, so she helped me get her ready for bed. Jessi wanted to wear a T-shirt and her diaper.

When it was time for bed, Randy hugged Jessi and kissed her. I couldn't bear to look into Randy's eyes at that moment. I got into bed with Jessi. We rolled around the bed, giving each other hugs and kisses. Jessi turned my face with those soft hands and kissed me several times on my left cheek. "It's okay, Momma," she said, comforting me as she had heard me comfort her so many times in the past when she bruised her knee or scraped her elbow. Now Jessi was taking care of her mother, nurturing her as she had been nurtured.

As I told Jessi once again about what was to happen in the morning, Jessi couldn't talk about it. She started a monologue about her T-shirt: "Well, when I was a little baby . . . well, I weared dis. I was a little baby. I had slippers on. I was born with dis shirt on, with the crocodiles on it." I asked Jessi if I could have a kiss. "Ya, sure," she said. She was getting too active for bedtime, so I asked her to calm down. She responded so well, rolling over to tuck Brea into bed. "Night-night, Brea," Jessi said as she pulled the cover over Brea.

Jessi held her bottle as I read a story, and occasionally she would laugh as we turned the pages. Jan reminded Jessi one more time about our love and asked her where she could find us. Jessi pointed to her heart. Jan's eyes welled up and he kissed his sweet daughter on the forehead. "You're such a bright little girl," he said. "I want you to always know that your mommy and daddy love you, and if you ever need us we will be there for you always." Jessi asked, "Can I sleep in dis bed?" I told her that was a good idea, because we had to pack up her bed to send to Iowa. "I'm going to sleep in it," she said.

"Yes, Jessi, you'll be sleeping in it in your new house."

"No! Dis is my house!" she proclaimed. "No new house!" I told her that everything would be okay in her new house, and

Jessi just drifted off the subject. She didn't want to hear about it now. She opened her arms to us, wanting one big hug. As we embraced I felt the strong union of three souls who knew each other well and loved each other profoundly.

Jessi asked me to sing "Rock-a-bye, Baby," and as I did, she drifted off to sleep. Randy was having a glass of wine in the kitchen, and Jan went down to talk with her for a while. I stayed upstairs, not wanting to leave my little Jessi. I held her tight, whispering in her ear that I loved her more than life itself and I wanted her to find happiness in her new home. Not wanting to wake Jessi, knowing that tomorrow would be a very hard day for her, I tiptoed out of the room to go down and have a glass of wine with Randy. Jan kissed me good night and went back upstairs to be with his little Sweet Pea.

Randy and I reminisced about Jessi, the joy she had brought into our lives, the happy times we had all shared, the growth we had all experienced together. Around two in the morning, I walked Randy down to her house. Most of the media had disappeared. It felt good to get some fresh air. I walked back from Randy's house sobbing. Our neighbor Cleo stepped outside with her family, wrapped a blanket around me, and told me to go home and go to bed; she was afraid that I would become very sick.

I walked in the door and went right upstairs to ask Jan if he could come down for a minute. "Robby, you have to get some sleep. This isn't going to help you any," he said.

"Jan, I can't sleep. I want to paint a message to Dan and Cara on the house. Will you help me?" Jan took my hand, led me upstairs, and told me to go to bed.

"Robby, I won't paint on the house. I'll get some cardboard out of the garage and paint a sign, and tape it to the house, okay? It's three o'clock in the morning. You need to lie down with your Sweet Pea. She needs all of your love." I gladly climbed into bed to hug my little Jessica. It was as if she had been waiting for me. The moment I hit the pillow, she rolled over and climbed on top of me and gave me a great big bear hug in her sleep. She was hugging me so tight, it was as if she was scared to death that tomorrow would come. She slept soundly until seven o'clock, never letting go of me. As we slept, Jan made the sign and hung it outside for the world to see. He painted a broken heart and the words "Dan and Cara, Please Don't Take Our Little Jessica Away."

August 2

Unable to fall back asleep after hanging the sign, Jan went downstairs to continue packing Jessi's things. At seven o'clock Jessi woke up, planting a kiss on my cheek and saying, "Momma, time to wake up!" I looked into her eyes and for a split second I did not remember that today was August 2. Her face looked so bright, so full of the expectation of another day about to begin. Suddenly I remembered what was about to happen and I could not speak. My throat was completely constricted as I looked at Jessi's beautiful face.

"Momma, let's read this book!" Jessi said, picking up *Mama, Can You Turn On the Moon?* by Chris Barton. I told myself that I had to find a way to read it, even though I feared I would become hysterical if I tried to utter a sound. I took a deep breath and slowly exhaled. "Okay, Pooh," I said, "let's read together." I managed to read all the words while my mind was racing at breakneck speed about how to make it through this. How could I let go of Jessi? How could she let go of Jan and me? How could any of us make it through this day? I held her close to me as I read, trying to memorize the feeling of her body leaning on me. I smelled her skin, touched her fine silky hair, listened to her rhythmic breathing. With all my senses, I tried to soak in these last moments with my daughter.

Just as Jessi and I finished the book, we heard Christine arrive. "Momma, there's Christine!" said Jessi, getting up and scurrying to the stairs.

"Go ahead down and see her, Pooh. I'll be there in a minute," I said. I listened to the familiar sound of Jessi's quick descent on the stairs as I went into the bathroom to wash up before going down. I was scared to go downstairs; I felt as if going down would start the inexorable process of saying goodbye to Jessi.

I finally had to come down as Jessi called to me, "Momma! Come see Christine!" I came down and hugged Christine while Jessi ran around the room after Miles. She told me she had been shocked to see the media outside our house. As she heard Jessi talking in the other room, Christine said, "I will cherish forever that sweet voice and the sound of Jessi's laughter." I looked at her and nodded, unable to speak. She asked how she could help us to prepare for the day's events, and I told her that we had a ten o'clock appointment with Jessi's pediatrician, Dr. Dumont. We wanted Dan and Cara to know that Jessi was in good health and had been well cared for. I was hoping Christine might play with Jessi a bit as I prepared breakfast and a tubby.

Jessi asked Christine to go in the other room to play with her puzzles. I stood in the kitchen waiting for the water to boil; it seemed to take hours. Norm called on the phone: "Hi, Robby, I'm outside. Will you pick up?" I didn't want to talk to anyone; it was too early. I left him talking into the machine. Just as the water finally boiled, I heard Norm say, "Robby, open the door!" His voice startled me. He had walked around to the kitchen window. When I let him in, he said he wanted to go over some plans for the day. I told him I couldn't deal with any of it and he would have to talk to someone else. Jessi and I had planned a nice tubby time, and that was all I could think about right then.

Jessi and I lingered in the tub for one last time. I knew I was supposed to tell her once more that this was the day she would be leaving, but Jessi kept on ignoring me when I would bring up the subject. After the bath, Christine dressed Jessi in her pink-and-white flowered dress and combed her hair for the last time while I got ready to go to the doctor's office. Jessi looked like a spirited angel with those electric eyes and that mischievous grin. When I returned to the room, Christine asked Jessi how her mommy looked and Jessi responded, "Momma's so beautiful." She reached up for my arms to hold her.

I called Suellyn and asked her to meet us at Dr. Dumont's office. As we walked outside, the press was everywhere. Norm escorted us to our car while John held back the throngs of people. Norm drove our car, with John following behind in his. Members of the media also trailed behind us, thinking that we were going to the point of transfer.

When we arrived, Dr. Dumont was waiting for us. For the first time ever, Jessi shied away from him. He gave Jessi a full examination. She wanted me to hold her. I knew from her behavior that she knew what was going on today, even though I had been unable to articulate it earlier. While we were there, Dr. Dumont prescribed Benadryl for Jessi, to be taken right before she left. He said that it would help her to sleep on the plane, making the trip easier for her.

On the way home I told Norm that I wanted to pick up

Randy and go to the park. The Schmidts had hired someone to watch us that day; he tried to follow us, but John blocked one of the streets as we disappeared into the park. Jan and John met us there shortly afterward.

We swung for a while, and then Jan sat and talked with Jessi by the river. John called our house to see how things were going there. Suellyn answered and told him it was time for us to come home. She said that during our absence Mom, Joan, Bridget, and Steve had arrived. John looked at us with deep compassion and said, "Robby, Jan— We have to go now. It's time."

Overcome by the stress, Jan started getting sick near the edge of the river. I held Jessi, telling her that Daddy would be okay. "He be okay? He be all better soon?" Jessi asked. When Jan felt well enough, we left the park. On the way home, Jessi wanted to sing "Skinnamarink-a-dink-a-dink." Jessi loved it when we got to the last line: "I love you in the evening and underneath the moon." We would stretch out "moooooon," and then Jessi would say, "Do it again!" Jessi's smile came back as we sang. She was happy for the first time that day.

As we approached the house around noon, the swarm of media had increased. The driveway was blocked by the Ann Arbor police and other members of the security team. Jan noticed members of the Justice for Jessi committee standing in the yard, but felt too devastated to stop and talk with them. I helped Jessi out of her car seat and carried her into the house. I was completely focused on Jessi, unable to see anyone else around me, unable to greet friends and family who had gathered in our living room. "Look, Jessi, Christine made lunch for you!" I said as Jessi climbed up onto the stool. She noticed a large container of bubbles on the counter and, in her fun-loving way, was more interested in playing with the bubbles than with eating. "Christine, we blow bubbles?" she said. Christine smiled and told her that would be just fine. Bridget and Mom came into the kitchen to be with Jessi. When Bridget tried to help Jessi open the bubble bottle, Jessi said with determination, "I do it!" She blew a great big bubble. "Gamma, Gamma, see the bubbles!" We all clapped and encouraged her to blow more.

Christine brought out lunch and told Jessi it was time to put away the bubbles. Jessi told her that she wanted to eat grapes and the muffins that Grandma had brought. She ate very little, but talked all through lunch, asking her usual inquisitive questions. "Do you like muffins? Do you like grapes?" Dropping a grape, she said, "Where'd it go?" Miles, always our faithful mealtime assistant, tried to clean up the floor. Jessi said, "Myse a good boy. He find it!" Much to her delight, Miles gobbled up the grape. As Jan and I busily packed the remainder of Jessi's books, I heard her ask Christine, "Why's Mommy sad? Where's Daddy?"

The mood in the living room resembled that of a wake. Family and friends sat in a daze, stunned by the reality which loomed before them. The scent of fresh-cut flowers permeated the room. It seemed that the only thing living in this room today was the basket of violets sent to us by Patti, my college roommate.

Stephanie called from next door. "Hello, Joan, can someone help me get into the house? The driveway is blocked by so many people. Is there someone there who could walk me in? The crowd is overwhelming! It's very intimidating." Joan asked John and Norm if they could help. As John was escorting Stephanie across the street, Kerry arrived and joined them. We had planned to have Kerry go with Suellyn to help Jessi through the transfer.

When she finished her lunch, Jessi asked to go outside. Christine, Bridget, and Joan said they would take her. I decided to stay inside to continue packing things for Jessi. I wanted her to have everything she needed. Deep inside I knew that I could never pack what she really needed—Jan and me, her home, her family. I looked at the piles of boxes all around me. We had packed twenty of them already. Jan was in the driveway with Steve, carrying some of the boxes to Norm's van. Peeking her head out the door, Jessi said to Jan, "I come outside, Dad!" Jan came to the door and picked her up and brought her into the backyard.

I stopped packing to look at Jessi through the window. She and Joan were rocking slowly back and forth on the two-seated swing. I said aloud "Oh my God, Jessi . . ." and started to sob. Kerry put her arm around me and gently ushered me into the living room. Piles of pictures sat on the tables and the floor. "Kerry, I don't know what to do," I cried. "Jan and I want to send pictures with Jessi, but we don't know what Dan and Cara will do with them."

Kerry said, "Robby, you need to do what you think is best for Jessica. You can't be concerned about what Dan and Cara's reaction will be. You have no control over that. The focus should be on Jessica and her needs. The photos will only benefit Jessi as she mourns her loss of you."

Stephanie circulated through the room, encouraging people to express their feelings and acknowledge their loss. She was an excellent listener. She was most adept at drawing people out and helping them work through their emotions. As I drifted through the room, I could see her talking to Mom and Randy. They were discussing Mom's plans for later that day. Mom was telling her that Irene was coming into town to be with her. Barry and Jerry had chosen not to come today, finding it to be too difficult. They wanted their memories of Jessi to be unscathed by the tragedy of this day. I noticed her doll Gramps sitting on the sofa, and wondered aloud, "Oh, Gramps, who can fix you?" He was in dire need of surgery before leaving for his new home. His back had split open some time before from too much love. Suellyn reluctantly accepted the job and through misty eyes patched Gramps up for his long journey.

I called to Jan to bring Jessi in for her nap. As they came toward the house, Jessi ran around the car, saying she didn't want to go in. One of the private investigators pulled a balloon out of his pocket and magically transformed it into a dog. Jessi paid little attention, running toward the front yard to investigate what everyone was doing. Christine nabbed her and brought her back into the house.

Jan and I took Jessi upstairs to lie down as Bridget and Joan followed. We lay on the bed quietly watching *Winnie the Pooh and the Blustery Day*. Jan and I spoke soothingly to Jessi, trying to calm her down for her nap. She just wasn't interested in sleeping. She engaged Bridget in a verse of "The Wonderful Thing About Tiggers," then came over to me and said she wanted to sit on my lap and be hugged. We talked about how much her Daddy and I loved her. We asked her, "Where is Mommy and Daddy's love?"

"Right here," she responded as she pointed to her heart.

Suellyn and Kerry entered the room and said it was time to go. Jessi clung to me tightly. Jan said, "It isn't time. We need a few more minutes." They said they would wait for us downstairs. Joan hugged each of us and gave Jessi a kiss. Finally I carried Jessi downstairs. Jan remained steadfastly by my side. As I held Jessi, Suellyn said it was time. I wanted Christine to have a chance to say goodbye, so I handed Jessi to her and they hugged and kissed. Jessi looked so confused and frightened. When Jessi was back in my arms, I felt I could not let go. Suellyn repeated, "It's time, Robby." When I hesitated, Suellyn said, "Robby, are *you* going to take her outside?"

"No! I just want to hold my baby. It isn't time!" Jan and I held Jessi between us. Grandma Jo kissed Jessi softly on the cheek and told her she loved her. Everyone else stood frozen in the room. Words cannot adequately describe the pain each of us felt. Jan and I could not bear to let go. As I held Jessi in my arms, she kissed my cheek, then looked down at Miles. He had started to whine. "Myse a good boy!" she said. Suellyn took Jessi in her arms and started for the door. Kerry held Brea, ready to go out the door with Suellyn and Jessi. Steve opened the door and they walked out onto the porch. Norm and John cleared the way for Suellyn and Kerry to walk through the crowd of photographers to the van.

Jessi was screaming, "Mommy! Mommy!" Christine and Joan had to physically restrain Jan and me as they shut the door. I fell to the floor screaming, crying, "Where are they taking my baby?" Jan was wailing and moaning "Jessi, Jessi . . ." as he held me. Then there was silence. We could not cry anymore. I felt as if I was drifting in and out of consciousness. Jan picked me up and carried me into Jessi big-girl bedroom.

The centers of our souls had been squeezed dry, our hearts ripped out. Our bellowing screams had drained us of what little life there was left inside us. "MOMMY! MOMMY! I WANT MY DADDY!" Jessi's cries resounded in my head. Jan and I had once thought we could give up our very lives to save Jessica. We felt ashamed for having followed the law. Why, why, dear God, why hadn't we run?

I slept on and off, awakening suddenly over and over again, horrified by the realization of what had just happened. I called for Stephanie to come into the room; I just had to ask her if she had heard me tell Jessi I loved her before she left. I needed to know that I had told her. Stephanie was very reassuring as she explained that I had kissed Jessi and told her that I loved her. She sat with me while I went in and out of sleep.

I kept asking for Jan. He was in the backyard with Steve, Joan, Bridget, and some of the Justice for Jessi people. I could hear their cries through the window. Joan and Bridget would come inside every few hours to check on me and see if I was still sleeping. Stephanie told the remaining few people that the next couple of weeks would not be "business as usual" and they should give themselves time to grieve and talk about their feelings. She gave Jan a hug and slipped out the door.

The following hours are still somewhat fuzzy in my mind. I have read that our minds protect us by throwing a heavy blanket over the memories that are too painful. We can lift the blanket at some point, when we can handle it. For now I share the entry that Maura was kind enough to write down for Jan and me in our diary.

Diary, August 2, 1993:

Dear Robby,

I know one day you will want to remember these last few hours of this day, so I thought that this might be the least I could do to help you in your healing process. I remember arriving at the house shortly after four. Barry and Jan were out in the garage and they decided that they would leave to go over to your mom's house. Jan asked if I could stay and keep an eye on you. After Jan left with Barry, I took a deep breath and walked into Jessi's room. I loved this room. I remember spending a rainy summer afternoon painting it with you and Jessi. Jessi was still so tiny she was sitting in her bouncy seat dozing while we worked. I now stood in the room with the memory of that day in the back of my mind. I looked under the windowsill and found the tiny little purple flowers I had drawn so long ago.

The little white dress Jessi had worn the night of her going-away party lay across the bed. An orange Popsicle stain that had dribbled down the front of the dress was the only presence of Jessi. That was the last time I saw her. She had crawled into our van and snuggled in between my twins sitting in their car seats. We had all enjoyed the wonderful Popsicle party, but it was time to say goodbye. Jessi kissed us all. It didn't seem fair that Caili, Christopher, and Jessi didn't understand that this goodbye was a final kiss. I gently laid the little dress back down on the bed as if she were still wearing it.

Grief hung in the air. It felt the same as the humidity

outside, heavy, inescapable, and thick. I sat down in one of the white wicker chairs in the sitting room. I looked at the dozens of flowers people had sent. Stacks of mail covered the table; messages of support and offers of prayers were everywhere. I felt so inadequate. What could I say to Robby that a million others hadn't all ready said? In the silent green room I prayed for wisdom, guidance, and acceptance. It was the first time I had ever been afraid to see my best friend. What if I said or did the wrong thing? Every window shade was pulled down, every door and window locked. My friend had either cocooned or entombed herself. I wasn't sure which.

Robby, you finally awoke and came downstairs. Your face was as white as a ghost and your eyes were haunted. You looked at me and wailed, "They took my baby," and doubled over. You repeated that sentence over and over again. I said nothing. I put my arms around your shoulder and walked you into a nearby chair. I had never experienced grief this deep. It was as if someone had blown a hole right through your soul.

I made some tea, and you asked if Jessi was okay and if the plane had landed in Iowa. You kept asking me to call and find out. I finally noticed that you could not take any more, so I walked you back upstairs. On the nightstand there was a thick stack of pictures. We sat on the bed and looked through a litany of memories: how Jessi loved to drive her little car, how much she loved talking on the phone. The sheer joy Jessi had brought to our lives. For my friend it was a comforting bedtime story, and she soon fell asleep again.

I walked back downstairs. What appeared to be lightning flashing announced Jan's return. I had forgotten about the media army outside. I was grateful for someone to talk to. I asked if we could sit in the backyard for a bit, so we did. He talked a lot about Jessi. He seemed so happy just to talk about her. I was amazed at how differently the two parents grieved.

About midnight I felt it was time to leave. I stepped out onto the little porch. A flash went off, almost blinding me—one last picture as I left Jessi's home after saying my goodbye.

With love and respect, Maura—

August 3

This was the day that was never supposed to come. The day after Jessi was gone, the first day of the forever that stretched out in a nightmarish road in front of us. Bridget woke us up with a cup of tea with honey. Jan got out of bed right away and went downstairs, but I could not. Bridget gave me a massage and said I had to get up, because *Good Morning America* camera crews were downstairs setting up.

Getting dressed was a major chore. I was searching for a dress as Suellyn arrived. I felt a surge of pain as I heard her voice, feeling such a bond with her in our loss. She came upstairs and we embraced. I wanted to talk about Jessi and the transfer, but I knew I couldn't at that moment. We had to be on-camera in fifteen minutes. Suellyn tried to help me prepare, ironing my dress on my broken antique ironing board. She laughed when I reported that I could not wear the periwinkle dress without my periwinkle bra, which was missing. My father had always said that every little bit of misery deserves a laughing moment. It was as if he were smiling down on me, saying, "Laugh a little. There's too much pain here."

Jan was as stoic as ever, pretending he could handle it all. He hardly shed a tear during the interview. I knew that inside he was broken in pieces that were sharp enough to cut through his soul. Charles Gibson asked me if there was a message I wanted to convey. I begged the world not to take away Jessica's identity. No matter what side they were on, I asked that they remember that Jessi was a person, a real human being, with a name. I begged them not to change her name.

After the camera crews had gone, Jan wept. He had held it in as long as he could. Soon Barry and Jerry arrived, and Jan went outside to spend some time with them. Suellyn, Bridget, and I sat in the kitchen having tea, talking about the ironing board and the bra. When Suellyn started to get up to leave, I felt very shaken and scared. I reached out to her, tears streaming down my cheeks. "Please don't go," I cried. "Don't leave me!" The moment of Jessica leaving my arms flashed through my mind.

Suellyn and I had become so close, so intimate. I needed her desperately at that moment, almost as if she were filling up the chasm inside me. She hugged me and told me everything would be okay. For the first time in our relationship, she wanted to stay with me through a desperately sorrowful moment without suggesting that I call Stephanie. She whispered lovingly that she wouldn't leave me, she would stay as long as I needed her. The attorney in her had disappeared. I had found the friend that I had looked for so long ago to help save Jessica.

Fifteen

I TOOK A DEEP BREATH and looked around the roomful of people, flowers, cards, and presents. Glancing down at the paper in my hand, I saw the words "Friends Meeting House," and reminded myself that I should take the word "Friends" to heart; all these people were here because they cared for us and for Jessi. Jan's brother, Richard, and his wife, Rhonda, had come from Iowa to be with Jan and me during this very difficult period.

The Justice for Jessi members had arranged this special event for us, "A Time for Grieving," so that we could gather with loved ones and supporters to share our loss, two days after Jessi left. It was a time for community, a time of reflection and prayer. It was as if, as a group, we would be better able to project our love and feelings of tenderness across the many miles which now distanced us from Jessica. The room was packed with people of all ages, most of whom I did not know. Many of them were sobbing, holding hands, shaking. Feeling faint, I thought I'd better go ahead and read the diary passage so I could go back and sit down. I read:

> *Jessi, we will always be by your side. We will caress your warm heart and give you strength. Hold on to your past, for it should carry you down the road to tomorrow. Never look back and blame yourself. Hold your head high and smile. You have given us the best two and a half years of our lives. Thank you. We'll always love you.*
>
> *Momma and Daddy—*

Everyone was crying. We had all lost something when Jessi left. Jan and I had lost our daughter; our family members had lost their grandchild, niece, or cousin; younger friends had lost a dear little playmate, and older ones, a breath of fresh air and a sweet companion. The committee members had lost a hard-fought struggle to change the system; and concerned well-wishers had lost their faith in our legal process. We had a lot to grieve over, and a lot to share.

We read a telegram which had come from Jan's family in Holland:

Dear Jan and Robby,

Although far apart and having not seen each other for years, we lived intensively with you through your sorrow. We know for sure that God was prayed to and begged to support you and to let you keep your daughter. On the morning of August 3, the newspapers in Holland published the loss of your daughter . . . We know that there are no words that can help you to overcome the tremendous grief, a grief that will last for years if not forever. Just remember in the coming months that here in Holland your faraway relatives grieve with you, think of you, and pray for you.

Love, Your Family in Holland—

The service provided some closure for Jan and me, as we were able to acknowledge what Jessica meant to us publicly and to thank the people who had reached out to us. It was a celebration of Jessi's life with us. Many people were able to speak, sharing their reasons for having come and their feelings about Jessi. At one point the children in the room were making a lot of noise, and some of the adults were trying hard to quiet them. I said, "Please don't ask the children to be quiet. To Jan and me, right now, the most beautiful sound in the world is a child's voice."

As we got up to leave, I glanced around the room and saw everyone looking at Jan and me as if they wanted to come up and talk with us. At first I felt I didn't have the strength to stay, but as people started to come up and hug us, I felt connected to them and loved by them, friends and strangers alike. We stayed on for quite some time. One woman said, through tear-filled eyes, that she would never forget the sound of Jessi's cries as she was taken away, that those cries would be the rallying call to the nation.

People all over the country would work tirelessly to keep this from happening to other children. Someone else said that each person in the room represented millions of people who wanted to reach out to Jessi, Jan, and me. Others said they had seen Jessi and me at the mall or in the park during these past months, and that the sight of a mother and daughter about to be ripped apart had just about killed them.

I saw the Justice for Jessi members talking with each person leaving the room, writing down phone numbers. Everyone wanted to help the committee, to work for changes that would give children a voice in our courts. My God, Jessi, I thought to myself, you've taught us all so much. Why did you have to be the one?

My brother Tom had contacted Mom prior to the transfer to say that he wanted to help us find a place where we could begin our healing, someplace outside of Michigan where people would let us have our privacy. He had friends who owned a condominium in Sun Valley, Idaho, and he thought that might be just the place. When Mom and Tom approached Jan with the idea, he told them that we were in such a state of grief that it didn't really matter to him where we were, but he would ask me about it. I refused. I didn't want to go anywhere. I didn't want to leave our home. My family got together and sat quietly in the kitchen with me trying to explain why they thought we should go. Joan said, "Robby, you would be all alone there with family. Tom, Kathy, and Mom plan to be with you for a few days. Here you will be facing reporters and phone calls every day. Lots of people have been dropping by while you've been asleep to wish you well and leave flowers or food. For your own sake, you have got to get out of here. You need the rest." Mom echoed her thoughts, adding that she feared for my health and that I had to take care of myself. I finally acquiesced, seeing that they were determined, and having no energy to put up a fight.

Jerry and Joan planned to drive us to the airport. I woke up in a panic. I didn't want to go. Why were they making me leave? I wanted to be home in case Dan and Cara called. I didn't want Jessi to think that we had forgotten her. Jan held me and said, "Robby, we are going to go. If anyone needs to reach us, they can leave a message. I'll call our machine to check messages every morning and night."

I boarded the plane reluctantly, not really knowing where we were going. I am sure they had told me, but I was completely numb at the time. I thought it might have been Montana or Utah. When I realized our destination was Idaho, I nearly fainted. No one else had realized what personal significance this would have for me. On our honeymoon twelve years before, when Jan and I had entered Boise, Idaho, I became very ill. It was there that Jan and I were first told that we might never be able to have children. I couldn't believe that this is where we would mourn the loss of our only child, Jessica.

As we sat looking out into the hills of Idaho, Jessi pervaded our thoughts. How could she survive without her family? The pain was too much to bear. I remembered Kerry saying that children don't know how to deal with the unknown. Jessi was dealing with such a vast unknown now that I didn't know how she could understand: that she had moved to Iowa and was not just visiting. Jessi would keep looking out the door wondering when Mommy and Daddy would be coming to pick her up.

I remembered Kerry's analogy of Jessi not being able to acknowledge that she had a different life and a different momma and daddy: "Take your hand and imagine you have a splinter, and you want to get it out. Now imagine trying to dig it out, and instead you keep pushing it deeper and deeper into the skin. By now the splinter is so deep that you can't reach it, so you just let it go, until one day it begins to get infected, and it forms a boil and eventually it needs to be surgically removed, and you need antibiotics to cure the infection that has spread throughout your body." This was now Jessi's life. We had told Jessi that the court had taken her away. Lucy had turned Jessi's reality around, by telling her she was just there to visit Dan and Cara for a little while so they could "cement their relationship." This lie, told to Jessi in front of Dan and Cara by a professional psychotherapist, only set the stage for further deception.

I found very little to smile about or take comfort in while we were in Idaho, but news from Ann Arbor helped to brighten one afternoon when committee member Annie Rose faxed us a letter recounting what had been going on with the committee:

Dear Robby and Jan,
I know it will not bring you much consolation in your time of sorrow and pain, but perhaps you will take heart in getting

some idea of just how many people are thinking of you and Jessi. At our first meeting the evening of August 2, the Ann Arbor police showed up to ask us if we could provide all our available phone numbers so they could give them out to callers from around the country. The police department's phones are so overloaded with calls, they cannot receive calls that must get through. The same thing is happening at all the television stations in this area, hospitals, newspapers, and the Child Advocacy Clinic at the University of Michigan. On August 2, the phone service for the committee documented that 46,000 callers had attempted contact with the Justice for Jessi group.

We have established an 800 number, thanks to donations from around the country. We're not sure how we'll be able to afford it in the long run, but for now we must have it, to handle the calls that pour in around the clock. We were very lucky to get a number that has meaning for all of us: (800) 4-R-JESSI. Between the 800 number and our own phone lines, we have been receiving between four and five thousand calls every day. Crates of mail are pouring in to the committee. We will do our best to answer all the calls and mail.

Of course we hold you in our hearts. We think of you, and of our dear little friend Jessi, constantly. All of our love to you.

Annie—

Jan went back to work immediately following our return from Idaho, needing to keep busy. To me, his first day back to work symbolized the beginning of our "life after Jessi." The last time Jan had been to work, Jessi was still here. I felt utterly cold and empty saying goodbye to him in the morning without Jessi. After he left, I turned on the radio. "Thanksgiving," by George Winston, was playing. It was as if Papa were reaching down and giving me the support and love which I so desperately needed. I could feel his presence all day long. I sat down and wrote in my diary:

Dearest Jessica,

I had a daughter, I am a mother.

Our time together was so precious. Now you are gone. Only pictures hang on the wall. They never go away, yet they only represent what once was. Something is missing. My little Pooh no longer lives here . . .

Christine stopped by that day. In our absence, she had been coming over to the house to take care of the mail. The post office had contacted a member of our family to say that they needed to put a container outside the door of our house to handle the overwhelming amount of mail. In the couple of weeks after Jessica left, we received over ten thousand letters, each one expressing sympathy over our loss of Jessica. We were very touched by the support and love that the letters conveyed. People we had never met poured their hearts out to us and helped, at least a little, to fill in the cavernous empty spaces left inside of us.

A woman from Newton, Pennsylvania, stated in her letter that as an attorney she was ashamed to be a part of a justice system that had failed three people so miserably. She had registered a star in Jessica's name because she knew that Jan took comfort in the moon and the stars. The International Star Registry assigned star number Lyra Ra 19h 16m 35s 42° 20″ to the name Jessica DeBoer. This name is permanently filed in the Registry's vault in Switzerland and recorded in a book which will be registered in the Copyright Office of the United States of America.

Another very special gift was the book *Goodnight Moon* sent to us by a woman in Hopewell Junction, New York. The book had a special addition—two inscribed brass plates. The first said, "FOR JESSICA," and the second, "May my spirit hold you strong against the wind, and God be with you, as I will always be. I love you, Jessi, Momma." In her letter the woman said, "Through all this, Jessica remains the most insightful of us all. She'll be back, just as she said she would."

Since I was unable to return thank-you letters to all the supporters, Joan helped me, sending out this note to many people:

> *"What is REAL?" asked the Rabbit one day, when they were lying side by side near the room. "Does it mean having things that buzz inside you and a stick-out handle?"*
>
> *"Real isn't how you are made," said the Skin Horse. "It's a thing that happens to you. When someone loves you for a long, long time, not just to play with, but really loves you, then you become Real." (Excerpt from* The Velveteen Rabbit)
>
> *To Momma, Dadda, Grandma Jo, Oma, Opa, many aunts and uncles, cousins, extended family, and to you . . . Jessica DeBoer was very real. Each day we think of her, pray for her,*

cry for her, miss her. We hold her close in our hearts, knowing that she needs us with her every day to face the darkness of the unknown. We know that as a family we strove to achieve what was best for Jessica. She deserved to laugh, to sing, to play, to be loved, to be held, to feel secure, to be a child. In our time together we experienced the ultimate joy of our lives. We experienced Jessi.

Jessi's Godmother and Aunt, Joan—

Media coverage continued as people all over the country reached out, proclaiming the injustice of the court system and questioning why Jessi should have to be the one to suffer.

Owner Doug Newton from Billy Martin's Western Wear in New York placed this poem in the New York *Times* on August 3:

*I am **Jessica**. Then,* **who?**
Black-robed judges and courts **will decide,**
not hearts and **what's** *right.*
Blood, it seems, is thicker than **love.**
Then who speaks for me? **Not me.**

Harvard Law School professor Elizabeth Bartholet wrote an article which also appeared in the New York *Times*. In it, she said:

Lawmakers in states throughout the country should take the DeBoer case as a signal to rethink the way their policies define family. Courts, legislatures and welfare agencies ought to recognize that families are tied together not by blood but by the bonds of love.

The Philadelphia *Inquirer* printed an article by Barbara Bennett Woodhouse, professor of family law at the University of Pennsylvania Law School. In part, she said:

Jessica's pain was the unnecessary cost inflicted by our failure to reform outdated laws. It is the fault of the grossly inefficient and underfunded court systems, where cases involving children drag on interminably while the human beings whose destinies are most at stake turn from infants to toddlers, to youngsters, putting down roots and becoming deeply attached to their "temporary custodians."

It is easy to point the finger at Cara and Daniel Schmidt or at Robby and Jan DeBoer for lacking the wisdom of Solomon.

The blame belongs squarely with us—the lawyers, legislators and judges who write the laws and run the courts that harm our children, and the citizens who tolerate them.

As Jan and I began the lengthy and difficult process of healing, supporters from the Justice for Jessi committee were going through their own healing process by dedicating themselves to continuing their work. They felt that the injustice they had witnessed over the past year was something that no child should ever again have to endure.

One evening as I sipped my tea in the kitchen, looking out the window and mentally drifting to scenes of Jessi in the backyard, Jan came in and related a conversation he had just had with Janet Snyder, one of the leaders of the committee, which was now called the DeBoer Committee for Children's Rights. "Robby, you just won't believe what's going on out there. It's phenomenal."

"Tell me about it," I said, not knowing if I could concentrate, but wanting to encourage the optimistic sound in Jan's voice.

"Well, Janet says that the mail has not slacked off at all, and the phone calls have increased. The 800 number rings twenty-four hours a day, every day. And seven or eight of the committee members are still receiving fifty to a hundred calls a day on their home phones. They've had to install extra phone lines and let their answering machines take the messages."

"What are all these people saying?"

He hesitated. I could see his enthusiasm turn to sadness. He waited a moment before responding. "I guess a lot of them say they want to help us get Jessi back." We both broke down in tears and cried for what seemed like hours.

When I was able to speak again, I wanted to hear more about the committee. "Jan, what else are the callers saying?"

"That's the amazing thing. Janet says that almost all the callers say the same thing, that they've never been so affected by anything before. They can't sleep or eat. They can't bear the thought of what happened to Jessi. They can't believe it actually happened, that the courts actually took her away. And they want to find a way to make sure that it stops happening to children throughout the country."

"I wonder how the committee members can do all of this from their own homes. Are they still getting together for meetings?"

"Robby, I forgot to tell you! The committee has an office now, which is being donated for the time being; also, some office equipment has been supplied. A couple from Chicago came to install a phone system to handle the huge volume of calls. People have donated a fax machine, a copier, and all kinds of supplies. The office is up and running! And across the country, people are setting up chapters of the committee to work in their own areas."

"My God!" I was amazed. What had started as a small group of supporters was turning into a nationwide movement. I felt a wave of intense pain. All this work, all this support and love, all these people caring about one child . . . and still she was taken away. "Jan, do you think the committee can really make a difference? Just think, they collected a quarter of a million signatures for Jessi, they had rallies and wrote thousands of letters, and it didn't make any difference!"

"I'll tell you what Janet told me. A lot of lawyers and social workers have been calling. What they are saying is that children have been going through this kind of thing for a long time, but the public didn't know about it. They say that if the public continues the pressure, if the committee expands its work throughout the country and lets its voice be heard, children's voices will eventually be heard, too. Because of Jessi . . ."

We looked at each other and could no longer speak.

Inspired by our conversation, my next diary entry turned to thoughts about the struggle that children in general were going through.

Diary, September:

> *Many wars have been fought by this country. More blood has been shed than could ever be imagined for the purpose of freedom and justice. And now a new battle has begun, one that does not necessarily make us bleed outside, but slices through the blood vessels of our souls. Our ignorance has caused this war. To choose sides is the foolishness of our humanity. An alternative would be to unite in our efforts to find a way for a child's voice to be heard, to be recognized and to be honored. I think columnist Mary McGrory said it best: "If we're going to save this country, we've got to save our children."*

Jan found some solace in writing in the diary as well.
Diary, October:

Dearest Jessi,

My life with you, although it seems so brief now, has been the greatest joy I've ever experienced. You have given us a gift of love that cannot be surpassed. I search for an answer to this madness called "justice." In your case, they never considered you to be an individual with rights. Your mom and I know differently. Maybe we made a huge mistake, but I don't think so. As parents we did what we thought was best for you. I would do it all over again given the same circumstances. What really breaks my heart is that you had to be the sacrificial lamb. At night I look into the heavens and see the stars and the moon, and it brings back the memory of you and the last night we spent together.

Love, Daddy—

It was almost inconceivable that after all of the legal processes we had been through, we still had to face one more. Our last day to file a brief to the U.S. Supreme Court was October 2, 1993. Although we had been turned down for a stay, we still had the right to file a case. The time required by the court to consider a case like ours was quite lengthy; if we were to win custody of Jessica, it would be after months and months of her living in Iowa with Dan and Cara. We decided that this would not be in Jessica's best interest. We had agreed that once Jessica was removed from our home we would not disrupt her life further by pursuing the case. We felt that this would only increase the tension and complications in the Schmidts' lives, taking their energies away from Jessica. We wanted their focus to be on Jessica's psychological welfare; we wanted them to seek ongoing assistance from an objective therapist. Jessi would only suffer more if we should win, being torn from her new home and new family. Jan and I could not do that to her. We would wait to see if Jessi would come home on her own when she got older.

Even though we were firm in our decision, it did not come without great heartache. Knowing that we were passing up whatever tiny chance there was of having Jessi back tore our hearts out all over again. I could almost feel her in my arms; I could hear Jan and me saying to her, "Jessi, you are home again. We're all back together again." It was not to be.

That day Joan and I drove to Manchester, a small town near

Ann Arbor noted for its antiques. I was looking for a trunk in which we would store Jessica's baby books, clothing, and other personal belongings. Jan and I hoped that one day she would return for them. The woman who sold us the trunk began to cry when we told her how it would be used. She told Joan and me that she prayed for Jessi often.

When we got home, we placed the trunk where Jessica's bed had once been. Joan opened the lid and tenderly wiped the inside, almost as if she were wiping Jessi's back after a bath. We worked in complete silence, folding outgrown clothes and laying them in the trunk. As each piece of clothing passed through my hands, I saw Jessi passing through our lives, lying in my arms as an infant, pushing herself across the bed as a three-month-old, zipping across the room in her walker as an eight-month-old, walking, talking, loving . . . and leaving.

On November 1, Cara called. We were not home at the time, but she did leave a message. It was the first communication we received from the Schmidts.

> *Hi, this is Cara. Just thought we would call and let you know how Jessi is doing. She's doing wonderfully. We're potty-trained. We skipped over the training pants and wear big-girl underwear. Not very many accidents. No "passies" anymore. She just gets along great. Adores Chloe. Loves us all. Likes to go through the whole family tree. Loves to go to church, dressing up in all her new dresses. I think she has a little crush on Pastor Renfrew, I don't know, she's so funny. Um . . . I trust you'll keep this call confidential and act responsibly for once because Jessi doesn't need to be the freak show that you turned her into anymore. Um . . . you have Mom and Dad's number if you ever need to call. Bye.*

We were disappointed and frustrated that we didn't get to speak to Cara directly. We did not take Cara up on her suggestion to call her parents' home. We did not want our communications to go through anyone else. We felt that until Cara and Dan felt comfortable giving us their home number we would wait. We did write to them the following day.

> *Dear Dan and Cara,*
> *Jessi has the ability to love. The love she shows to Chloe,*

the enjoyment of a newfound friend in a pastor, fancying a new dress and also the extension of loving both of you. Jessica has all these capabilities and more. Please love her enough to acknowledge that Jessica has loved in the past, and has lived a life of joy once before. Watch over her always and may God bless you all.

Please hug and kiss Jessica for us. We miss that beautiful smiling face and the joy she spread throughout our lives. All of Jessica's other family tree send their love to her, especially Grandma Jo, Oma and Opa, Aunt Joan, Uncle Chuck, her cousin Scott, Uncle Jerry, Uncle Barry, Randy and the boys, Aunt Nelli, Gina and Christine . . . the list goes on and on . . .

We appreciate your initiating this. We wanted to give you space. You may call anytime. Thank you again.

Jan and Robby DeBoer—

Sadness was a part of every day for us, but we were unprepared for the morose feelings that overwhelmed us as Thanksgiving approached. It was the season for family togetherness. Christmas shopping, holiday cheer. I felt bombarded by the Christmas decorations. What used to be such a joy was now a knife in my heart.

We received a package just before Thanksgiving from Harmony House, containing Linda Ronstadt's new CD. On it a song, written by Emmylou Harris, "A River for Him," was dedicated to Jessica. The dedication read: "To Baby Jessica and all the children whose voices are too small to plead for mercy from the court." We were so moved by the dedication that we were actually scared to listen to the song at first. We were big fans of both Linda Ronstadt and Emmylou Harris, so we knew we would love the song. We sat on the sofa holding hands and listening to the beautiful words and melody, thinking of our sweet daughter. "I hope Jessi hears the song someday," I whispered to Jan.

Our attorney in Iowa called to tell us that a hearing had been set for December 3 to address the contempt of court charge and warrants for our arrest that accompanied the charges. We had requested that the warrants be dropped, agreeing to pay the fines. The Schmidts' Iowa attorney, however, had another plan altogether. She requested that the judge add new language to the file, so that we would never again have any contact with Jessi.

The judgment for contempt of court was usually a five-hundred-dollar fine, but now it was to be turned into a thousand-dollar fine per person and payment of attorneys' fees, in addition to an ironclad agreement that Jan and I knew we could never keep.

It seemed totally unreasonable for this judge to attempt to make such a ruling unless she had proof that we had harassed Dan and Cara or had shown intent to see Jessi, neither of which had happened. Did "contact" mean sending Jessi cards or presents? The contempt charge was first put into place a year before because we did not bring Jessi back. That was now a moot issue because Jessi was back in Iowa with Dan and Cara. Now the contempt charges were being redesigned, and we would have no part of it. We advised our lawyer that we would not agree to the new terms, and the hearing was set aside.

Later that night I could hardly breathe. I felt as if I were going to have a heart attack. I started to remember part of what I had suppressed from August 2. I could feel Jessica being taken out of my arms, screaming. I woke up in a cold sweat, gasping for air. I had held back these feelings for so long; I couldn't believe the pain we had all been put through that day. Why? Why did this all have to happen? I fell back asleep and began dreaming again.

Jessi was in my arms. She was kissing my cheek as she used to do all the time. When I turned to look into her eyes, she disappeared. It was my first vision of Jessica. It seemed so real. I felt great comfort. The love Jessi was sending was so pure and deep.

Christmastime was very somber, but we tried to make the best of it. Jan bought a Christmas tree, and we decorated it a few days before the holiday. A large package came from a woman in North Carolina. As Jan and I unwrapped it we began to cry. It was a magnificent portrait of Jessica, in the little white old-fashioned frock dress. The detail was incredible. Jessi's eyes looked right at us. It was almost as if she were in the room—she was so angelic.

We had sent Jessi a sled just like Graham's for Christmas and a little outfit. We never received word from Dan or Cara, but later discovered that they had given them to Jessi when we saw both gifts in a television report.

Christmas morning I crept downstairs at about seven o'clock and lay on the couch looking at the Christmas tree in the dark. I must have dozed off to sleep when Jessi appeared again in the same position in my arms, giggling and kissing my face. This time I heard her say, "It be okay, Momma, it be okay," and then she kissed me on the lips. I tried to keep Jessica in focus but she disappeared just as quickly as she had come into my sight. I thanked God for letting me see Jessi. Later that morning, Jan and I took a wishbone that we had been saving for a couple of years; we sat down next to the Christmas tree and made a wish. We counted to three and said the wish aloud simultaneously. We both wished Jessi safety, happiness, good health, and a good life. The wishbone had broken into three parts; the top cracked off, leaving Jan and me with equal halves.

The weeks between Christmas and Jessi's birthday were difficult for us. Having missed her desperately throughout the Christmas season, we anticipated her third birthday with heavy hearts. The emptiness in our home mirrored the emptiness in our hearts. One night I woke up to a bright light shining in the room. The sky was gray and full of clouds, but the light was almost blinding. Within minutes the light had softened and there in its place was a quarter-moon. I felt Jessica in my heart. The night had been brightened with her presence.

Stephanie and Kerry both advised us to send Jessi a birthday present, to let her know that she was not forgotten. Kerry explained that we had to do what was right for Jessi, knowing that Jessi now feels as if we have abandoned her. Cara had told Jan at the last visit that we could send Jessi presents. Jan called Toys "R" Us in Cedar Rapids and had them deliver a Little Tikes cottage to Jessi. Sending the gift lifted our spirits and gave us a feeling of hope.

Later we were to read in a magazine interview that Dan and Cara had returned the gift to the store. Jan and I felt despair over Dan and Cara's decision, and wondered how they could tell the world that they talked openly about Jessi and her life back in Ann Arbor and at the same time deprive her of something that would give her a sense of not being abandoned.

The evening of Jessi's birthday was beautiful, crisp, and snowy, bringing back wonderful memories of that day so long ago when my mother and I went to meet Jessi for the very first time. Jan and I went out to dinner to celebrate Jessi's birth and to remember the wonderful times we had spent together. When we went to leave the restaurant, our tears began to fall.

Shortly after Jessi's birthday, Jan and I felt that the time had come to pack up all Jessica's photos and put them away. We needed to start moving on into the life ahead of us. It was a difficult step to take, but we felt we needed to do it. Stephanie had said to try to make it a special night, so we wouldn't feel so empty-hearted afterward. We lit some candles that night and celebrated Jessi being in our lives, reminiscing about the wonderful times captured in the photos.

The compensation we received for the ABC television movie went to pay our legal bills and to establish a college fund for Jessica.

Both Dan and Cara have weathered the storm, the long-drawn-out fight to retrieve their daughter. For Jan and me this was never a personal battle. We were stunned by the lack of responsibility that the courts showed for a child. We feel very strongly that Dan and Cara have the ability to love Jessica. We have said all along that we hope they get professional help for Jessi so that she will be able to trust the world again. We still pray every day that the Schmidts will put their feelings for us aside and help Jessi down the road to recovery. We also hope that they will tell Jessi that she is there to stay, and not let her falsely hope that one day, during her childhood, she will return to us.

Cara was recently quoted in an Associated Press article: "I can say with absolute conviction that had I been counseled, if someone had made me sit down and listen to how I might feel, to make me hear how I would be punishing Dan by taking the easy way out, I wouldn't be here today" (speaking about her views on adoption issues to legislators). Dan has said, "Don't hold my past actions against me." Jan and I advocate that Dan and Cara start being responsible for their actions, and stop putting the blame on so many other people. We pray for Jessica's sake that they take this step soon and not let it affect any more of Jessica's life. She has suffered enough.

Cara has a heart within her. At one time, I believed it was the heart of an angel. She bestowed unconditional love upon her child, as only a parent can, when she gave up her daughter so that she could have a better life than she was able to provide at the time. Cara was willing to walk away from her child, to let her go, at her own emotional expense, in the name of love. The pain that any mother feels from such a loss is tremendous. She sealed with a kiss a letter written in such a poetic manner to her beautiful daughter that you could feel her love and never forget it. It is time for Cara to recapture that feeling of unconditional love and to let Jessi acknowledge that Jan and I are not just strangers who live on Pear Street. We were Jessica's parents, and Cara should be able to allow Jessi to feel the love that she once felt for us and not deprive her of her memories.

When I look back to the time when we first went public with our story, I see the anger we felt toward a man that we did not know. Although Jan and I did not name him, we must take responsibility for the fact that his past was brought to the public's attention. Dan, too, has a heart. Jan and I have both seen his expressions of love for Jessi. We now ask that Dan act on this love by allowing Jessi to know that she was loved in the past, by her momma and daddy, and by letting Jessi remember her love for us without feeling inhibited. She needs to express this love.

The time has come to acknowledge Dan and Cara as Jessica's parents. Each of us must be supportive, so that Jessi will be raised in a healthy, stable environment. All parents need a sense of support to be successful in caring for their children. Our efforts should be directed toward changing the laws to consider the best interest of all children.

Dear Jessi,

My father was French: strong-willed and well seasoned with character. I wish you could have known him. He would have been a wonderful grandfather to you. The following was a passage he wrote and distributed to all his children. I believe it will convey to you an idea of what the foundation of your life was. You, too, Jessica, are strong in character. Your momma and daddy hope that what we built together will continue to flourish within you. Never blame yourself for that which has happened in your life. Always hold your head high, like my papa, and enjoy life!

Love, Momma—

IF YOU LIKE TO
EAT,
DRINK,
SLEEP,
LAUGH,
RUN,
JUMP,
PLAY,
THINK,
TALK,
READ,
LEARN,
DREAM,
LOVE,
YOU HAVE A LOT IN
COMMON WITH ME.

Jan and I truly love Jessica, and would give the world to her. We have received her love back tenfold. Jan and I pray for Jessi's happiness with the Schmidts. We hope Jessi finds love within her new world. We will have to wait many years before the last chapter of this book is written. Our future may one day bring another child into our lives, but for now we are just grateful we were able to love Jessica, and we will continue to do so for a long time to come. Jan, as always, counts the moons, waiting for his daughter's return.

God bless our little Jessi.
Love,
Momma and Daddy